# Family Treasures

## Cookbook

### Recipes from the Heart

**For additional copies of this cookbook
visit your local bookstore or contact:**

Mrs. Freeman Yoder
7850 Dutch Bethel Rd.
Freedom, IN 47431
812-828-9660

First Printing – April 1999
Second Printing – July 1999
Third Printing – January 2000
Fourth Printing – November 2000
Fifth Printing – September 2001
Sixth Printing – December 2002
Seventh Printing – February 2004
Eighth Printing – January 2007

**Carlisle Printing**
WALNUT CREEK

2673 Twp. Rd. 421
Sugarcreek, OH 44681

# Introduction

Our family wishes to welcome you to our new *Family Treasures* cookbook, featuring over 600 recipes.

In our Amish homes today, life is often centered around our kitchens. With this thought in mind, my aunts, sisters, mother-in-law, sisters-in-law, grandmothers, mom and I have compiled this cookbook. Some of these recipes are special and treasured, that have been handed down through the generations; some are new and unusual, but simple to make, plus many other tried and true favorites.

I want to thank family and friends, and each one who contributed to the publication of this cookbook in any way.

I hope you will enjoy using this recipe book and that it will be a blessing to all busy cooks of the present and future generations.

Last but not least, a very special thank-you to my husband Freeman who helped with the artwork. He drew the roses, and daughter Charlene did some of the other artwork. To daughter Amy, who helped so willingly to put the recipes in alphabetical order. May God bless you all!

Mrs. Freeman (Mabel) Yoder

# Table of Contents

*Please Note: Perma-Flo and clear jel are thickeners similar to cornstarch and can be bought at Amish bulk food stores.*

## Abbreviations

| | |
|---|---|
| **Cup = c.** | **Teaspoon = t.** |
| **Pint = pt.** | **Tablespoon = T.** |
| **Quart = qt.** | **packet = pkt.** |
| **Gallon = gal.** | **envelope = env.** |
| **Ounce = oz.** | **dozen = doz.** |
| **Pound = lb.** | **package = pkg.** |

# *Appetizers,*

# *Beverages,*

# *& Dips*

*Scatter some sunshine*
*Forget about yourself*
*Put all your worries*
*Away on a shelf!*

*Whether therefore ye eat, or drink, or*
*whatsoever ye do, do all to the glory of God...*
*1 Cor. 10:31*

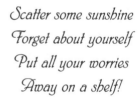

# Rules For Daily Life

### 1. BEGIN THE DAY WITH GOD;
Kneel down to Him in prayer;
Lift up thy heart to His abode
And seek His love to share.

### 2. OPEN THE BOOK OF GOD,
And read a portion there;
That it may hallow thy thoughts,
And sweeten all thy care.

### 3. GO THROUGH THE DAY WITH GOD,
Whatever thy work may be;
Where'er thou art - at home, abroad,
He still is near to thee.

### 4. CONVERSE IN MIND WITH GOD;
Thy spirit heavenward raise;
Acknowledge every good bestowed,
And offer grateful praise.

### 5. CONCLUDE THE DAY WITH GOD,
Thy sins to Him confess;
Trust in the Lord's atoning blood
And plead His righteousness.

### 6. LIE DOWN AT NIGHT WITH GOD
Who gives His servants sleep;
And when thou tread'st the vale of death,
He will thee guard and keep.

## Banana Brunch Punch

*Mrs. Herman (Elsie) Mullett*

6 med. ripe bananas
1 can (12 oz.) frozen orange juice
    concentrate (thawed)
1 can (6 oz.) frozen lemonade
    concentrate (thawed)
3 c. warm water
2 c. white sugar
1 can (46 oz.) pineapple juice
2 bottles (2 liters ea.) lemon
    lime soda

Mash the bananas in a salsa master; add orange juice and lemonade. Mix the warm water and sugar together. Then mix to banana mixture. Put in large freezer container; cover and freeze until solid. One hour before serving, take punch out of freezer. Just before serving, place in a large punch bowl. Add pineapple juice and soda. Stir until well blended. Yield: 2½ gal.

## Cappuccino Mocha Mix

*Mrs. Freeman (Mabel) Yoder*

4 c. coffee creamer (non-dairy)
2½ c. non-fat dry milk
2 c. sugar
⅔ c. cocoa
¾ c. instant coffee
½ c. chocolate drink mix (Nestle's is good)
½ c. powdered sugar
dash of salt
1 lg. box or ⅔ c. instant
    vanilla pudding
1 lb. French Vanilla Cappuccino

Mix in a lg. bowl. To serve, mix 3 heaping teaspoonfuls to a cup of boiling water; stir well. *Optional: May add a small handful of marshmallows & ¼ t. vanilla extract.* Store mix in an airtight container. Delicious!

## Cocoa Mix

*Regina Miller*

1 box (8 qt.) dry milk
8 oz. jar powder non-dairy creamer
1 lb. instant chocolate (Nestle's
    Quik)
2 c. powdered sugar

**Variation:** ½ t. salt added to above if desired.

Mix together. Use ⅓ c. cocoa mix for 1 c. hot chocolate.

## Eggnog

*Mrs. Freeman (Mabel) Yoder*

**All ingredients must be cold.** Beat 4 eggs until thick and lemon colored. Add ⅓ c. sugar, ⅛ t. nutmeg, 2 t. vanilla , and ⅛ t. salt. Add ½ c. cold cream and 4 c. milk. Beat with eggbeater.

*Don't be afraid to try new recipes.*
*The worst that can happen is - you'll have to eat them yourself!*

## Golden Wedding Punch

*Mrs. Freeman (Mabel) Yoder*
*Mrs. Leland (Orpha) Yoder*

**2 (12 oz.) cans frozen orange juice concentrate**
Mix as directed on cans, in a large container. Add:

**2 (46 oz.) cans pineapple juice**
**1 can frozen lemonade concentrate**
**2 c. water**
**1 lg. bottle ginger ale**

**2 lg. bottles Upper 10 or Spring Mist, something similar to Mountain Dew (Upper 10 is hard to find)**

Mix well, then chill before serving. I usually add 1 c. sugar and a few more cups of water. A very refreshing drink; serves 50-60.

## Mocha Punch

*Mrs. Freeman (Mabel) Yoder*
*Mrs. Sam (Viola) Miller*

**1½ qts. water**
**½ c. instant chocolate drink mix**
**½ c. sugar**
**¼ c. instant coffee granules**

**½ gal. vanilla ice cream**
**1 c. whipped cream**
**chocolate curls for garnish (opt.)**
**2 c. milk**

In a large saucepan, bring water to a boil. Remove from the heat. Add drink mix, sugar, and coffee; stir until dissolved. Cover and refrigerate for about 4 hours or overnight. About 30 min. before serving, put into a punch bowl. Add ice cream by scoopsful; add milk; stir until partially melted. Garnish with whipped cream and chocolate curls.

## Orange Slush

*Sister Elvesta*

**2 c. sugar**
**3 c. water**
Boil together, then cool. Add:

**1 (6 oz.) frozen orange juice**
**6 bananas, chopped**

**1 qt. chopped peaches**
**1 (No.2) can crushed pineapple**

Put in a bowl and stir often while freezing. Take out of freezer and thaw partially before serving. Good for breakfast or anytime.

## Rhubarb Drink

*Mrs. Freeman (Mabel) Yoder*

**2 qts. rhubarb**
**2 qts. rhubarb juice**
**1 (12 oz.) can frozen lemonade concentrate**

**3½ qts. water**
**1 pkg. raspberry Kool-Aid**
**2 c. sugar**
**46 oz. pineapple juice**

**1 (12 oz.) can frozen orange juice concentrate**

In 4 qt. kettle, cook 2 qt. rhubarb until soft. Let set for a half hour, then drain. You should have 2 qts. juice or a little more; add the rest of ingredients; stir well. Makes close to 7 qts. This can be canned when the water is omitted, and added when the jars are opened.

## Rhubarb Nectar

*Mrs. Noah (Amanda) Lehman*

8 qts. cut-up rhubarb
8 qts. water
1 (46 oz.) pineapple juice
1 box cherry Jell-o
5 c. sugar

Cook rhubarb until juice is out. Strain; add juice, sugar, and Jell-o. Cook until dissolved; can or freeze. Serve with 7-Up; this can be omitted.

## Sherbet Punch

*Mrs. Freeman (Mabel) Yoder*

½ gal. lime sherbet, softened
1 liter ginger ale
4 c. grapefruit juice or citrus soda
2 c. lemon lime soda

Stir all together until sherbet is almost all dissolved; raspberry or orange sherbet may be used instead of lime. Makes approx. 5 qts.

## Tea to Freeze

*Mrs. Mervin (Emma) Yoder*

4 qts. boiling water
4 c. tea leaves, such as homegrown peppermint, balsam, mint, etc.
4 c. sugar

Put tea in water. Let set 15 min. Remove leaves. Add sugar and cool. Put in 1 qt. boxes and freeze. Add 3 qts. water when ready to serve.

## Wedding Punch (Serves 100)

*Mrs. Elmer (Wilma) Beechy*
*Mrs. Sam (Viola) Miller*

4 (46 oz.) cans pineapple juice
1 (46 oz.) can grapefruit juice
1 (46 oz.) can orange juice
2 lg. frozen orange juice concentrate
lots of ice!
5 c. sugar
5 qts. water
2 (2 liter) Mt. Dew, Sprite, or Lemon-Lime
1 gal. sherbet of your choice

Mix in a large container, add ice, and add sherbet last.

## Caramel Fondue (Fruit Dip)

*Mrs. Glen (Lydia Mae) Miller*

¾ c. white sugar
½ c. corn syrup
¼ t. salt
¼ c. oleo
½ c. cream

Cook all ingredients over low heat, stirring, to soft ball (234°). Cool to 220° and add another ½ c. cream. Bring to a boil, remove from heat and add ½ t. vanilla. Serve with any fresh fruit, apples, oranges, bananas, etc.

*When the day is dying in the west,*
*Heaven is touching earth with rest.*

## Cheese Log
Mrs. Sam (Viola) Miller

1 (8 oz.) cream cheese
1 (8 oz.) bacon flavored cheese
1 pkg. dried beef, cut fine

1 t. Worcestershire sauce
1 t. minced onion (opt.)
a little Lawry's seasoning salt

Velveeta or mild or sharp cheddar may be used instead of bacon flavored cheese. If you do, add 2 t. imitation bacon bits. Shred cheese fine, then let set by stove till fairly soft. Also let cream cheese soften before mixing. Mix well and roll into finely chopped nuts and form a log. Sprinkle with parsley flakes and refrigerate a few hours before serving. Serve with a variety of crackers.

## Chip Dip
Mrs. Andy (Dorothy) Miller

1 c. mayonnaise
1 c. sour cream
¼ t. onion salt
¼ t. garlic salt

¾ t. parsley flakes
¾ t. dill weed
½ t. Accent

Combine all ingredients together, mixing thoroughly. Chill well! Any kinds of chips, carrots, celery, etc. is very good dipped into this mixture. Keep refrigerated. Yield: about 1 qt.

## Cottage Cheese
Mrs. Vern (Irene) Schlabach

1 gal. milk (cows' or goats')
½ to ¾ c. vinegar (depending on its strength)

Heat milk until it is almost boiling. Remove from heat and add vinegar. The milk will curdle immediately. Stir it gently, then let set until cool. Drain through a cloth or colander, allowing the curds to drip until they are dry. Run water through the curds to rinse off the whey. Allow to dry. Place in a bowl and add cream or milk to moisten the curds. Add salt to taste.

## Fresh Vegetable Dip
Mrs. Noah (Amanda) Lehman

1 - 1½ c. (12 oz.) sour cream
¾ c. mayonnaise
1 T. dried minced onion
1 t. dried dill weed

1 t. dried parsley flakes
1 t. garlic salt
dash of Worcestershire sauce
fresh vegetables

In a small bowl combine sour cream, mayonnaise, onion, dill, parsley, garlic salt, and Worcestershire sauce. Chill for at least 1 hour. Serve with fresh vegetables. Yield: 2 cups.

*Any housewife no matter how large her family can always get some time alone; by doing the dishes.*

## Frozen Fruit Salad (Slush)

*Mrs. Christie (Anna) Yoder*

2 c. sugar
3 c. hot water
6 bananas, mashed
6 oz. frozen orange juice
1 (#2) can crushed pineapple
fresh peaches

Combine sugar and hot water. Cool and add the rest of the ingredients to the syrup. Freeze. Thaw to icy slush before serving. Very refreshing!

## Fruit Dip

*Mrs. Lonnie (Norma Mae) Bontrager*

1 (8 oz.) pkg. cream cheese
1 c. brown sugar
1 t. vanilla

Mix together. Use as a dip with your favorite fruit. Especially good with apples.

## Fruit Slush

*Mrs. Lloyd (Edna) Raber*

2 c. sugar
3 c. boiling water
1 can (12 oz.) frozen orange juice
6 to 8 bananas, sliced
1 can (20 oz.) crushed pineapple
18 oz. 7-Up

Dissolve sugar in boiling water. Add orange juice concentrate, bananas, and pineapple. Stir until orange juice is dissolved. Stir in 7-Up then pour into large container or several small containers and freeze. Thaw approximately 1 hour or until slushy before serving.

## Mozzarella Cheese

*Mrs. Vern (Irene) Schlabach*

4 gal. whole milk
5 t. citric acid powder dissolved in ½ c. cold water

Stir into cold milk. Mix well, heat to 98.6°, remove from heat and add **2 t. rennet (or 10 junket tablets) dissolved in ½ c. cold water.** Stir well. Let set undisturbed for ½ hour, not longer, then cut into 1" squares. Let set another 5 - 10 min. until whey separates from curds. Heat to 110°. Keep well stirred to keep curds sticking together. Remove from heat and stir another 20 min. or so. Drain in colander for 15 min.

Heat **1 gal. water with 1 c. salt** to 170° - 180°. Pull cheese apart into small chunks and put in hot water. Using a wooden spoon, stretch cheese upward until nice and soft (all melted together in one piece). Place in mold and set in cold water.

I use an ice cream pail with holes poked in bottom and around sides a few inches up, put cheese in there and weigh down with another ice cream pail on top of cheese. Put a gal. of water or rocks inside second pail to press. I set it in cold water a few hours then refrigerate, or eat right away.

## Tartar Sauce

*Mrs. Martin (Katie) Wickey*
*Ola Bontrager*

¾ c. mayonnaise
3 T. pickle relish
1 T. lemon juice

1 T. finely chopped onion
½ t. prepared mustard
salt & pepper to taste

Combine all ingredients in a mixing bowl. Cover and chill until used.

## Vegetable Dip

*Mrs. Merlin (Mary) Lehman*

⅔ c. mayonnaise
⅔ c. sour cream
1 T. dry onion flakes
1 T. parsley flakes

1 t. dill weed
1 drop Tabasco sauce
1 t. Accent

Mix and chill; serve with fresh veggies or chips.

## Vegetable Dip

*Mrs. Marvin L. (Erma) Miller*

1½ c. mayonnaise
2 T. parsley flakes
2 t. Lawry's salt
4 drops Tabasco sauce

1½ c. sour cream
2 T. onion flakes
2 t. Accent

Mix together with a wire whip.

## Yogurt

*Mrs. Freeman (Mabel) Yoder*
*Mrs. Sam (Viola) Miller*

1 gal. milk
3 T. or 3 pkgs. unflavored gelatin
½ c. cold water
fruit of your choice, opt.

2 t. vanilla
6 T. plain yogurt, store-bought
1½ c. sugar
¾ c. non-fat dry milk

Mix non-fat dry milk with the 1 gal. milk, then heat milk to 190°. While heating, soak gelatin in the cold water; add to milk when it reaches 190° then cool to 130°. Add vanilla, yogurt, and sugar. Beat until smooth with beater. Cool to 118° to 120° in a *'Yogotherm' or an ice cream pail and cover and put in oven with just the pilot light on overnight or 7 to 8 hours. Chill well. Before adding fruit, take out a little more than 6 T. for your next batch. This may be eaten without fruit added. Do not use your own yogurt to start another batch more than 6 - 8 times for contamination and bacteria reasons. You should start over with fresh boughten yogurt. Making half batches works very well too. *(*A Yogotherm is an insulated container purposely for yogurt making.)*

# Yogurt

*Mrs. Eldon (Katie) Nisley, Mrs. Milo (Lorene) Yoder*

Heat **1 gal. milk** to 180°. Let cool to 130°. While milk cools, soak 2 T. plain gelatin in ½ c. cold water. When milk has cooled add gelatin (stir some warm milk into gelatin mixture to dissolve), ½ c. starter, 2 T. vanilla, 1 heaping c. sugar. Beat all ingredients well. Put into glass or plastic containers. To make a different flavor you can add jello to a few of the containers; stir until jello is dissolved. Put in oven with a pilot light for 4 to 8 hours. Refrigerate till cold and set. Skim off layers that form on top before serving.

You will have to buy yogurt for a starter or get some from someone that has made some already, then keep ½ c. of your own for your next batch. *Variations: Honey or maple syrup may be used instead of sugar.*

*Do not be like the rooster who thought
the sun rose to hear him crow!*

# Breads &

# Rolls

---

*A lot of kneeling keeps you in
good standing with God*

*Matthew 6:9-13*

After this manner therefore pray ye:

Our Father which art in heaven,

Hallowed be thy name.

Thy kingdom come. Thy will be done

In earth as it is in heaven.

Give us this day our daily bread.

And forgive us our debts,

as we forgive our debtors.

And lead us not into temptation, but deliver us from evil:

For thine is the kingdom, and the power,

and the glory forever. Amen.

Man shall not live by bread alone, but by every word that

proceedeth out of the mouth of God. *Matthew 4:4*

## 100% Whole Wheat Bread
*Mrs. Christy (Anna) Bontrager*

⅓ c. sorghum or honey
1 T. lecithin
1 T. oil
1 T. yeast
2 c. lukewarm water
2 t. salt
6 c. whole wheat flour

Dissolve yeast in warm water. Add oil, lecithin, salt, & honey. Add the flour slowly, mixing in well. When it becomes too stiff to stir with a spoon, turn out onto a well floured surface, and knead in the rest of the flour (or as much as you need). Put into a greased bowl; cover and let rise until double. Punch down. Divide into equal parts; flatten with a rolling pin. Shape into loaves and place into greased pans. Let rise until almost double. Bake at 300° for 30 min. Makes 2 or 3 loaves, depending on the size of your pans.

## Apple Bread
*Mrs. Lester (Verna) Bontrager*

2 c. sugar
1 c. oil or oleo, melted
3 c. flour
1 t. soda
1 t. salt
1 t. cinnamon
3 eggs, beaten
2 t. vanilla
3 c. chopped apples
1 c. chopped nuts, opt.

Mix oil or oleo and sugar. Add flour, soda, salt, and cinnamon. Beat all together, then add beaten eggs and beat again. Add chopped apples and nuts; fold in. Pour into 2 greased and floured loaf pans and sprinkle with sugar. Bake at 325° for 50 - 60 min. or until knife inserted in center comes out clean.

## Banana Bread
*Mrs. Allen (Elsie) Bontrager*

2 c. sugar
1 c. shortening
6 ripe mashed bananas
4 eggs
½ t. vanilla
2½ c. flour
1 t. salt
2 t. soda

Cream sugar & shortening (do not melt, and I usually use softened oleo or butter). Add mashed bananas, eggs, and vanilla and beat well. Then stir in flour, salt, and soda. Bake at 325° or 350° (depends on your oven, but not too hot) for 45 to 50 min. Moist and delicious. Makes 2 lg. loaves or 3 small ones.

## Banana Bread
*Grandma (Mary) Bontrager*

3 very ripe bananas
¾ c. white sugar
pinch of salt
1 egg
¼ c. butter
1 t. soda
1 T. water
2 c. pastry flour

Mash bananas with fork. Blend in sugar, salt, and beaten egg. Melt butter and mix in banana mixture. Dissolve soda in water and add with sifted flour. Add nuts if preferred. Mix and bake in loaf pan for 45 min. at 375°.

## Basic White Bread
*Mrs. Freeman (Mabel) Yoder*

4 c. warm water
¼ c. sugar
½ c. oil

1½ T. salt
1 T. yeast
6 - 8 c. flour*

*Some wheat flour may be used for brown bread. In a large bowl, mix water and yeast together. Let set for 5 min., then add sugar, salt, oil, and 3 c. flour. Stir well with a spoon, then keep adding flour and knead with hands until soft and elastic. The longer you knead, the softer your bread will be. Cover and let rise until double in size, punch down and let rise again until double. Then divide evenly into 3 large loaves or 4 smaller ones. Let rise. Bake at 325° for 15 min., then increase heat to 350° for 25 - 30 min. or till golden brown.

## Best-Ever Banana Bread
*Mrs. Freeman (Mabel) Yoder*

1¾ c. all-purpose flour
1½ c. sugar
1 t. baking soda
½ t. salt
2 eggs

1 c. (2) ripe med. bananas, mashed
½ c. vegetable oil
¼ c. buttermilk
1 t. vanilla
1 c. chopped nuts

In a large bowl combine eggs, bananas, oil, buttermilk, sugar, and vanilla; add flour, salt, and soda. Mix just until blended; fold in nuts. Pour into a greased 9x5x3" baking pan. Bake at 325° for 1 hour and 20 min. or until bread tests done. Cool on wire rack. Recipe does not double well. Can be divided into 2 pans.

## Bread
*Mrs. Lester (Mary) Lehman*

¾ c. sugar
4¼ c. warm water
3 T. yeast
12 c. flour

1 T. salt
½ c. oil
4 T. instant mashed potatoes

Dissolve all ingredients except flour in warm water; let set a few minutes; add the flour. Knead for 10 min. Cover and let rise until double in size. Knead a few minutes and let rise until double in size again. Form 4 loaves; let rise some more and bake at 325° for 35 to 40 min. or until golden. *I use 3 c. whole wheat flour for brown bread.*

*The grass is greener on the other side, but it's just as hard to mow!*

## Bread
*Mrs. Herman (Elsie) Mullett*

6 t. yeast
2 t. sugar
1 c. lukewarm water
¼ c. brown sugar
¼ c. white sugar
¼ c. honey
¼ c. oil
¼ c. lard
3 t. salt
2 c. hot tap water
1½ c. whole wheat flour
7 c. flour

Mix yeast and sugar; add 1 c. water; set aside. Then mix brown sugar, white sugar, honey, oil, lard, and salt. Add your hot water to dissolve. Work in flour. Let rise 2 times for 45 min. Bake at 350° for 35 min.

## Bread
*Mrs. Edwin (Annie) Ropp*

4½ c. warm water
¾ c. sugar or honey
2 T. yeast
3 t. salt
½ c. vegetable oil
12 c. flour

Put warm water in a large mixing bowl. Add sugar and yeast. Let set until foamy. Add the salt, oil, and 4 c. of the flour. Beat well until it is smooth. Add rest of the flour and knead. Let rise for 1 hour; punch down. Let rise again for ½ hour. If you want brown bread, I add 4 c. whole wheat flour before I add any white flour. Makes 5 loaves. Bake 40 min. at 325°.

## Brown Bread
*Mrs. Eldon (Katie) Nisley*

1 T. salt
⅔ c. vegetable oil
⅔ c. honey or molasses

Add 3 c. boiling or hot water; stir until salt is dissolved. Add 2 c. cold water. Stir in 5 c. whole wheat flour and 1 round T. yeast; stir well then let set until bubbly, ½ to 1 hour. Add 5 c. white flour and stir well. Add 4 more c. white flour and knead until smooth. Let rise and knead down 3 times, divide into 5 loaves and let rise again and bake at 325° for 40 min. I do not preheat oven, but turn on the oven and put bread in right away. When removing from oven, rub butter or oleo over top of loaves.

## Corn Bread
*Mom (Rosa) Bontrager*

2 c. flour
2 c. cornmeal
½ c. brown sugar
¾ c. white sugar
4 t. baking powder
2 eggs
1 t. salt
1 t. vanilla
5 T. melted oleo

Stir in milk until the right consistency (approx. 1¼ c.). Bake at 350° for 45 min. or an hour.

## Delicious Bread
*Mom (Rosa) Bontrager*

1 c. mashed potatoes
5 T. lard
1½ qt. water, lukewarm
3 T. salt
½ c. sugar
5 t. dry yeast

Mix potatoes, lard, salt, & sugar into water. Sprinkle yeast on top and let set for 10 min. Then work in flour until it doesn't stick to your hands or the bowl. Let rise for 2 hours, work down and let rise again for 2 hours. Work out in pans. Let stand in pans for 1½ hours or until right size. Bake at 325° for 45 min. Makes 6 loaves. *Note: Add 5 - 6 c. wheat flour for brown bread.*

## Homemade Bread
*Mrs. Marvin L. (Erma) Miller*

½ c. warm water
2 T. yeast (regular)
1 c. milk
2 T. salt
5 T. sugar
4 T. lard
3 c. warm water
3 c. whole wheat flour
8 - 9 c. white flour

Mix the yeast with the warm water and let soak. Scald the milk; add salt, sugar, and lard. When melted, add the 3 c. warm water. Mix with the 3 c. (optional) whole wheat flour and let set for 10 min. Mix all together and add as much of the flour as possible. Turn out on a flat surface and knead the rest in. Put in covered bowl and let rise for 1 hour. Punch down and let rise ½ hour; repeat 2 more times, every ½ hour. Divide into 4 equal parts and roll out. Put in greased bread pans. Let rise until 1 inch above pan. Bake at 350° for 25 - 30 min.

## Homemade Bread
*Mrs. Mervin (Gertie) Eash*

3 c. very warm water
⅓ c. lard or oil
½ c. sugar
4 t. salt
1 egg, beaten
2 c. whole wheat flour
1½ T. dry yeast
white bread flour

Stir together water, oil, sugar, salt, and egg in a large bowl. Mix yeast with whole wheat flour and 2 c. white flour. Then add to liquid. Stir vigorously for a min. Add white flour to make a soft dough. Grease sides of bowl and let rise for an hour. Then punch down and turn over in bowl. After the second hour, do the same. The third hour, shape into 4 loaves. Let rise until double in size. Bake in 325° oven for 30 min.

*You are never fully dressed*
*until you wear a smile.*

# Honey Oatmeal Bread

*Mrs. Mervin (Emma) Yoder*

5 c. water
4 c. oatmeal
½ c. yeast
2 c. lukewarm water
2 T. sugar
2 c. honey
1½ c. vegetable oil
¼ c. salt
8 eggs
4 c. wheat flour
18 c. white flour, more if needed

Bring 5 c. water to a boil; add oatmeal. Cool slightly. Dissolve yeast in 2 c. lukewarm water and sugar. Mix together with remaining ingredients for 10 min. Let rise; punch down. Let rise again. Put in pans. Makes 8 loaves. Bake as usual bread at 325° - 350° for approximately 45 min. to 1 hour.

# Oatmeal Bread

*Mrs. Ivan (Arlene) Bontrager*

½ c. shortening or margarine
2 c. quick oatmeal
3½ c. boiling water

Pour boiling water over oatmeal and shortening. Let stand for 10 min. Mix **2 c. white flour and 3 T. instant yeast** in another bowl.

Beat **4 eggs.** Add **4 t. salt.** To the oatmeal mixture add **½ c. molasses, ½ c. honey,** the eggs and salt. Mix well. Mixture should be about lukewarm by now. Add the flour-yeast mixture and beat well. Gradually add approximately 8 to 10 more cups of flour - either white all-purpose flour or a mixture of white and whole wheat flour. When dough hangs together, grease bowl and ball of dough generously. Cover with plastic wrap and set in warm place. Let rise for 30 - 45 min. Knead dough and let rise again. Knead and form loaves. Put into greased loaf pans. Grease tops and cover again. Let rise until double. Bake in 325° oven for approx. 30 min. A loaf that is done will not be too hot to hold in your hand when you remove it from the pan immediately after taking it out of the oven. If done, return to pan and brush tops with butter. Let cool in pans for 10 to 15 minutes. Remove and finish cooling. Store in plastic bags.

# Parmesan Garlic Bread

*Mrs. Freeman (Mabel) Yoder*

¼ c. margarine, softened
¼ c. vegetable oil
¼ c. grated Parmesan cheese
1 t. garlic powder
½ t. parsley
½ t. lemon pepper
8 thick slices homemade bread
or French bread

In a small mixing bowl, blend margarine, oil and Parmesan cheese. Add garlic, parsley, and lemon pepper; mix until smooth. Spread mixture evenly on both sides of the bread; place on a cookie sheet. Cover with foil. Bake at 400° for 15 - 20 min. Serve warm. This is a good way to use up old bread.

## Pumpkin Bread

*Mrs. Freeman (Mabel) Yoder*

3½ c. flour
2 t. baking soda
1 t. salt
1 t. cinnamon
1 t. nutmeg
3 c. sugar
1 c. vegetable oil

4 eggs, beaten
¾ c. buttermilk
1 t. vanilla
1 t. butter flavoring
1 can (16 oz.) pumpkin
1 c. raisins
1 c. chopped pecans

In a large mixing bowl, sift together flour, soda, salt, cinnamon, and nutmeg. Add sugar, oil, eggs, and buttermilk. Mix well. Stir in flavorings, pumpkin, raisins, and pecans. Pour into two greased bread pans. Bake at 350° for 60 - 65 min. or until done. Let stand for 10 min. before removing from pans. These freeze well.

## Raisin Bread

*Mom (Rosa) Bontrager*

5 c. lukewarm water
¾ c. vegetable oil
3 T. yeast
¾ c. sugar
5 eggs, beaten

2 T. salt
3 c. raisins, cooked & drained, cooled
approx. 15 to 17 c. flour

In a large bowl, dissolve yeast in warm water. Add sugar, salt, veg. oil, and beaten eggs. Then add raisins. Stir in flour until too thick to stir, then work in the rest of the flour with your hands; knead 15 to 20 min. Add only flour to make a soft elastic dough. Cover and let rise. Punch down and let rise until double. Divide dough into 6 loaves; roll out and spread with butter; sprinkle on brown sugar and cinnamon. Roll up and pinch edges together. Let rise 1" above bread pans then bake at 350° for 45 min. *Optional: Glaze with your favorite frosting.*

*Thank God for dirty dishes,*
*They have a tale to tell;*
*While others may go hungry,*
*We're eating very well.*
*With home, health, and happiness,*
*I shouldn't have to fuss,*
*For by the stack of evidence,*
*God's been very good to us.*

## Whole Wheat Bread
*Mrs. Ervin (Clara) Yoder*

3 c. very warm water
½ c. honey
1½ T. salt
⅓ c. oil (canola preferred)

3 c. whole wheat flour
5 c. white flour
1 egg
2 T. dry yeast

Put water in large bowl; add honey, oil, salt, whole wheat flour, and yeast. Whisk all together with wire whip until nice and smooth. Then add egg and whisk it in. Add 3 c. white flour and stir in with wooden spoon. Work the rest of the flour in with your hands. It may not take all of it. But knead until smooth and elastic. Grease bowl then flip dough so greased side is up. Cover and let rise ½ hour. Knead again and flip dough. Let rise until double. Then knead and divide into 3 loaves. I like to grease a Tupperware lid and form my loaves on it. Put into greased pans and let rise until double. Bake 35 to 40 min. in 375° oven. You may use more whole wheat flour and less white if you wish. I don't grease my bread when I take it out of the oven, but you can if you like. I always put the loaves in plastic bags while still warm to soften the crusts.

## Zucchini Bread
*Mrs. Owen (Verna) Hershberger*

1 c. white sugar
1 c. brown sugar
1 t. salt
¼ t. baking powder
2 t. cinnamon
2 c. unpeeled chopped zucchini

1 c. oil
3 c. flour
1 t. soda
1 t. vanilla
1 c. chopped nuts
3 eggs

Mix all together then put in bread pans. Makes 2 small loaves or 1 large. Bake at 350° for 50 - 60 min.

## Bar-B-Q Buns
*Mrs. Freeman (Mabel) Yoder*

2 c. warm water
2 pkg. (T.) yeast
¼ c. sugar

1½ t. salt
¼ c. vegetable oil
6 to 7 c. flour

Dissolve yeast in warm water; stir until dissolved. Add sugar, oil, salt, and 3 c. of the flour. Then add the rest of the flour gradually and knead 8 to 10 min. Let rise in warm place till doubled. Divide dough into 20 to 22 pieces. Shape into hamburger sized buns; press down to flatten. Place on greased cookie sheets 2 inches apart. Let rise, optional. Make a mixture of 2 egg whites and 4 T. water and brush tops. Sprinkle with sesame seeds. Bake at 400° for 15 to 20 min. Brush with margarine. Split buns and serve with your favorite sloppy joes.

## Biscuit Mix

*Mrs. Leland (Orpha) Yoder*

8 c. flour
1/3 c. baking powder
8 t. sugar
2 t. cream of tartar
2 t. salt
1 c. powdered milk
1¾ c. shortening

Sift together the dry ingredients and cut in shortening. Pack loosely in airtight container. To use mix: **1 c. dry mix to 1/3 c. water.** Bake 10 to 12 minutes at 450°. Powdered milk can be omitted, then milk added instead of water.

## Biscuits Supreme

*Mrs. Sam (Viola) Miller*

2 c. flour
½ t. salt
4 t. baking powder
½ t. cream of tartar
2 t. sugar
½ c. shortening
2/3 c. milk

Mix dry ingredients; cut in shortening until mixture is crumbly. Add milk and just stir until dough follows fork around bowl. Drop by spoonfuls on ungreased cookie sheet and bake at 450° for 10 - 12 min.

## Blueberry Muffins

*Mrs. Lester (Verna) Bontrager*

2 c. flour
2/3 c. sugar
1 T. baking powder
½ t. salt
2 eggs
1 c. milk
1/3 c. butter or margarine, melted
1 t. nutmeg
1 t. vanilla
2 c. fresh or frozen blueberries
additional sugar and melted butter

In a bowl, combine flour, sugar, baking powder, and salt. In another bowl, beat eggs. Blend in milk, butter, nutmeg, and vanilla; pour into dry ingredients and mix just until moistened. Carefully fold in blueberries. Fill greased or paper-lined muffin cups 2/3 full. Bake at 375° for 20 - 25 min. Brush tops with melted butter and sprinkle with sugar. *(If using frozen berries, rinse and pat dry before adding to batter.)*

*A slip of the foot you can soon recover,*
*but a slip of the tongue you may never*
*get over.*

## Bread Sticks
*Mrs. Noah (Amanda) Lehman*

Heat: **1 c. milk**  **1 t. salt**
**¼ c. sugar**  **4 T. butter or margarine**

Remove from heat as soon as butter is melted. Then add:

**3½ c. flour**  **¼ t. oregano**
**½ T. yeast**  **1 egg, beaten**
**⅛ t. garlic powder**

Roll out and cut the size you want. Makes two 13 x 9" pans full. Melt 4 T. butter or margarine in each pan and sprinkle pizza seasoning over it. Then roll bread sticks in this mixture and bake for 15 to 20 min. at 350° or until done.

They can be dipped in pizza sauce or cheese sauce when eating if you like. For cheese sauce heat ⅓ c. milk and 10 slices cheese. Very good!

## Butter Crescents
*Mrs. LaVern (Martha) Yoder*

**½ c. milk**  **1 pkg. active yeast**
**½ c. butter, softened**  **½ c. warm water (105°-115° F)**
**⅓ c. sugar**  **1 egg, lightly beaten**
**½ t. salt**  **3½ - 4 c. flour**
Glaze:
**1 egg, lightly beaten**

In a saucepan, heat milk until bubbles appear around edge. Combine sugar, butter, and salt, add hot milk, and stir well. Cool to lukewarm (95°-100° F). In a small bowl, dissolve yeast in warm water; let stand until foamy. Beat yeast and egg mixture in milk mixture; beat in 2 cups of flour. Mix in enough remaining flour until dough pulls away from sides of bowl. Knead until smooth and elastic, 2 - 3 min. Place in a large greased bowl and cover with damp cloth. Let rise for 1 hour; punch down and let rise 10 min. Then roll out half of the dough into 12" circle, cutting circle into 6 wedges. Roll up into crescents and put on baking sheets. Let rise then bake at 400° for 15 min.

*Cleaning house while children are growing
is like shoveling snow while it is still snowing.*

## Butterscotch Breakfast Ring

*Mrs. Ivan (Arlene) Bontrager*

1 c. butterscotch morsels, divided
2 T. butter
2 T. unsifted flour
1/8 t. salt

1/2 c. chopped pecans
8 oz. pkg. refrigerated quick
   crescent dinner rolls
7 t. corn syrup

Preheat oven to 375°. Melt over hot (not boiling) water, 1/2 c. of the butterscotch chips and the butter. Remove from heat. With fork, mix in flour, salt, and pecans. Set aside. Separate crescent roll triangles. On greased cookie sheet, arrange crescents, overlapping edges to form a circle on the inside with a 4" diameter. (Long pointed ends should point outwards.) Spread 2 rounded teaspoonfuls of butterscotch mixture onto each triangle. Roll up triangles toward center. Slash inside half of each roll. Bake for 15 min. Cool and drizzle with glaze.

Glaze: Melt over hot, but not boiling, water, the remaining 1/2 c. of the butterscotch morsels with the corn syrup. Mix well. *Note: Instead of using crescent rolls, mix up your favorite sweet roll dough; roll out into a rectangle about 6" by 14". Spread with butterscotch mixture; roll up and place onto a cookie sheet, forming dough into a circle. Slash outer edge to aid in forming a circle. Proceed as above.*

## Cherry Treat

*Mrs. Lonnie (Norma Mae) Bontrager*

1 T. yeast
1/2 c. scalded milk
1/4 c. sugar
1 t. salt
2 eggs, beaten

1/4 c. lukewarm water
1/2 c. oleo
2 1/2 c. flour
4 c. cherry pie filling

Let dough rise double in size, then roll out half of dough; put in bottom of cake pan. Put in your pie filling, roll out rest of dough and put on top. Let rise 1 hour or until doubled in size. Bake at 350° for 35 to 40 min. When done, frost. Mix together:

1 c. sugar
1/2 c. flour
1 c. milk
3/4 c. margarine

1/2 t. almond flavor
1 t. vanilla
1/2 t. salt

Mix together flour, sugar, and milk in saucepan. Heat slowly until it thickens. Cream margarine, almond, vanilla, and salt into it. Spread on top of cake.

*"He that followeth me . . . shall have the light of life."*

# Cinnamon Rolls

*Mrs. Orva (Marietta) Yoder*

1 c. scalded milk
1 c. lukewarm water
4 t. yeast
½ c. shortening

½ c. sugar
2 eggs, beaten
5 c. flour
1½ t. salt

Scald milk and pour over sugar, salt, and shortening. Dissolve yeast in warm water. When milk has cooled, add yeast and beaten eggs. Beat well. Add flour gradually, beating well. Place in well greased bowl, and let rise until double in size. Roll dough out; spread with butter, brown sugar, and cinnamon. Roll and cut into 1" thick pieces. Put in pan and let rise a little. Bake at 350° until browned. Frost with your favorite frosting.

# Cinnamon Rolls

*Mrs. Clarence (Anna Marie) Miller*

2 c. sugar
1½ c. oleo
4 t. salt
4 eggs, beaten

4 T. yeast
5 c. warm water
12 c. flour

Melt oleo; add sugar and salt. Put yeast in water with 1 t. sugar per T. yeast. Let set for 5 min. Then add oleo mixture; add eggs and flour; knead well. Let rise until double. Roll out and spread with butter, cinnamon, and brown sugar. Let rise again until almost doubled. Bake at 375° for approximately 15 min.

# Cinnamon Rolls

*Mrs. Melvin (Mary Esther) Shrock*

2¼ c. sugar
2¼ c. warm water
1 T. salt
1 t. nutmeg
1½ t. ReaLemon
1⅛ c. lard or oleo, melted

4 eggs
2¼ c. scalded milk
⅓ c. yeast, instant, heaping full
16 - 16½ c. flour, or until easy
  to handle

In a large bowl, add warm water, eggs (beaten), sugar, salt, ReaLemon, oleo, and nutmeg; mix well. Cool scalded milk and add to this. Add yeast to 6 c. of the flour and mix until smooth. Add the rest of the flour gradually. Knead 100 times, let rise, work down and roll out in amounts easy to handle. Add butter, brown sugar, and cinnamon. Roll, cut, and put on greased cookie sheet. Let rise and bake at 325° - 350° for 20 - 25 min. or until done.

For frosting cook together:

2 c. brown sugar                    2 c. cream

Cook for 5 min. then cool. Add **powdered sugar** until thick. Then add **maple flavor**. Makes 7 - 8 dozen.

## Cinnamon Rolls

*Mrs. Glen (Lydia Mae) Miller*

1 pkg. dry yeast
1 c. lukewarm water
1 c. milk
6 T. sugar
6 T. shortening (oleo)
1½ t. salt
1 egg, beaten
6 c. flour

Soften yeast in warm water. Scald milk; while cooling add sugar, shortening, and salt. When cool add to yeast; add egg and flour to handle nicely. Let rise until double in size. Then make into rolls; roll out to desired thickness and spread with butter, cinnamon, and brown sugar. Let rise again and bake at 400° for 15 min. Yield: 3 dozen.

## Classic Shortbread

*Mrs. Christy (Anna) Bontrager*

½ c. butter, room temp.
⅓ c. powdered sugar
¼ t. vanilla
1 c. flour, unsifted

Cream the butter until it is light. Cream in the powdered sugar, then the vanilla. Now work in the flour. Knead the dough on an unfloured board until it is nice and smooth. Spray the shortbread pan very lightly with a non-stick vegetable oil spray. Firmly press dough into pan. Prick with a fork and bake at 325° for 30 - 35 min. or until very lightly browned. Cool for 10 min. then loosen the edges with a knife and flip onto cutting board. Cut while still warm.

## Coffee Rolls

*Mrs. Eli (Martha) Mullet*

Soften 1 T. yeast in ¼ c. warm water. Then combine:
¾ c. scalded milk
3 T. Crisco
2 T. sugar
1½ t. salt

Cool to lukewarm. Stir in yeast. Add 2½ - 3 c. flour. Let rise until double in size. Pinch off small pieces of dough; dip in 1 c. melted butter and then in cinnamon mixture:
¾ c. sugar
¼ c. brown sugar
2 t. cinnamon
¾ c. chopped nuts

Let rise until double in size. Bake at 350° for 25 - 30 min. Drizzle with powdered sugar glaze.

## Cornmeal Cheddar Biscuits

*Mrs. Freeman (Mabel) Yoder*

1½ c. flour
½ c. yellow cornmeal
2 t. sugar
1 T. baking powder
¼ to ½ t. salt
½ c. butter or margarine
½ c. shredded cheddar cheese
1 c. milk

In a bowl, combine dry ingredients; cut in butter until crumbly. Stir in cheese and milk, just until moistened. Drop by ¼ cupfuls onto an ungreased baking sheet. Bake at 450° for 12-15 min. or until light brown. Serve warm. Makes 1 dozen.

## Delicious Rolls

*Mrs. Daniel A. (Ida) Miller*

1 pkg. dry yeast
¾ c. lukewarm water
1 T. sugar
1 c. scalded milk
2 t. salt

3 T. sugar
4 T. shortening
1 well beaten egg
6 c. bread flour

Put together yeast, warm water, and 1 T. sugar. Let set for 10 min. Put salt, 3 T. sugar, and shortening into scalded milk. When milk is lukewarm, add yeast mixture and the egg. Add flour and knead (a softer dough than for bread). Let rise in a warm place until double in size. Fold down and let rise again. Roll dough out and spread with butter. Sprinkle with brown sugar and cinnamon. Roll together like a jelly roll. Cut with sharp knife about ¼" to ½" thick. Let rise in greased pan until double. Bake at 400° for 15 to 20 min. Put on your favorite icing. Makes 2 pans full. I use string to cut them instead of a knife.

## Easy Dinner Rolls

*Mrs. Ivan (Arlene) Bontrager*

¾ c. scalded milk
⅓ c. shortening
1½ t. salt
¼ c. sugar

¾ c. water
1 egg
4 c. flour
1 T. instant yeast

To scalded milk mix shortening, then salt and sugar until all is dissolved. Add water. Put egg into an empty 8 oz. yogurt cup or anything with a tight-fitting lid, put lid on, and shake well. (A quick way to beat an egg slightly, and no beater to clean up.) Mix egg with first mixture. Mixture should be lukewarm by this time. Add half of the flour and the yeast. Mix well. Gradually add rest of flour. Cover bowl and let rise in warm place until double. Grease 2 muffin pans. Stir dough and drop by spoon into muffin cups. Let rise and bake at 375° for 15 - 20 min. or until golden. Brush with butter. Serve warm.

## Homemade Bisquick Mix

*Mrs. Freeman (Mabel) Yoder*

8 c. flour
1½ c. non-fat dry milk
½ c. baking powder

1 T. salt
1½ c. solid shortening

Mix all dry ingredients together then cut in shortening until crumbly. Makes 3 lbs. This can be used wherever a recipe calls for store-bought Bisquick mix; it works the same.

*Why should a man have more dollars than sense?*

## Hot Potato Rolls

*Mrs. Marvin (Ruby) Shrock*

2 c. milk
½ c. sugar
2 eggs
1 T. salt
1 c. potatoes, mashed
½ c. shortening
2 pkg. yeast dissolved in ½ cup warm water
8 c. flour or more

Pour scalded milk over shortening, sugar, and salt. Add mashed potatoes; cool to lukewarm. Dissolve yeast in warm water and add to first mixture. Then add eggs and flour. Knead until smooth. Let rise until double in bulk. Shape into rolls and let rise again. Bake at 350° for 20 - 25 min.

## Icebox Rolls

*Mrs. Ezra (Mary) Miller*

1 c. sugar
1½ t. salt
1 c. shortening
2 eggs, beaten
6 c. flour
1 cake yeast or 1 pkg. dry yeast
1 c. warm water
1 c. boiling water

Pour boiling water over sugar, shortening, and salt. Let yeast stand in luke-warm water until it starts to rise and gets bubbly. Add to mixture then add beaten eggs and flour; blend well. Place in a large bowl, grease dough and cover. May be stored in refrigerator up to 10 days if you don't want to use it all right away. It will rise in refrigerator so use large bowl. Roll out as for cinnamon rolls and spread with melted butter, brown sugar, and cinnamon. Roll dough up and slice. Place in pans and let rise until light. Bake at 400° for 12 to 15 min. *Note: Dough is real soft but do not use more flour. Just flour hands when working with dough.*

## Cappuccino Muffins

*Mrs. Freeman (Mabel) Yoder*

**Muffins:**
2 c. flour
¾ cup sugar
2½ t. baking powder
½ t. salt
1 t. ground cinnamon
1 c. milk
2 T. instant coffee
½ c. butter, melted
1 egg
1 t. vanilla
¾ c. small chocolate chips

Combine all dry ingredients for muffins. In another bowl, stir coffee into milk until dissolved. Add butter, egg, and vanilla; mix well. Stir into dry ingredients just until moistened. Fold in chocolate chips. Fill greased muffin cups two-thirds full. Bake at 375° for 18 to 20 min. or until tests done. Cool. Serve with following spread.

**Coffee Cream Cheese Spread:**
8 oz. cream cheese (softened)
2 T. sugar
2 t. instant coffee
½ t. vanilla
½ c. small chocolate chips or milk chocolate candy coating cut in bits

Combine all spread ingredients and beat well. Refrigerate until serving. Cut muffins in half and spread generously with filling.

# Lemon Cream Cheese Braid

*Mrs. Freeman (Mabel) Yoder*

1 pkg. or T. yeast
3 T. warm water
½ c. butter or margarine, melted
¼ c. sugar

⅓ c. milk
2 eggs
½ t. salt
3 - 3½ c. flour

Filling:

2 pkgs. cream cheese, softened, 1 (8 oz.) and 1 (3 oz.)
½ c. sugar
1 egg

opt. 1 t. grated lemon peel

In a bowl, combine and dissolve yeast and warm water. Let stand for 5 min. Add sugar, milk, butter, eggs, salt, and 2 c. flour. Mix well; stir in enough of remaining flour to form a soft dough. Knead on a floured surface until smooth and elastic, about 6 - 8 min. Place in a greased bowl, turning once to grease top. Cover and let rise in a warm place until double. Meanwhile, beat filling ingredients in a mixing bowl until fluffy; set aside. Punch dough down. On a floured surface, roll into a 14 x 12" rectangle. Place on a baking sheet; spread filling down center third of rectangle. On each long side, cut 1" strips, 3" into center. Starting at one end fold alternating strips at an angle across filling. Seal end. Cover and let rise for 30 min. Bake at 375° for 25 - 30 min. or until golden brown. Cool. Combine ½ c. powdered sugar, 2 - 3 t. milk and ¼ t. vanilla, then drizzle over cheese braid.

# Melt-in-Your-Mouth Biscuits

*Mrs. Andy (Dorothy) Miller*

2 c. flour
2 T. sugar
2 t. baking powder
¾ t. cream of tartar

½ t. salt
½ c. shortening
⅔ c. milk
1 egg, unbeaten

Mix dry ingredients together and cut in shortening until mixture resembles coarse meal. Pour milk in slowly, mixing well after each addition. Add egg and stir well. Bake 10 - 15 min. in a 450° oven. Yield: 1 dozen.

# Oatmeal Muffins

*Mrs. Ezra (Mary) Miller*

1 c. quick oats
1 c. sour milk
1 egg
¾ c. brown sugar
1 c. flour

1 t. baking powder
1 t. salt
¾ t. soda
⅓ c. shortening

Mix all together and bake in muffin tins. Bake at 350° for 20 - 25 minutes.

## Overnight Rolls

*Mrs. Toby (Martha) Yoder*

1 c. boiling water
½ c. sugar
1 pkg. yeast
4 c. flour
½ c. butter
½ t. salt
2 eggs, beaten

Mix water, sugar, butter, and salt. Cool to lukewarm. Mix ½ t. sugar, 2 T. warm water, and yeast. Stir to dissolve, then add to first mixture. Add eggs. Stir in 2 c. flour and beat 3 min. Add remaining 2 c. flour and beat. Refrigerate until cold. Roll out for rolls. Brush with melted butter; sprinkle with brown sugar and cinnamon. Roll up and cut. Put in a greased pan. Let set on cupboard overnight. In the morning bake at 375° for 15 min. Glaze.

## Pizza Hut Dough

*Mrs. Lester (Mary) Lehman*

1 c. warm water
½ T. yeast, dissolved in warm water
¼ t. salt
⅛ c. oil
2½ c. Robin Hood flour or your favorite flour
black pepper

Place dough in a greased bowl; let rise for ½ hour. I usually knead in enough flour until dough is no longer sticky. 1 batch is enough for 1 pan.

## Pizza Hut Dough

*Sister Mary Yoder*

2 T. yeast
2 t. sugar
⅔ c. warm water

Mix ingredients and let stand 5 min. till bubbly.

2 c. cold water
2 T. sugar
3 c. flour
3 T. vegetable oil
1 T. salt
½ t. oregano
¼ t. garlic salt or powder

Beat batter until smooth. Then beat in yeast mixture. Add **3½ c. more flour;** work until elastic. Let rise until double; put ¼ **c. vegetable oil** on pan. Then press dough on pan. Let rise 5 to 10 min. Add **sauce;** bake at 400° for 10 to 15 min.

*Sorrow looks back,*
*Worry looks around,*
*Faith looks up.*

## Raised Doughnuts
*Mom (Rosa) Bontrager*

4 c. milk
½ lb. margarine
1 T. vanilla
1 T. salt
5 eggs, beaten
Glaze:
2 lbs. powdered sugar

6 c. flour
½ c. lukewarm water
1 c. sugar
5 T. yeast
6 c. flour

2 T. cornstarch

Mix with water to a thin glaze. *Optional: ½ t. maple flavoring.*

Scald milk; remove from heat and add margarine. Cool to lukewarm. Put into a large mixing bowl; add vanilla, salt, and eggs. Gradually add 6 c. flour; beat well. Then mix yeast with warm water. Mix in sugar and add to above mixture; stir well. Add 6 more cups of flour and knead to a smooth elastic dough. Let rise in a warm place until doubled. Roll out to desired thickness and cut with a doughnut cutter. First ones will be ready to deep fat fry by the time the last ones are rolled out. Glaze while warm.

## Soft Biscuits
*Mrs. Clarence T. (Ruby) Yoder*

2¼ c. warm buttermilk (110° - 115°)
2 T. active dry yeast
2½ c. all-purpose flour
2½ c. whole wheat flour
1 T. salt

1 T. baking powder
1 t. soda
⅓ c. sugar or honey
1 c. melted butter or margarine

Dissolve yeast in warm buttermilk; set aside. In a large mixing bowl, combine flour, salt, baking powder, soda, and sugar. Stir in melted butter and the milk with yeast. Mix well. Turn out onto a lightly floured surface. Knead lightly - roll to a ½ inch thickness. Cut with a 2½ in. biscuit cutter (or 4 in. for larger biscuits). Place on a lightly greased baking sheet. Cover and let rise a little in a warm place. Bake at 450° for 8 - 10 min. Lightly brush tops with melted butter (if desired). Yields about 2½ dozen. *This is a favorite in our family. It can be made quickly to take the place of bread if the bread is all gone and not enough time to bake.*

*Happiness is not having what you want,
but wanting what you have.*

## Stickie Quickie Buns

*Mrs. Eldon (Katie) Nisley*

1½ c. flour
1 pkg. yeast
¾ c. milk
¼ c. oil
½ c. water
Topping:
¾ c. butter or oleo
1 c. brown sugar
1 t. cinnamon

¼ c. sugar
1 t. salt
1¾ c. flour
1 egg
1½ c. raw chopped apple (opt.)

¾ c. nuts (opt.)
1 T. light corn syrup
1 T. water

In a large bowl, mix 1½ c. flour and yeast. Heat milk, oil, water, sugar, and salt until warm. Pour into yeast mixture; add egg. Beat on high speed for 3 min. by hand. Stir in 1¾ c. flour (add apple); cover and let rise for 30 min. While dough is rising, mix topping.

Heat all ingredients in pan until melted. Pour in a 13 x 9" pan or 2 large pie pans. Stir down batter and drop by T. on topping. Bake 20 min. at 375°. Cool 1 min. then cover with cookie sheet and invert to remove pan. Makes about 25 buns. This recipe can be prepared the night before if it is covered and refrigerated.

## Stickie Quickie Buns

*Mrs. Simon (Martha) Schmucker*

1½ c. flour
1¾ T. yeast
¾ c. milk
½ c. water
¼ c. butter
Topping:
½ c. butter
1 c. brown sugar
1 t. cinnamon

¼ c. sugar
1 t. salt
1 egg
1½ c. flour

⅓ c. pecans
1 T. Karo
1 T. water

Combine 1½ c. flour and yeast; heat milk, water, butter, sugar, and salt until warm. Pour into yeast mixture. Add beaten egg; beat well. Stir in 1½ c. flour; cover. Let rise for 30 min. Combine the topping in a saucepan; heat until melted. Pour into a 9 x 13" pan. Stir down and drop by T. on topping. Bake at 350° for 15 - 20 min. When done flop on cookie sheet so the topping is on top. Best when served warm; can be made in 1 hour.

## Yeast Pizza

*Mrs. Allen (Elsie) Bontrager*

1 pkg. dry yeast
1 c. warm water
3 c. flour

1 t. sugar
1½ t. salt
¼ c. vegetable oil

Dissolve yeast in warm water; add sugar, salt and oil. Mix thoroughly, add half of flour and beat until no lumps. Gradually add remaining flour; knead dough for 5 min. Roll out on flat sheet and add pizza sauce and your favorite toppings. Bake at 425° for 20 min. or until edges are golden.

# Cookies
# & Bars

*Keep your words soft and sweet.*
*You never know when you'll have to*
*eat them.*

*Trust in the Lord with all thine heart; and lean not unto thine own*
*understanding. In all thy ways acknowledge Him,*
*and He shall direct thy paths.*
*Proverbs 3:5,6*

# Take Time

Take time to think ... It is the source of power.

Take time to play ... It is the secret of perpetual youth.

Take time to read ... It is the fountain of wisdom.

Take time to pray ... It is the greatest power on earth.

Take time to love and be loved ... It is a God-given privilege.

Take time to be friendly ... It is the road to happiness.

Take time to laugh ... It is the music of the soul.

Take time to give ... It is too short a day to be selfish.

Take time to work ... It is the price of success.

Take time to do charity ... It is the key to heaven.

Both our attitude and our behavior must reflect
God's love for us.

**Note:** Keeping a piece of bread in your cookie
container keeps the cookies nice and soft.

## $250 Cookies

*Mom (Elsie) Yoder*

2 c. butter, softened
2 c. white sugar
4 eggs, beaten
2 c. brown sugar
1 t. salt
2 t. soda
2 t. baking powder
2 t. vanilla
4 c. flour
5 c. oatmeal
24 oz. chocolate chips
3 c. nuts
1 (8 oz.) Hershey bar, cut up

Stir all together in a bowl. Use a cookie spatula; a spoon will do. Bake at 375° for 8 to 10 min. Makes 5 dozen cookies. *This cookie recipe has a story behind it! A lady was in a restaurant where they served these cookies. The lady asked for the recipe. The waitress said it cost $250. The lady came up with $2.50 but then it was two hundred and fifty dollars. So that's where it got its name!*

## Apple Butter Cookies

*Mrs. Freeman (Mabel) Yoder*

½ c. butter or margarine, softened
2 c. packed brown sugar
2 eggs
1 c. quick-cooking oats
1 c. apple butter
2 c. flour
1 t. soda
1 t. baking powder
1 t. salt
4 T. milk
1 c. nuts
1 c. raisins

In a large bowl, cream butter and sugar. Beat in eggs, oats, and apple butter. Combine dry ingredients; gradually add to creamed mixture along with the milk. Beat until blended. Stir in nuts and raisins. Chill well. Drop by teaspoon onto lightly greased cookie sheets. Bake at 350° for 15 min. Glaze.

## Buttermilk Cookies

*Mrs. Herman (Elsie) Mullett*

4½ c. white sugar
3 sticks oleo + 1½ c. shortening
  or 6 sticks oleo
1½ T. soda
1½ t. salt
7 eggs
2 c. buttermilk (or 1 T. vinegar
  to 1 c. milk)
1½ T. vanilla flavoring
14½ c. flour
1½ T. baking powder

Butter Icing:
melt ¼ c. butter (no substitute)
3 T. boiling water
½ t. vanilla
2 c. powdered sugar

Stir until smooth.

Beat eggs; add sugar, oleo, and shortening together. Then add rest of ingredients. Works best if chilled overnight. Roll out on floured board and use a cookie cutter. Bake at 350° for 15 min. Makes 98 to 100 cookies. *These are best when they are 3 to 4 days old. If I bake them for church, I bake them on Thursday already.*

## Brown Sugar Cookies
*Grandma (Mary) Bontrager*

2 c. brown sugar
¾ c. shortening, butter or lard
2 eggs
1 c. milk

2 t. soda
2 t. baking powder
vanilla
4 c. flour - 2 c. Robin Hood &
2 c. New Rinkle

Cream shortening and sugar thoroughly. Add eggs; add milk alternately with dry ingredients. Bake at 350°.


## Butterscotch Oatmeal Cookies
*Mom (Rosa) Bontrager*

¾ c. packed brown sugar
¼ c. white sugar
1 c. butter, softened
1 box instant butterscotch pudding
2 eggs

1 t. vanilla
1½ c. flour
1 t. soda
3½ c. quick oatmeal
butterscotch chips

Roll into balls the size of walnuts and roll in powdered sugar. Bake at 375°.


## Chocolate Bit Cookies
*Mrs. Edwin (Annie) Ropp*

2 c. brown sugar
1 c. white sugar
2 c. butter flavored Crisco
6 eggs
1 T. vanilla

2 t. salt
4 t. soda
4 t. cream of tartar
7 c. flour
3 pkg. choc. chips

Mix well in order given. I add one egg at a time and stir it until it is fluffy. Drop by t. on cookie sheet. Bake at 375° for 10-12 min. You can add nuts to the mixture if you wish. Don't bake these till they are brown or they will not be as good.


## Chocolate Chip Cookies
*Mrs. Freeman (Mabel) Yoder*

4 c. sugar
4 c. brown sugar
1 c. softened margarine or butter
3 c. lard or vegetable shortening
4 t. vanilla
1½ c. nuts, optional
8 eggs

3 t. soda
1 t. cream of tartar
4 t. salt
10 c. flour
2 - 6 oz. boxes instant vanilla
pudding
2 pkgs. chocolate chips

Mix sugars, eggs, and shortenings. Add rest of ingredients and mix well. Bake at 350° until set. Remove from oven just before they "go down".

## Chocolate Chip Cookies

*Mrs. Mervin (Gertie) Eash*

1½ c. brown sugar
½ c. white sugar
1 c. shortening
2 T. milk
3 eggs
1 T. vanilla

4 c. flour
2 t. soda
2 t. cream of tartar
1 t. salt
1½ c. choc. chips

Cream together shortening and sugars. Add milk, eggs and vanilla. Stir until smooth. Sift dry ingredients and add to creamed mixture. Add choc. chips. Place on greased cookie sheet. Bake at 400° for 10 min.

## Chocolate Chip Cookies

*Mrs. Noah (Amanda) Lehman*

2¾ c. Wesson oil
2 c. white sugar
4 t. baking soda
1 T. cold water
3 c. choc. chips
2 t. salt

8 eggs, beaten
2 c. brown sugar
2 t. baking powder
9 c. flour
2 t. vanilla
nuts (optional)

Mix sugars then add oil, eggs, vanilla, flour, etc. Bake at 350°. Take out when a little soft. Very good!

## Chocolate-Covered Marshmallow Cookies

*Mrs. Glen (Lydia Mae) Miller*

1¾ c. sifted cake flour
½ t. salt
½ t. baking soda
½ c. unsweetened cocoa
½ c. shortening
1 c. sugar
Frosting:
2 c. sifted powdered sugar
5 T. unsweetened cocoa
⅛ t. salt

1 egg
1 t. vanilla
¼ c. milk
18 large marshmallows, halved
36 pecan halves

3 T. butter or marg., softened
4 to 5 T. light cream

Sift together flour, salt, soda and cocoa. Set aside. In a mixing bowl cream shortening and sugar; add egg, vanilla and milk. Add dry ingredients and mix well. Drop by heaping t. about 2 in. apart onto greased cookie sheets. Bake at 350° for 8 min. Do not overbake. Remove cookies from the oven and top each with a marshmallow half. Return to oven for 2 min. Remove cookies to wire racks to cool. Meanwhile beat all frosting ingredients together. Spread frosting on each cookie and top with a pecan half. Yield: 3 doz.

## Chocolate Crinkles

*Mrs. Clarence (Anna Marie) Miller*

1 c. cocoa
½ c. veg. oil
2 c. sugar
4 eggs
2 c. flour
2 t. baking powder
2 t. vanilla
½ t. salt

Mix oil, cocoa, and sugar. Blend in eggs one at a time. Add vanilla, flour, baking powder and salt. Chill dough several hours or overnight. Drop by t. or make balls. Roll in powdered sugar then in granulated sugar. Bake in a 350° oven very slowly. Will burn easily on bottom if oven is too hot.

## Chocolate Peanut Butter Cookies

*Mrs. Clarence (Anna Marie) Miller*

1 c. shortening
1 c. peanut butter
2 c. white sugar
4 eggs
1 t. soda
3 c. flour
2 t. salt
½ t. cinnamon
1 c. water
2 c. quick oats
1 12 oz. pkg. choc. chips

Cream shortening, peanut butter and sugar until light. Beat in eggs. Add dry ingredients and water. Fold in oatmeal and choc. chips. Drop by t. onto a cookie sheet. Bake at 375° for 12 min. Roll in sugar while still warm.

## Chunky Chocolate Chip Peanut Butter Cookies

*Mrs. Ezra (Mary) Miller*

2½ c. all-pupose flour
1 t. baking soda
1 t. ground cinnamon
1 t. salt
1½ c. or 3 sticks marg.
1 c. packed brown sugar
1 c. granulated sugar
1 c. creamy peanut butter
2 eggs
2 t. vanilla
4 c. choc. chips
1 c. peanuts, walnuts or pecans

Combine flour, baking soda, cinnamon and salt in a small bowl. Beat butter, brown sugar, granulated sugar and peanut butter in large mixer bowl until creamy. Beat in eggs and vanilla. Gradually beat in flour mixture. Stir in choc. chips and nuts. Drop dough by rounded T. onto ungreased baking sheets. Press down slightly. Bake in preheated 375° oven for 7-10 min. or until edges are set but centers are still soft.

*See Jesus in everything and in
everything find happiness.*

# Coffee Cookies

*Mrs. Andy (Dorothy) Miller*

3 c. brown sugar
1½ c. lard
3 eggs
1½ c. coffee (as for drinking)
2 t. vanilla flavoring
Caramel Frosting:
3½ T. milk
2 t. vanilla
¾ c. brown sugar
⅓ c. butter or oleo

1 t. lemon flavoring
1½ t. baking soda
4½ t. baking powder
6 c. flour

2½ c. powdered sugar or
enough to make a spreading
consistency

Mix together sugar and lard and stir in the rest of the wet ingredients. Combine baking soda, baking powder and flour. Stir into first mixture and mix well. Drop by t. on cookie sheet 2 in. apart. Bake in 350° oven for about 10 min. Frost each cookie individually with caramel frosting, putting wax paper between each layer to keep from sticking together. Store in airtight Tupperware container. Yield: 5 doz.

# Cowboy Cookies

*Mrs. Ivan (Arlene) Bontrager*

1 c. soft marg. (from a tub)
½ c. sugar
1½ c. brown sugar
2 eggs
2 c. flour
1 t. soda

½ t. salt
1 T. vanilla
2 c. uncooked oatmeal
1 c. coconut (optional)
1 pkg. (12 oz.) choc. chips
(optional)

Blend marg. and sugars with fork or pastry blender. Add eggs; beat well. Mix in remaining ingredients. Drop by t. onto greased cookie sheet and bake at 350° about 15 min. Tips to avoid hard cookies: Do not melt marg. Add coconut, chips, nuts or raisins. Do not overbake.

# Cup of Everything Cookies

*Mrs. Ora (Susie) Miller*

1 c. marg.
1 c. Rice Krispies
1 c. sugar
2 eggs
1 t. baking soda
½ c. nuts

1 t. cream of tartar
1 c. brown sugar
1 c. coconut
1 c. oatmeal
3½ c. flour
1 c. cooking oil

Mix all together and drop on ungreased pan and bake at 350° for 10 min.

## Dishpan Cookies

*Mrs. Vernon (Polly) Beechy*

2 c. white sugar
2 c. brown sugar
2 c. shortening
4 eggs
Mix together until smooth then add:
1 t. vanilla
5 c. quick oats

2 t. baking powder
1 t. salt
choc. chips, raisins or nuts
   may be added if desired

3½ c. all-purpose flour
2 t. soda

Fix-and-mix bowl from Tupperware is big enough. Bake at 375° until slightly brown. Remove from oven before they are completely set.

## Double Orange Cookies

*Mrs. Freeman (Mabel) Yoder*

1½ c. sugar
1 c. butter or marg., softened
1 c. sour cream
2 eggs
1 can (6 oz.) orange juice
  concentrate, thawed
  save 2 T. for frosting

4 c. flour
1 t. baking powder
1 t. soda
1 t. salt
2 T. grated orange peel
  (optional)

Frosting:
3 oz. pkg. cream cheese, softened
1 T. butter or marg. softened
2 c. powdered sugar

1 T. orange peel (optional)
2 T. milk

In a large bowl cream sugar and butter until fluffy. Add sour cream and eggs. Beat until well blended. Add the remaining concentrate with the dry ingredients to the creamed mixture; mix well. Stir in orange peel. Drop by rounded t. onto lightly greased cookie sheets. Bake at 350° for about 10 min. or until edges just begin to brown. When cookies have cooled combine frosting ingredients and spread a thin glaze over each cookie.

## Golden Carrot Cookies

*Mrs. Freeman (Mabel) Yoder*

¾ c. sugar
¾ c. shortening
1 egg
1¼ c. raw, grated carrots
2 c. sifted flour

½ t. salt
1 t. baking soda
1 t. vanilla
½ t. lemon flavoring

Cream sugar, egg and shortening; beat well. Stir in carrots then add flour, salt, soda and flavorings. Bake at 350° until cookie springs back when touched.

# Grandma's Sugar Cookies

*Mrs. Elmer (Martha) Yoder*
*Submitted by Mabel Yoder in*
*memory of Grandma (Polly) Bontrager*

4 eggs
3 c. sugar
½ c. butter or marg.
½ c. shortening
1 c. milk

1 c. cream
4 t. baking powder
4 t. soda dissolved in 3 T. hot
water
7 c. flour

In a large bowl cream together the first four ingredients. Add the rest and refrigerate or put in a cool place overnight, then roll out on a floured surface. Cut into desired shapes and bake at 350° until cookie springs back when lightly touched.

# Holiday Cutouts

*Mrs. Christie (Anna) Yoder*

2 c. butter
3 c. white sugar
5 eggs
1 c. sour cream
1 t. salt

1 t. soda
1 t. vanilla
1 t. baking powder
¼ c. boiling water
7 c. flour

Cream butter and sugar. Add other ingredients. Mix well. Chill dough. Roll and cut out. Bake at 375° for 8 min. Don't overbake. The longer they sit the better.

# Holstein Cookies

*Regina Miller*

½ c. marg., softened
¼ c. sugar
¾ c. packed brown sugar
1 t. baking soda
1 t. vanilla

2 eggs
2½ c. flour
1 pkg. choc. chips
1 box vanilla pudding (instant)
1 box choc. pudding (instant)

To make the two color cookies, make one batch of cookie dough with vanilla pudding and also one batch of cookie dough with choc. pudding. Then take a little of each dough and roll together, then roll into white sugar before baking. Bake at 350°.

*The foundation of understanding is the willingness to listen.*

## Honey Sugar Snaps

*Mrs. Freeman (Mabel) Yoder*

2 c. white sugar
2 c. brown sugar
4 eggs
6 t. soda
9 c. flour
1 c. softened butter or margarine

1 c. precreamed shortening
1 c. honey
2 t. nutmeg
1 t. salt
*1 c. sugar
*2 t. cinnamon

In a large bowl combine sugars and shortenings. Add eggs and beat well. Add honey and dry ingredients. If mixture is too dry to mix with a spoon, mix with hands. *In a small bowl combine the 1 c. sugar and 2 t. cinnamon. Shape dough into balls and roll into sugar-cinnamon mixture and bake at 350° until golden brown. The dough is very light brown and the cookies will be a very deep golden brown, and crinkly on top when done. A very good cookie to dip into coffee, cappuccino or milk.

## Iced Oatmeal Raisin Cookies

*Mrs. Ivan (Arlene) Bontrager*

2 c. raisins                          1½ c. water

Stew raisins by cooking with water until water is almost gone. Put in large bowl and add:

2 c. brown sugar
2 c. white sugar
4 c. oatmeal
2 c. lard or shortening (heated)

1 t. salt
1 c. hot water
2 t. soda

Mix well and let stand 5-10 min. Then add:

6 eggs
2 t. cinnamon
2 t. cloves

½ c. milk
1 c. chopped nuts (optional)

Mix. Last add:

6 c. flour                          4 t. baking powder

Drop by t. onto a greased cookie sheet. Bake at 375° for 10 min. When cool ice with the following:

3 c. powdered sugar
6 T. milk

¼ t. maple flavoring
1 t. vanilla

## Monster Cookies (small batch)

*Mrs. Noah (Amanda) Lehman*

1 stick oleo
1 c. brown sugar
1 c. white sugar
1 t. vanilla
2 t. soda
1¾ c. flour

3 eggs
1½ c. peanut butter
1 t. light Karo
3 c. quick oats
¼ lb. choc. chips
¼ lb. M&M's

Mix in order given and bake at 350°. Do not overbake.

## No-Bake Chocolate Oatmeal Cookies

*Mary Miller*

2 c. white sugar
½ c. butter
2 T. cocoa
½ c. choc. chips
½ c. milk

Boil one min. then mix with 3 c. quick oats. Let stand for one hour before eating them. Yield: 45 cookies.

## Oddy's Cookies

*Mrs. Vern (Irene) Schlabach*

3 c. brown sugar
2 c. shortening
1 pkg. choc. chips
4 eggs
2 c. oatmeal
½ c. coconut
½ c. nuts
4 c. flour
2 t. baking soda
1 lb. dates or raisins
vanilla
1 t. salt

Combine the dry ingredients with the eggs and shortening. Stir in choc. chips and dates or raisins. Drop on cookie sheets and bake in 350° oven 8 min. or little less.

## Old-Fashioned Apple Cookies

*Mrs. Daniel (Esther) Yoder*

½ c. butter
1¼ c. brown sugar
1 egg
¼ c. milk
1 t. vanilla
3 c. quick oats
1 c. flour
¼ t. nutmeg
1 t. cinnamon
½ t. soda
½ t. salt
1 c. chopped apples
¾ c. raisins (optional)
¾ c. walnuts (optional)

Mix together and bake 10 min. at 400°. Do not overbake.

## Outrageous Chocolate Chip Cookies

*Mrs. Milo (Lorene) Yoder*

2 c. sugar
1½ c. brown sugar
2 c. oleo or butter
2 c. peanut butter
2 t. vanilla
4 eggs
4 c. flour
2 c. oatmeal
4 t. soda
1 t. salt
12 oz. choc. chips

Mix together and roll in balls and press on cookie sheet. Bake at 350° for 10-15 min. till done. This can also be spread on cookie sheets and be baked as bars.

*When God measures men,*
*He puts the tape around the heart,*
*not the head.*

## Overnight Cookies

*Gandma (Mary) Bontrager*

6 c. flour
1 t. soda
1 T. cream of tartar
4 eggs

1 c. butter (half & half oleo & butter)
3 c. brown sugar

Sift 6 c. New Rinkle flour; add 1 T. soda, then sift again. Then add 1 T. cream of tartar and sift once more. Mix 1 c. butter well with flour. Beat 4 eggs; add 3 c. brown sugar. When sugar is dissolved, add to the flour. Shape into a roll. Let stand in fridge overnight. Then cut in slices and bake at 350°. Yield: 3 doz.

## PBO Snackers

*Mrs. David (Rachel) Plank*

1 c. brown sugar
1 c. white sugar
2 eggs
½ c. oleo
½ c. veg. oil
¾ c. peanut butter
1 t. vanilla

3 c. oatmeal
1 c. flour
1 t. cinnamon (optional)
¼ t. nutmeg
1 t. soda
½ t. salt
1½ c. choc. chips

Mix all ingredients in first column well. Add dry ingredients. Bake at 350° for 12 min.

## Peanut Butter Chocolate Chip Cookies *Mrs. Milo (Lorene) Yoder*

1 c. oleo
1 c. white sugar
1 c. brown sugar
1 c. peanut butter
2 eggs

1½ t. soda
1 t. baking powder
½ t. salt
1 c. choc. chips
2½ c. flour

Beat together first 5 ingredients, then add the rest. Drop by t. on cookie sheet and bake until done.

## Peanut Butter Fingers

*Mrs. Sam (Martha) Schrock*

½ c. marg.
½ c. white sugar
⅓ c. peanut butter
1 c. pastry flour
**Mix together and add:**
½ t. soda
**Blend and add:**
1 c. quick oats

½ c. brown sugar
1 egg, beaten
¼ t. salt

½ t. vanilla

Spread in 9 x 13 in. cake pan and bake at 350° for 20 min. Do not overbake. Sprinkle **1 c. choc. chips** over top. Mix **½ c. powdered sugar, ¼ c. peanut butter, and 2 - 4 T. milk.** Drizzle this mixture over top. It takes 1½ batch for 1 cookie sheet.

# Pecan Fingers

*Mrs. Christie (Anna) Yoder*

¾ c. shortening (half marg.)
¾ c. confectioner's sugar
1 ½ c. Gold Medal flour
2 eggs
2 T. flour
1 c. brown sugar
½ t. baking powder
½ c. flaked coconut
½ t. salt
½ t. vanilla
½ c. walnuts

Heat oven to 350°. Cream shortening and confectioner's sugar. Blend in 1 ½ c. flour. Press evenly in bottom of ungreased 13 x 9 x 2 baking pan. Bake 12-15 min. Mix remaining ingredients. Spread over hot baked layer and bake 20 min. longer.

# Pride of "Wisconsin" Cookies

*Mrs. Harry (Edna Mae) Bontrager*

1 c. brown sugar
1 c. white sugar
1 c. precreamed shortening
2 eggs
2 c. flour
1 t. salt
1 t. soda
1 t. baking powder
1 t. vanilla
1 pkg. choc. chips
3 c. quick oats

Cream together sugars and shortenings. Add well beaten eggs and mix well. Add one cup flour, salt, soda, vanilla and baking powder. Stir well again. Add choc. chips and 2 c. oatmeal and mix well. Then add one more c. flour and 1 more cup oatmeal and mix in with your hands. Drop on cookie sheets with cookie dispenser or roll into balls and flatten a little bit. Bake at 375° until light brown. When storing them add a piece of bread to keep them nice and soft.

# Pudding Cookies

*Mrs. Ivan (Arlene) Bontrager*

1 c. Bisquick
1 pkg. instant pudding
   (3 oz.), your fav. flavor
¼ c. veg. oil
1 egg
1 t. baking powder

Heat oven to 350°. Mix all ingredients till dough forms a ball. Drop by t. onto greased cookie sheets. Press down to flatten balls of dough. Bake approx. 8 min. These are easy for children to make or handy for a very busy day. Takes about 10 min. to make and bake.

*Some people treat God like a lawyer;*
*they only go to Him when they are in trouble.*

## Soft Chocolate Chip Cookies

*Mrs. Lloyd (Edna) Raber*

4 c. brown sugar
2 c. shortening
4 eggs
4 T. hot water
1½ T. vanilla
7 c. flour
1 T. baking powder
½ t. salt
2 (12 oz.) pkg. choc. chips
1 large box instant vanilla
  pudding

Beat the first five ingredients with mixer for 10 min. or until creamy. Stir in the rest until well blended. Drop by t. onto greased cookie sheet. Bake at 375° for 10 - 12 min. Do not overbake. These freeze very well. Makes 6 dozen.

## Soft Christmas Cookies

*Mrs. Leland (Orpha) Yoder*

1 c. shortening
1½ c. white sugar
3 eggs
1 c. sour cream
1 t. baking powder
½ t. salt
3 t. soda
4 c. flour

Cream shortening and sugar; add eggs and the sour cream. Stir together the baking powder, salt, baking soda and the flour and add to creamed mixture. Roll and cut in desired shapes. If I'm in a hurry I just drop by t. on a cookie sheet and press down with the bottom of a cup which was made wet and then dipped into sugar. After each cookie you have to dip back into the sugar again. Bake at 350° for 10 min. Ice with powdered sugar icing and decorate.

## Soft Oatmeal Cookies

*Mrs. Lonnie (Norma Mae) Bontrager*

1 c. oil
2 eggs
1¼ c. sugar
⅓ c. molasses
1¾ c. flour
1 t. soda
1 t. salt
1 t. cinnamon
2 c. quick oats
1 c. raisins
½ c. nuts

Mix the first four ingredients. Sift together and add flour, soda, salt and cinnamon. Mix and add raisins, nuts and oatmeal. Drop by spoonful onto greased cookie sheet. Bake 10 min. at 400°.

## Sour Cream Sugar Cookies

*Mrs. LaVern (Martha) Yoder*

2½ c. brown sugar
2 c. white sugar
½ c. oleo
1⅓ c. lard
3 eggs
1 c. milk
1 T. vanilla
2 c. sour cream (commercial)
10 c. flour
2 t. soda
1 t. salt

Mix sugar, oleo, lard and eggs. Mix well then add rest of ingredients and drop by t. into flour. Shape into balls and bake at 350° just until done.

## Sour Cream Cookies

*Mrs. Lloyd (Edna) Raber*

¾ c. shortening
1½ c. brown sugar
2 eggs
½ t. baking powder
1 t. soda

1 t. vanilla
½ t. salt
2½ c. flour
1 c. thick sour cream

Mix sugar, vanilla and shortening. Add eggs and sour cream. Next add dry ingredients. Bake at 375°.

**Golden Icing:**
Brown ½ c. butter; stir in 1 c. powdered sugar and 1 t. vanilla. Add hot water until right to spread.

## Sour Cream Raisin Bars

*Mrs. Lloyd (Edna) Raber*

1¾ c. oatmeal
1¾ c. flour
1 c. sugar (½ white & ½ brown)
1 c. oleo
**Filling:**
4 egg yolks
1 c. white sugar
1 T. cornstarch

1 t. soda
1 t. baking powder
pinch of salt
½ t. vanilla

2 c. sour cream
2 c. raisins

Mix sugar and oleo. Add other dry ingredients. Pat ⅔ of crumbs in a 9 x 13 in. cake pan. Bake 15 min. at 325°. Cool. Filling: Mix together and boil. Stir often. Pour over crumbs and cover with remaining crumbs. Bake another 20 min.

## Whoopie Pies

*Mrs. Vern (Irene) Schlabach*

4½ c. flour
2 c. sugar
1 c. shortening
2 eggs
1 c. sour milk
**Filling:**
4 c. powdered sugar
1 T. vanilla
4 T. flour

1 c. hot water
2 t. vanilla
1 t. salt
2 t. soda
½ c. cocoa

2 egg whites
1½ c. shortening

Cream together sugar, eggs and shortening. Sift flour, cocoa and salt. Add to creamed mixture alternately with sour milk and vanilla. Add soda to hot water and add gradually to the dough. Drop by t. on cookie sheets and bake at 400° until cookie springs back when lightly touched. For filling beat egg whites and blend in the rest, and cream well. When cookies have cooled put filling between two cookies. Variations: Flour may be omitted and 6 T. milk added to filling, and cookies baked at 350° - 375°. To make sour milk add 1 T. vinegar to 1 c. milk.

## Apple Squares

*Mrs. Freeman (Mabel) Yoder*

2 eggs
2 c. sugar
¾ c. veg. oil
2½ c. flour
1 t. cinnamon

3 c. diced, peeled tart apples
1 c. chopped nuts
¾ c. butterscotch chips
3 t. baking powder
1 t. salt

In a bowl combine sugar, eggs, oil, baking powder and salt and mix well. Stir in flour and cinnamon (batter will be thick). Stir in apples and nuts. Spread into a greased 13 x 9 in. pan. Sprinkle with chips. Bake at 350° for 35-40 min. or until golden and toothpick inserted in middle comes out clean. Cool before cutting. This is very moist and delicious!

## Bridge Mix Bars

*Mrs. Lonnie (Norma) Bontrager*

3 T. butter
½ pkg. white or yellow cake mix
1½ c. miniature marshmallows
1 c. choc. chips

1 c. flaked coconut
1 c. nuts, chopped
1 can Eagle Brand milk

Heat oven to 350°. Melt butter in 9 x 13 in. pan in oven. Spread evenly. Sprinkle dry cake mix over butter; layer marshmallows, choc. chips, coconut and nuts over cake mix. Spread milk evenly over the top. Bake 20-30 min. or until golden brown.

## Brownies

*Mrs. Toby (Martha) Yoder*

**Sift together:**
¾ c. flour
2 T. cocoa

¼ t. baking powder
¼ t. salt

**Combine:**
½ c. shortening

¾ c. sugar

Cream well. Blend in 2 eggs one at a time and add dry ingredients. Add: **1 t. vanilla.** Spread in greased 9 x 13 in. pan. Bake at 350° for 15 min. Remove from oven and place 12 large marshmallows cut in half or 2 c. mini marshmallows on top. Return to oven for 3 min. till marshmallows are soft. Spread with the following frosting.

**Combine:**
½ c. brown sugar, ¼ c. water, 2 T. cocoa (heaping). Bring to a boil and boil for 3 min. Add **3 T. butter, 1 t. vanilla and 1½ c. powdered sugar.** Spread over marshmallows and cut.

*It is better to fill a little place right
than a big place wrong.*

## Brownie Mix

*Mrs. Lester (Mary) Lehman*

6 c. all-purpose flour
4 t. baking powder
4 t. salt
Mix and store in container.
**To make brownies:**
2½ c. brownie mix
2 eggs, beaten
Bake at 350°.

8 c. sugar
1 8 oz. can cocoa
2 c. Crisco

1 t. vanilla
1 c. chopped nuts

## Cappuccino Bars

*Mrs. Freeman (Mabel) Yoder*

3 c. flour
1¼ c. sugar
1 c. butter or Crisco all-
   veg. shortening
¼ c. corn syrup or reg.
   pancake syrup
2 eggs
1 t. vanilla

1 t. rum extract
2 T. instant espresso or
   coffee powder
¾ t. baking powder
½ t. soda
½ t. salt
1½ c. mini semisweet
   choc. chips

Heat oven to 350°; grease a 10 x 15 in. pan. A reg. 9 x 13 pan may also be used. Set aside. Combine sugar and shortening in a large bowl. Blend well; add eggs, syrup, vanilla and rum extract. Beat until light and fluffy. Combine flour, coffee powder, baking powder, soda and salt. Add gradually to creamed mixture at low speed. Mix until just blended. Do not beat. Spread dough in an even layer on bottom of pan using a spatula. Sprinkle with choc. chips. Bake 30-35 min. DO NOT OVERBAKE. Place pan on a cooling rack. Cool 10 min. before cutting into bars. Makes 32 bars.

## Caramel Turtle Brownies

*Mrs. Freeman (Mabel) Yoder*

1 - 16 oz. tub soft caramel dip
   or 14 oz. pkg. caramels
⅔ c. evaporated milk
¾ c. butter or marg., melted

1 box German choc. cake mix
1 c. choc. chips
1 c. chopped nuts

Preheat oven to 350°. In heavy saucepan combine caramels and ⅓ c. of the evaporated milk. Cook over low heat until caramels are melted. Set aside. In a large bowl, combine dry cake mix, butter, ⅓ c. evaporated milk and nuts if desired. Stir until well blended then press half of dough in a greased 13 x 9 in. cake pan. Bake at 350° for 6 min. Remove from oven and spread choc. chips over baked crust. Spread on caramel mixture and crumble the other half of dough over caramel mixture. Bake 15 - 18 min. Refrigerate 30 min. before serving.

## Cherry Bars

*Mrs. Allen (Elsie) Bontrager*

1¾ c. sugar
4 eggs
1 t. vanilla
1 c. oleo
3 c. flour
1½ t. baking powder
1½ t. salt
cherry pie filling

Cream sugar and oleo until fluffy. Add eggs and vanilla. Beat well. Sift in dry ingredients, stirring until blended. Spread dough in 15 x 10 in. baking sheet. Save a little dough. Spread with pie filling and dot or drizzle with rest of dough. Bake at 350° for 45 min.

**Lemon Frosting:**
1¼ c. powdered sugar
2 T. lemon juice
1 T. melted oleo

Mix and drizzle on bars while warm.

## Chocolate Chip Cream Cheese Bars *Mrs. Herman (Elsie) Mullett*

1 white or choc. cake mix
2 eggs
⅓ c. oil
8 oz. cream cheese
⅓ c. white sugar
¾ c. choc. chips

Mix cake mix, one egg and the oil together until crumbly. Reserve one c. of the mixture and put the rest into a 9 x 13 in. cake pan. Bake at 350° for 15 min. Mix remaining ingredients together and add on top of baked layer. Put reserved crumbs on top. Bake for another 25 min.

## Chocolate Chip Zucchini Bars

*Mrs. Orva (Marietta) Yoder*

½ c. butter
½ c. oil
1¾ c. sugar
2 eggs
1 t. vanilla
¼ c. cocoa
¼ c. choc. chips
1 t. soda
½ t. salt
½ t. cinnamon
2 c. shredded zucchini
2½ c. flour
½ c. sour milk
¼ c. chopped nuts

Cream butter, oil and sugar. Add eggs, vanilla and milk. Add dry ingredients and beat well. Stir in zucchini and ¼ c. choc. chips. Spread in a greased 11 x 17 in. pan. Sprinkle nuts and additional ½ c. choc. chips on top of batter. Bake at 325° for 40 - 45 min.

*Love in your heart wasn't put there to stay;*
*love isn't love till you give it away.*

## Chocolate Mint Brownies
*Mrs. Orva (Marietta) Yoder*

1 c. brown sugar
1 c. butter,
  no substitute
2 T. cocoa
1 egg
½ c. milk
1¾ c. flour
½ t. soda
1 c. walnuts
1 t. vanilla

Mix sugar and cocoa; add egg and melted butter. Add flour alternately with milk. Bake in 350° oven for 15 - 20 min.

**Filling:**

2 c. powdered sugar
1 T. water
3 drops green food color
½ c. butter (softened),
  no substitute
½ t. mint extract

Combine filling ingredients in a med. mixing bowl and beat until creamy. Spread over completely cooled brownies. Soften butter but do not melt it; set in room temp. Refrigerate until set.

**Topping:**

1 10 oz. pkg. choc. chips    9 T. butter

Melt choc. chips and butter over low heat. Let cool for 30 min. or until lukewarm, stirring occasionally. Spread over filling and chill before cutting. Store in refrigerator. Delicious!

## Chocolate Pecan Brownies
*Mrs. LaVern (Martha) Yoder*

¾ c. flour
¼ t. baking soda
¾ c. white sugar
⅓ c. butter
2 T. water
1 12 oz. pkg. choc. chips
1 t. vanilla
2 eggs
½ c. chopped pecans

Preheat oven to 325°. Grease a 9 in. square baking dish. Mix flour and soda. Bring to a boil sugar, butter and water; when it comes to boil remove from heat and stir in 1 c. of choc. chips and vanilla. Stir until smooth. Cool completely then add eggs 1 at a time, beating well after each addition. Gradually stir in flour mixture then add choc. chip mixture and pour into pan and bake for 30 - 35 min.

*When the outlook is not good, try the uplook.*

# Double Choc. Chip Brownies  *Mrs. Lonnie (Norma Mae) Bontrager*

2 c. choc. chips
½ c. butter or marg.
3 eggs
1 ¼ c. flour

1 c. white sugar
¼ t. baking soda
1 t. vanilla
½ c. nuts

Melt 1 c. choc. chips and butter in large saucepan over low heat; stir until smooth. Remove from heat. Add eggs; stir well. Add flour, sugar, baking soda and vanilla; stir well. Stir in remaining choc. chips and nuts. Spread in greased 13 x 9 in. baking pan. Bake at 350° for 18 to 22 min.

# Double Choc. Crumble Bars  *Mrs. Alvin (Katie Mae) Yoder*

½ c. butter
¾ c. sugar
2 eggs
1 t. vanilla
¾ c. all-purpose flour
Topping:
2 c. miniature marshmallows
1 pkg. (6 oz.) choc. chips

½ c. chopped pecans
2 T. cocoa
¼ t. baking powder
¼ t. salt

1 c. creamy peanut butter
1 ½ c. crispy rice cereal

Cream butter and sugar. Beat in eggs and vanilla. Set aside. Stir together flour, nuts, cocoa, baking powder and salt. Stir into egg mixture. Spread in bottom of greased pan (9 x 13). Bake at 350° for 15 - 20 min. Sprinkle marshmallows evenly on top. Bake 3 min. more then cool. Combine choc. chips and peanut butter. Cook and stir over low heat until choc. is melted then stir in cereal. Spread mixture on top of cooled bars. Chill and cut in bars. Refrigerate. Yield: 3-4 doz.

# Dreamy Fudge Bar Cookies  *Mrs. Marvin (Ruby) Shrock*

1 c. shortening
2 eggs
1 t. soda
3 c. rolled oats
Chocolate Filling:
1 14 oz. Eagle Brand milk
1 c. choc. chips

2 c. brown sugar
2½ c. flour
dash salt

1 T. butter
1 c. walnuts

Cream shortening and sugar and beat in eggs. Add dry ingredients and set aside. In saucepan melt choc. chips, milk and butter over low heat. Stir until smooth; cool slightly and add walnuts. Press ¾ of oatmeal mixture in bottom of jelly roll pan and cover with chocolate mixture. Sprinkle remaining oatmeal mixture on top and flatten slightly. Bake at 350° for 20 min. or until golden brown.

## Frosted Brownie Pizza

*Mrs. Freeman (Mabel) Yoder*

¾ c. flour
⅛ t. salt
2 squares unsweetened choc. (1 oz. each)

½ c. butter (no substitute)
1 c. sugar
2 eggs, beaten

Frosting:
1 c. powdered sugar
⅓ c. creamy peanut butter

1 ½ t. vanilla
2 to 4 T. milk

Toppings:
¾ c. M&M's
½ c. coconut

½ c. chopped pecans
1 ½ c. miniature marshmallows

In a heavy saucepan over low heat melt butter, choc. and sugar. Remove pan from heat and stir in flour until smooth. Add eggs and beat until smooth. Spread onto a greased 12" pizza pan. Bake at 350° for 15 min. or until a toothpick near the center comes out clean. Cool completely. For frosting: In a mixing bowl mix powdered sugar, vanilla, peanut butter and enough milk to spreading consistency. Spread over crust. Sprinkle with toppings and return to oven for 2-3 min., enough to melt marshmallows lightly.

## Fudge Nut Bars

*Mrs. Christy (Anna) Bontrager*

2 c. brown sugar
1 c. butter
2 eggs
2 t. vanilla

2½ c. flour
1 t. salt
1 t. soda
3 c. quick oats

Cream butter, sugar, eggs and vanilla. Sift together dry ingredients and add to creamed mixture. Last add oatmeal. Place ⅔ of mixture in pan.

Melt:
12 oz. choc. chips
1 can Eagle Brand milk
2 T. butter

½ t. salt
2 t. vanilla
1 c. nuts

Spread over mixture in pan. Sprinkle the remaining crumbs over all. Bake at 350° for approx. 20 min.

*Swallow your pride occasionally; it's not fattening.*

## Granola Bars
*Mom (Elsie) Yoder*

1½ lbs. marshmallows
¼ c. butter
¼ c. oil
½ c. honey
¼ c. peanut butter
8 c. Rice Krispies

2 c. oatmeal
1 c. peanuts
1 c. coconut
1 c. graham cracker crumbs
1 c. choc. chips or M&M's
1½ c. raisins

Melt marshmallows with butter. Add oil, honey and peanut butter. Add rest of ingredients and press into pan.

## Hawaiian Delights
*Mary Miller*

1 c. butter
1 c. white sugar
1 egg
1 t. vanilla
1 c. quick oats

2 c. flour
2 t. baking powder
½ t. salt
1 c. crushed pineapple, drained
Save juice for icing.

Mix in order given then drop by t. on ungreased cookie sheet. Bake at 350° 5 - 10 min.

**Icing:**

⅛ c. butter, softened
1 c. powdered sugar

⅛ c. pineapple juice

## Hershey Choco Peppermint Log
*Mrs. Merlin (Mary) Lehman*

4 eggs, separated
1 t. vanilla
⅓ c. cocoa
½ t. baking powder
⅛ t. salt

½ c. white sugar
⅓ c. white sugar
½ c. flour
¼ t. soda
⅓ c. water

Line a 15½ x 10½ x 1 in. jelly roll pan with foil then oil the foil. Beat egg whites until foamy. Gradually add ½ c. sugar, beating until stiff peaks form. Set aside. Beat egg yolks with vanilla on high about 3 min. Gradually add ⅓ c. sugar, beating 2 min. Combine dry ingredients then add to egg yolk mixture alternately with water. Fold choc. mixture into egg whites. Spread evenly in pan. Bake at 375° for 12 - 15 min. Put on towel with powdered sugar and roll up.

**Peppermint Filling:**

Beat **1 c. Rich's topping** then add ¼ c. powdered sugar, ¼ c. crushed peppermint candy or 1 t. mint extract and a few drops of red food color.

**Choc. Glaze:**

Melt **2 T. butter** in saucepan over low heat. Add **2 T. cocoa** and **water,** stirring constantly until it thickens. (Do not boil.) Cool slightly. Blend in **1 c. powdered sugar and ½ t. vanilla.**

## Holiday Squares

*Mrs. Freeman (Mabel) Yoder*

1½ c. sugar
1 c. butter or marg.
4 eggs
1 t. salt
2 c. flour

1 t. lemon flavoring
1 can cherry, blueberry,
raspberry or pie filling
of your choice

Cream butter and sugar till light and fluffy; beat in eggs one at a time. Beat in flour, flavoring and salt. Pour batter into a well greased 10 x 15 in. pan. Mark off 20 squares and place a heaping T. of filling on each square. Bake at 350° for 40 - 50 min. Make a thin frosting of ½ **c. of powdered sugar** and **2 T. milk** and drizzle over bars while still warm. Or sift **powdered sugar** over while still warm.

## Marble Squares

*Mrs. Lester (Mary) Lehman*

1 c. melted oleo
¾ c. white sugar
⅔ c. brown sugar
2 eggs
½ t. salt

1 t. soda
1 t. vanilla
2¼ c. flour
1 c. choc. chips

Mix all ingredients except choc. chips and spread in 9 x 13 in. pan. Sprinkle choc. chips on top and bake at 350° for 3 min. Remove and cut through batter with knife for marble effect. Put in oven and bake 20 - 30 min. Do not overbake. Cut in squares while still warm. Add nuts if desired.

## Marshmallow Chip Bars

*Regina Miller*

¼ c. oleo
½ c. butterscotch chips
¾ c. flour
⅓ c. brown sugar
1 t. baking powder
1 beaten egg

1 t. vanilla
1 t. salt
1 c. choc. chips
1 c. mini marshmallows
¼ c. nuts (optional)

Melt oleo and butterscotch chips over low heat, stirring constantly. Cool then add and mix well the flour, sugar, baking powder, egg, vanilla and salt. Fold in choc. chips, nuts and marshmallows. Bake in 9" pan for 15 min. at 325°. Do not overbake.

*Pray earnestly; you can't expect a thousand-dollar answer to a ten-cent prayer.*

## Mint Brownies Supreme
*Mrs. Toby (Martha) Yoder*

21½ oz. pkg. fudge brownie mix
½ c. water
½ c. oil
1 egg
½ t. mint extract

**Filling:**
½ c. marg., softened
3 oz. cream cheese
2½ c. powdered sugar
3 T. creme de menthe syrup
green food coloring if desired

**Frosting:**
1 c. choc. chips
⅓ c. marg.

Heat oven to 350°. In a large bowl combine brownie ingredients; beat 50 strokes with spoon. Spread in a greased 9 x 13 in. pan. Bake 30 min. or so. Do not overbake. Cool completely. In a med. bowl combine margarine and cream cheese; beat until light and fluffy. Add powdered sugar and creme de menthe syrup and 1-2 drops food coloring. Beat until fluffy. Chill. Melt margarine for frosting on low heat; add choc. chips and stir constantly until melted. Spread over chilled brownies. Keep refrigerated. *I don't usually have brownie mix so I make my own brownie recipe and add ½ t. mint extract.*

## Nutrition Bars
*Mrs. Clarence T. (Ruby) Yoder*

Combine:
1 c. soft butter
1 c. honey
Add:
1 t. salt
1 t. soda
2 c. oatmeal
3 c. whole wheat flour
1 c. coconut

4 eggs, beaten
2 t. vanilla

½ c. sunflower seeds
  (or nutmeats)
½ c. carob chips
½ c. raisins

Mix together well and press into a cookie sheet. Bake at 350° for 20 - 25 min. Let cool and cut into bars. Delicious!

*There is no limit to what man can do if he doesn't care who gets the credit.*

## Peanut Butterscotch Fudgies

*Mrs. Ivan (Arlene) Bontrager*

Cookie Dough:

| | |
|---|---|
| 1 c. butter or margarine | 2 c. all-purpose flour |
| 1½ c. brown sugar | 1 t. soda |
| 1 egg | 1 t. salt |
| 1 T. vanilla | 2½ c. quick oatmeal, uncooked |

Beat butter and sugar together until light and fluffy. Blend in egg and vanilla. Add flour, soda, and salt. Mix well; stir in oats.

Filling:

| | |
|---|---|
| 1 (15 oz.) can sweetened condensed milk | 2 T. butter or margarine |
| | ½ t. salt |
| 1 (6 oz.) pkg. (1 c.) butterscotch flavored morsels | 1 t. vanilla |
| 1 c. chunky-style peanut butter | |

Melt first 5 filling ingredients in heavy saucepan over low heat, blending until smooth. Add vanilla.

Press half of cookie dough into greased 13 x 9" baking pan. Spread filling evenly over dough in pan. Arrange remaining dough on top and press down slightly. Bake in 350° oven for 35 to 40 min. Cool; cut into squares. Yield: 1 panful.

## Pecan Squares

*Mrs. Andy (Dorothy) Miller*

Crust:

| | |
|---|---|
| 3 c. flour | 1 c. butter or oleo, softened |
| ½ c. sugar | ½ t. salt |

Filling:

| | |
|---|---|
| 4 eggs | 3 T. melted butter or oleo |
| 1½ c. light or dark corn syrup | 1½ t. vanilla |
| 1½ c. sugar | 2½ c. chopped pecans |

Blend together the crust ingredients until mixture resembles coarse crumbs and press into a greased 13 x 9" cake pan. Bake at 350° for 20 min. Meanwhile, combine the first 5 ingredients of the filling and stir in the pecans. Spread evenly over hot crust and bake at 350° for 25 min. or until set. Cool and cut into squares. Store in airtight container. Yield: 2 dozen.

*Love is space and time measured by the heart.*

## Pecan Tarts

*Mrs. Glenn (Lydia Mae) Miller*

1 pkg. (3 oz.) cream cheese,
  softened
½ c. butter or oleo, softened
Filling:
1 egg
¾ c. packed brown sugar
1 T. butter or oleo (melted)

1 c. all-purpose flour
¼ t. salt

1 t. vanilla
⅔ c. chopped pecans
maraschino cherry halves (opt.)

In mixing bowl, beat cream cheese & butter. Blend in flour and salt; chill for 1 hour. Shape into 1 inch balls; press into the bottom and up the sides of greased mini muffin cups. For filling, beat the egg in small mixing bowl. Add brown sugar, butter, and vanilla; mix well. Stir in pecans. Spoon into shells. Bake at 325° for 25 - 30 min. Cool in pan on wire rack. Put maraschino cherries on top if desired. Yields about 20.

## Pumpkin Bars

*Mrs. Leroy (Sara) Yoder*

4 eggs, beaten
1 c. salad oil
2 c. sugar
1 c. pumpkin
½ t. salt

2 t. cinnamon
1 t. soda
1 t. baking powder
2 c. flour

Combine all ingredients and pour into greased and floured long cookie sheet. Bake at 350° for 20 - 25 min. or center springs back when touched.
Frosting:

3 oz. cream cheese
4 T. oleo
¾ lb. powdered sugar

1 t. vanilla
1 t. milk

I use this if I happen to have cream cheese. If not, other frosting is alright too. It is the best with cream cheese.

## Raisin Puffs

*Mrs. Mervin (Emma) Yoder*

1 c. water
1½ c. raisins
3½ c. flour
1 t. baking soda
1½ c. sugar

1 c. margarine, softened
2 eggs
1 t. vanilla
½ c. sugar
1 t. cinnamon

In saucepan cook raisins in boiling water; boil until water is gone. Cool; combine flour, soda, and ½ t. salt; beat together sugar and margarine until combined. Add eggs and vanilla; beat well. Add dry ingredients to beaten mixture; beat until blended. Stir in raisins. Combine the ½ c. sugar and cinnamon. Shape dough into 1 inch balls; roll in cinnamon sugar. Place on ungreased cookie sheets. Bake at 375° for 8 min. Makes approx. 70.

## Reese's Peanut Butter Cups

*Mrs. Freeman (Mabel) Yoder*

½ c. peanut butter
½ c. butter
½ c. brown sugar
½ c. sugar
1¼ c. flour

½ t. salt
½ t. vanilla
¾ t. baking soda
1 egg
1 bag small Reese's peanut butter cups (24 - 30)

Mix all ingredients together. Roll into 1" balls. Drop balls into greased mini-tart tins. Bake at 350° for about 12 min. Press Reese's cups into center. Let cool and dump out.

## Rhubarb Dream Bars

*Mrs. Daniel (Esther) Yoder*

1½ c. flour
⅔ c. powdered sugar

¾ c. butter or oleo

Mix like pie crust. Press into a 9 x 13" cake pan. Bake 15 min. at 350°.

3 eggs
2 c. sugar
½ c. flour

½ t. salt
3 c. rhubarb

Mix and pour on crust. Bake 35 min. at 350°.

## Salted Peanut Chews

*Mrs. Merlin (Mary) Lehman*

1 box yellow cake mix
⅓ c. oleo, melted

1 egg, beaten

Mix until crumbly. Press into 13 x 9" pan. Bake at 350° for 12 - 18 min.; remove from oven and top with **3 c. mini marshmallows**. Return to oven for 2 min. While base cools, mix topping:

⅔ c. corn syrup
¼ c. oleo

2 t. vanilla
10 oz. butterscotch chips or peanut butter chips

Heat until all is melted. Add **2 c. rice cereal or 2 c. salted peanuts**. Spread over marshmallows.

## S'more Bars

*Mrs. Freeman (Mabel) Yoder*

3 c. crushed graham crumbs
½ c. brown sugar
3 c. miniature marshmallows

1 c. melted margarine
1 c. mini chocolate chips

Combine cracker crumbs, margarine, and sugar. Mix well; press ¾ of mixture into a greased 9 x 13" cake pan. Sprinkle marshmallows and choc. chips over crumbs. Spread with remaining crumbs and bake at 375° for 10 min. Press down firmly with a spatula then cool completely before cutting. Yummy! More like candy than bars.

## Soft Granola Bars

*Mrs. Milo (Lorene) Yoder*

1 c. brown sugar
1 c. oil
2 eggs
1½ c. whole wheat flour
¼ t. salt
2 c. oatmeal

1 t. soda
1½ t. cinnamon
1½ t. cloves
1 c. raisins or dates
1 c. nuts or coconut

Honey Glaze:
¼ c. honey                   2 T. butter

Heat until butter melts and mixture is heated thoroughly.

Mix the first 3 ingredients until smooth. Then add the rest; spread on 15½ x 10½ x 1" pan. Bake at 350° for 17 to 22 min. Cool 15 min., then drizzle with glaze. Cool completely and cut into bars.

## Speedy Brownies

*Mrs. Sam (Viola) Miller*

2 c. sugar
1¾ c. flour
½ c. baking cocoa
1 t. salt

5 eggs
1 c. veg. oil
1 t. vanilla
1 c. semisweet choc. chips

In a mixing bowl, combine the first 7 ingredients. Pour into greased baking pan. Sprinkle with choc. chips. Bake at 350° for 30 min. This is a very simple, easy, & quick dessert if you're in a hurry, but still delicious!

## Twinkies

*Mrs. Martin (Katie) Wickey*

1 box yellow (choc.) cake mix
1 sm. box instant vanilla pudding
½ c. Crisco

4 eggs
1 c. water

Cream shortening, add dry ingredients, beat eggs and add eggs and water. Beat until batter is smooth and creamy. Divide batter in two small cookie sheets. Use wax paper for one. Bake at 350° for 15 - 20 min.

Filling:
5 T. pastry flour               1 c. milk

Cook until thick and set aside to cool. Stir occasionally. Be sure it is cold before adding the following mixture.

½ c. butter                     1 c. powdered sugar
1 t. vanilla                    ¼ t. salt

Cream butter, add the remaining ingredients and beat until fluffy. Add cooked mixture and beat again until fluffy. Spread on one cake and put other cake on top.

# Cakes &

# Frostings

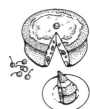

*Trust Him when dark doubts assail thee;*
*Trust Him when thy strength is small;*
*Trust Him when to simply trust Him*
*Seems to be the hardest thing of all!*

*He gives food to all flesh,*
*for His steadfast love endures forever.*
*Psalm 136:25*

# Hints For Cakes & Frostings

- Have all ingredients at room temperature.
- Fill cake pans about ⅔ full and spread batter well into corners and to the sides, leaving a slight hollow in center.
- The cake is done when it shrinks slightly from the sides of the pan or if it springs back when touched lightly with the finger.
- After a cake comes from the oven, it should be placed on a rack for about 5 min. Then the sides should be loosened and the cake turned out onto rack to finish cooling.
- Cakes should not be frosted until thoroughly cooled.
- Roll fruits and raisins in flour before adding them to the cake batter so they will stay distributed throughout the cake.
- When adding dry and wet ingredients, such as flour and milk, begin and end with the dry ingredients, beating well after each addition for a smoother batter.
- If eggs are not beaten well, or ingredients not thoroughly mixed, a coarse-grained cake will result.
- For an interesting flavor, add a melted chocolate mint to chocolate cake batter.
- To keep chocolate cakes brown on the outside, dust the greased pan with cocoa instead of flour.
- If baking in glass dishes, decrease the oven temperature 25° to prevent overbrowning.
- Use the circular cardboards from the bottom of frozen pizzas when transporting a cake. Cover with foil first.
- If a layer cake comes out lopsided, insert marshmallows between the bottom layer and the cake plate, or wherever they are needed.
- Stir 3 oz. of chocolate chips into 7-minute frosting while it is still hot to make it creamy and delicious.
- When frosting a cake, place strips of waxed paper beneath the edges of the cake. They can easily be removed after frosting.
- For a different frosting, mix 2 T. of pineapple and 2 T. of orange juice. Add enough powdered sugar to stiffen.
- Sprinkle applesauce cake or banana cake generously with granulated sugar, coconut, and chopped nuts before baking. It makes a crunchy topping.
- When melting chocolate, grease pan in which it is to be melted.
- When you are creaming butter and sugar together, it's a good idea to rinse the bowl with boiling water first. They'll cream faster.

## 7-Minute Frosting

*Mrs. Freeman (Mabel) Yoder*

2 egg whites
3 T. water
⅛ t. salt
1½ c. sugar

1 T. corn syrup
2 c. marshmallows (miniature)
1 t. vanilla
½ c. powdered sugar

In top of double boiler, over boiling water, beat egg whites, sugar, water, salt, & corn syrup. Keep beating until soft peaks form; approx. 7 min. Remove from heat and add 1 t. vanilla and 2 c. marshmallows. Stir until marshmallows are almost all dissolved. Then stir in powdered sugar. Makes a large amount, enough for a tall angel food cake or 2 loaf cakes. Is nice and light for angel food cakes.

## A Love Cake for Mother

*Sister Mary Yoder*

1 can of "obedience"
several lbs. of "affection"
1 pt. of neatness
some holiday, birthday, and every-
    day surprises
1 can of "running errands" (willing brand)

1 box powdered "get up when I
    should"
1 bottle of "keep sunny all day
    long"
1 can "pure thoughtfulness"

Mix well; bake in a hearty warm oven and serve to "Mother" every day. She ought to have it in big slices.

## Angel Food Cake

*Mrs. Emmon (Edna) Schmucker*

2 c. egg whites
2 t. water
2 t. cream of tartar
1 t. salt

2 c. sugar
1½ c. flour
1 T. vanilla

For spice cake put in:
1 t. cinnamon
½ t. allspice

½ t. cloves

Mix with flour and add to mix.

For chocolate twirl mix: **2 t. cocoa with a little hot water.** For jello mix: **1 T. to flour.** Bake at 375° for 1 hour in angel food cake pan. Beat egg whites and water until stiff. Beat in the cream of tartar, salt, and sugar. Then fold in the flour.

*The person who never makes a mistake
must get tired of doing nothing.*

## Angel Food Cake

*Mrs. Lonnie (Norma Mae) Bontrager*

2 c. egg whites
1½ t. vanilla
2 t. cream of tartar
½ t. salt
1 c. white sugar
1 c. white flour
1¼ c. powdered sugar

Place egg whites in large bowl; add cream of tartar, salt, and vanilla. Beat at high speed of mixer until very stiff but still shiny and moist. Beat in white sugar, 2 T. at a time, and continue to beat until it holds stiff peaks.

Sift together white flour and powdered sugar two times. Fold sifted flour mixture in slowly and lightly. Bake in ungreased tube pan at 375° for 40 min. or until done.

## Angel Food Cake

*Mrs. Glen (Lydia Mae) Miller*

2 c. egg whites
2 t. angel cream
2 T. water
½ t. salt
1 t. vanilla
2 c. sugar
1½ c. flour

In a mixing bowl, beat together the first five ingredients until very stiff. Fold in 1¾ c. sugar, and put ¼ c. sugar to the flour and sift it. Then fold that in with the rest of the mixture - 2 T. at a time, sugar and flour both. Blend well, but stir slowly. Bake at 375° - 400° for 45 min. or until brown on top. Don't open oven door while baking. Yield: 1 cake.

## Apple Cake

*Miriam Yoder (in memory of Katie)*

2 eggs
2 c. sugar
pinch of salt
2 c. flour
½ c. oil
2 t. soda
2 t. cinnamon
1 t. vanilla
4 c. diced apples
1 c. nuts

Cream eggs and sugar - add the rest of ingredients and stir well. Pour in greased 9 x 13" pan. Bake at 350° for 45 min.
Frosting:

1½ c. powdered sugar
6 oz. cream cheese
3 T. butter
½ t. vanilla

Mix together well and put on cake when cool.

*Both our attitude and our behavior
must reflect God's love for us.*

# Apple Cake
### Mom (Rosa) Bontrager

2 c. finely chopped apples  
1 c. sugar  
1 egg  
1 c. flour  
½ t. cinnamon  
1 t. soda  
½ t. salt  
½ c. nuts  

Mix apples with sugar until sugar dissolves. Add remaining ingredients. Pour into 9 in. square pan. Bake at 350° for 30 to 40 min. Cool.

Topping:
⅓ c. brown sugar  
⅓ c. white sugar  
1⅔ T. flour  
⅔ c. water  
2 T. butter  
1 t. vanilla  

Combine sugars, flour, and water. Cook over medium heat until clear. Add butter & vanilla. Poke holes in top of cake; pour on topping. Let cool and serve. Good with ice cream.

# Apple Cake to Eat With Ice Cream
### Mrs. Christie (Anna) Yoder

½ c. butter  
1 box yellow cake mix  
½ c. coconut  
2½ c. sliced apples  
½ c. sugar  
1 t. cinnamon  
1 c. sour cream  
2 egg yolks or 1 egg  

Cut butter in cake mix (dry) until crumbly. Mix in coconut. Pat mixture lightly into ungreased 13 x 9" pan, building up slight edges. Bake 10 min. Arrange apple slices on warm crust. Mix sugar & cinnamon; sprinkle on apples. Blend sour cream and egg yolks. Drizzle over apples. Topping will not completely cover apples. Bake 25 min. or until edges are light brown. Do not overbake.

# Apple Dapple
### Mrs. Daniel (Esther) Yoder

2 eggs  
2 c. white sugar  
1 c. cooking oil  
2¾ c. flour  
½ t. salt  
1 t. soda  

Add sifted ingredients to egg mixture. Then add **3 c. chopped apples, vanilla, and nuts** (if desired). Bake in 13 x 9" cake pan for ½ hour at 350°.

Icing:
1 c. brown sugar  
¼ c. milk  
2 T. butter  

Cook 2½ min. Stir a little after removing from heat. Dribble over cake while icing and cake are still hot.

## Blue Ribbon Banana Cake

*Mrs. Herman (Elsie) Mullett*

¾ c. margarine

1½ c. white sugar

2 eggs

1 c. mashed bananas

2 c. flour

1 t. baking soda

1 t. baking powder

1 t. vanilla

½ c. buttermilk

½ c. coconut & ½ c. nuts

Creamy Nut Icing:

¾ c. sugar

3 T. flour

¾ c. cream

½ t. salt

3 T. butter

¾ c. chopped nuts

1 t. vanilla

½ c. coconut

Beat eggs; add sugar, margarine, bananas, buttermilk, soda, baking powder, vanilla, nuts, coconut, & flour. Mix all together and bake in a 9 x 13" cake pan at 350° for 45 min. or until toothpick comes out clean.

Icing: Mix everything together and cook until thick. Put on cake while still warm.

## Boston Cream Pie (Cake)

*Mrs. Reuben (Martha) Yoder*

1 c. sifted all-purpose flour

½ c. hot milk

1 t. baking powder

2 eggs

¼ t. salt

1 c. sugar

2 T. butter or margarine

1 t. vanilla

Sift together flour, baking powder, and salt. Add butter to hot milk. Keep hot! Beat eggs until thick and lemon colored. Gradually add sugar, beating constantly. Add vanilla; quickly add sifted dry ingredients to egg mixture. Stir just until blended. Stir in hot milk mixture; blend well. Pour into 2 greased and floured 8 in. layer cake pans. Bake in moderate oven (350°) for 25 - 30 min. Cool in pans for 15 min. Remove from pans and finish cooling on wire racks.

Now prepare cream filling. Combine in saucepan:

⅓ c. sugar

1 T. cornstarch

2 T. flour

1 t. salt

Gradually stir in 1½ c. milk. Cook over moderate heat, stirring constantly, until mixture boils and thickens. Cook and stir for 2 - 3 min. longer. Slightly beat 1 egg plus 1 egg yolk. Stir a little of the hot mixture into the beaten eggs; blend and return to the rest of hot mixture. Cook and stir until mixture just comes to boiling. Add 1 t. vanilla; cool. Beat smooth. Now spread over 1 of the cakes. Put the second cake on top. Now prepare glaze. Place 1 oz. square of unsweetened chocolate & 1 T. butter in small saucepan. Stir over low heat until chocolate melts. Remove from heat; add 1 c. powdered sugar & 1 t. vanilla. Blend in enough boiling water (approx. 2 T.) to make of drizzling consistency. Now drizzle over top of cake and serve.

## Brown Sugar Cake

*Mrs. Eldon (Katie) Nisley*

½ c. margarine
2 c. brown sugar
2 c. buttermilk or sour milk
3 c. flour
2 t. baking soda
1 t. vanilla

Cream together 2 c. sugar and margarine. Add buttermilk and soda, then flour and vanilla. Pour into greased cake pan and bake in 350° oven until toothpick inserted into center comes out clean.

Topping:
Combine **6 T. butter, 4 T. milk, 2 c. coconut, and 1 c. chopped nuts.** Spread over cake and bake an additional 10 min. If I don't have nuts, I use butterscotch chips which also makes it delicious.

## Caramel Apple Coffee Cake

*Mrs. Freeman (Mabel) Yoder*

3 eggs
2 c. sugar
1½ c. vegetable oil
2 t. vanilla
3 c. flour
1 t. salt
1 t. baking soda
3 c. chopped peeled apples
1 c. coarsely chopped pecans

Topping:
½ c. butter or margarine
¼ c. milk
1 c. packed brown sugar
⅛ t. salt

In a mixing bowl, beat eggs until foamy; gradually add sugar. Blend in oil and vanilla. Combine flour, salt, and baking soda. Add to egg mixture. Stir in apples and pecans. Pour into a greased 10 in. tube pan. Bake at 350° for 1 hour and 15 min. or when cake springs back when touched lightly with fingers. Cool before removing from pan. For topping, combine all ingredients in a saucepan; boil 3 min., stirring constantly. Slowly pour over cake; some topping will run down onto serving plate.

## Caramel Icing

*Ola Bontrager*

1 stick butter
1 c. brown sugar
¼ c. cream
1 t. vanilla
powdered sugar

Boil butter and sugar together in saucepan for 2 min. Remove from heat. Add cream; boil one or more minutes; let cool. Add vanilla and enough powdered sugar to spread. This is great on rolls or cakes.

*The beauty of life is to be
measured in thoughts that rise above the needs of self.*

## Chocolate Cake
*Grandma (Mary) Bontrager*

1½ c. white sugar
2 c. flour (1 c. New Rinkle &
  1 c. Gold Medal)
½ c. cocoa
2 t. soda
½ t. salt

½ c. butter
2 eggs
½ c. milk
1 t. vanilla
1 c. boiling water

Sift dry ingredients. Cream butter and sugar. Add eggs, 1 at a time. Blend in milk. Add vanilla. Sift in dry ingredients. Last add boiling water. Bake in a 9 x 13" pan for 30 - 35 min.

## Chocolate Cake
*Mrs. Freeman (Mabel) Yoder*

2 c. flour
1¾ c. sugar
3 T. cocoa
2 t. soda
1 t. baking powder
½ c. vegetable oil

*1 c. buttermilk or sour milk
1 t. vanilla
1 t. salt
2 eggs
1 c. boiling water
1 t. instant coffee

Combine sugar, salt, oil, vanilla, and eggs. Add flour, cocoa, soda, and baking powder. Gradually add milk; stir well. Mix coffee with boiling water and add to batter by ¼ cupsful. Bake at 350° for 35 - 40 min. or until toothpick inserted comes out clean. *To make sour milk, put 2 t. vinegar in a cup and fill with milk.* Bake in a 13 x 9" pan.

## Chocolate Cake
*Mrs. Eldon (Katie) Nisley*

3 c. flour
2 c. sugar
2 t. soda
6 T. cocoa
1 t. salt

2 t. vanilla
⅔ c. vegetable oil
2 T. vinegar
2 c. cold water

Mix in order given and beat well. Bake in 350° oven for 40 min.

*When you speak, always remember that*
*God is one of your hearers.*

## Chocolate Dream Cake

*Mrs. Mervin (Emma) Yoder*

1 - Chocolate Cake Layer
**1 box chocolate cake mix**
  Mix as directed on box, then bake and cool.
2 - Cream Cheese Layer
**1 (8 oz.) container Cool Whip**          **½ c. powdered sugar**
**8 oz. cream cheese**
  Mix together and set aside.
3 - Jam Layer
**1 c. sugar**                              **2 - 4 T. clear jel**
**1 qt. strawberries, sliced**             **1 qt. water**
**1 sm. (3 oz.) box strawberry jello**     **1 pkg. strawberry Kool-Aid**
  Heat water to boiling, then add Kool-aid, sugar and jello. Mix clear jel with water and use to thicken boiling mixture. Cool. Add strawberries.
  Spread cream cheese layer on cake. Add jam layer. May add Cool Whip on top for garnish.


## Chocolate Frosting

*Mrs. Lonnie (Norma Mae) Bontrager*

**¼ c. cocoa**                  **1 c. milk**
**¾ c. white sugar**            **1 T. butter**
**2 T. cornstarch**             **1 t. vanilla**

  Mix together cocoa, sugar, and cornstarch; then slowly add milk and cook until it thickens. (Stir all the time while cooking.) Remove from heat and add butter and vanilla. Spread on cake while hot.


## Chocolate Chip Cake

*Mrs. Ervin (Clara) Yoder*

**1¾ c. flour**                 **1 c. sugar**
**2 T. cocoa**                  **2 eggs, beaten**
**½ t. salt**                   **1 t. vanilla**
**1 t. soda**                   **1 c. lg. chocolate chips**
**1 c. boiling water**          **¾ c. chopped nuts**
**1 c. shortening**

  Sift together flour, cocoa, salt, & soda. Cream shortening and sugar. Add eggs & vanilla. Beat well; add water and flour mixture alternately. Beat until smooth. Spread in greased 13 x 9" pan. Sprinkle with chips & nuts. Bake at 350° for 45 min. No icing necessary.


*Be patient with the faults of others;*
*they have to be patient with yours.*

## Chocolate Zucchini Sheet Cake
*Mrs. Ray (LeEtta) Yoder*

2 c. sugar
1 c. vegetable oil
3 eggs
2½ c. flour
½ c. cocoa

1 t. soda
¼ t. baking powder
¼ t. salt
½ c. milk
2 c. shredded zucchini

Mix sugar and oil. Add eggs one at a time. Combine flour, cocoa, soda, baking powder, and salt. Gradually add, alternating with milk. Stir in zucchini and vanilla. Pour into a greased 10 x 15 x 1" pan. Bake at 375° for 25 min. While baking combine frosting & spread over the cake while it is still hot.

Frosting:

½ c. oleo
¼ c. cocoa
1 T. vanilla

6 T. evaporated milk
4 c. powdered sugar

## Chocolate Praline Cake
*Mrs. Freeman (Mabel) Yoder*

1 c. brown sugar
1 c. butter (no substitutes)
¼ c. whipping cream

¾ c. coarsely chopped pecans
1 box chocolate cake mix

Topping:

2 c. non-dairy ready-to-whip topping or real cream
½ c. powdered sugar        ½ t. vanilla
chocolate curls - opt.

In a saucepan, combine brown sugar, butter and cream. Stir over low heat until butter is melted. Pour into two greased 9 in. cake pans. Sprinkle with pecans. Set aside. Prepare cake mix according to pkg. directions. Carefully pour batter over pecans. Bake at 325° for 35 - 45 min. or until toothpick comes out clean. Cool in pans for 10 min. Invert on dinner plate; cool completely then beat cream; add powdered sugar and vanilla. Beat until stiff. Place half of whip cream on one cake, pecan side up; top with second cake layer and spread with remaining topping. Garnish with choc. curls if desired.

*Love never asks how much must I do,*
*but how much can I do.*

## Cinnamon Coffee Cake

*Mrs. Clarence T. (Ruby) Yoder*

1 c. butter or marg., softened
1½ c. sugar
2 t. vanilla
4 eggs, beaten
3 c. all-purpose flour
Crumbs:
½ c. sugar
½ c. chopped walnuts

2 t. baking powder
1 t. soda
1 t. salt
2 c. sour cream
   (we often substitute
   buttermilk)

2 T. cinnamon

In a large mixing bowl cream butter and sugar until fluffy. Add vanilla and eggs, beating well. Combine flour, baking powder, soda and salt. Add alternately with cream, beating just enough after each addition to keep batter smooth. Spoon ⅓ of batter into a greased 10 in. tube pan. Combine cinnamon, sugar, and nuts. Sprinkle ⅓ over batter in pan. Repeat layer 2 more times. Bake at 350° for 70 min. or until cake tests done. Cool for 10 min. then remove from pan to a platter to cool completely. Yield: 16 - 20 servings.

## Cinnamon Supper Cake

*Mrs. Lonnie (Norma Mae) Bontrager*

1½ c. sugar
½ c. oleo
2 eggs, beaten
1 c. milk

2 c. flour
3 t. baking powder
½ t. salt
2 t. vanilla

Cream together sugar and oleo. Add eggs and mix good, then add rest of ingredients. Bake at 350° for 20 - 25 min. When cake is done melt 2 T. oleo or butter and mix 6 T. powdered sugar and 2 t. cinnamon. Pour melted oleo over cake then quickly sprinkle on cinnamon and powdered sugar. Good with fresh strawberries, rhubarb or any other fruit.

## Coffee Cake

*Mrs. Allen (Elsie) Bontrager*

Put 1 c. hot water in bowl. Add 1 t. sugar. Stir, then add 1 T. yeast. Let set in a warm place. In separate bowl: Add 1 t. salt, 1 c. milk, 1 c. lukewarm water, ¾ c. veg. oil and 1 c. white sugar. Beat in 1 egg. Stir in yeast mixture. Mix in 3 c. flour. Slowly add more till mixture is smooth and elastic. Let rise till double, then punch down and work out in 4 round pans. Brush tops with melted or soft butter, then sprinkle with a cinnamon and sugar mixture. Bake at 350°. When cool, split in center. Fill with cream cheese filling.
Filling:
3 egg whites, beaten
3 t. vanilla
¼ t. salt

3 c. powdered sugar
8 oz. cream cheese, softened
1 c. butter, softened

Cream together then slowly add more powdered sugar till right consistency, about 3 c.

## Creamy Icing

*Mrs. Marvin L. (Erma) Miller*

¼ c. sugar
2 T. water
2⅓ c. powdered sugar
½ t. salt

1 egg (beaten)
½ c. Crisco
1 t. vanilla
cocoa (optional)

Boil the water and sugar together for 1 min. Mix powdered sugar, salt and egg. Blend the 2 together. Add Crisco, cocoa and vanilla. Beat until creamy. Enough for 1 cake.

## Cream-Filled Coffee Cake

*Mrs. Freeman (Mabel) Yoder*

1 c. milk, scalded
1 stick marg.
½ c. sugar
1 pkg. yeast or 1 T. soaked
  in ½ c. warm water

3½ c. flour
pinch of salt
2 eggs, beaten

Mix sugar, salt and eggs in a large bowl. Add milk, marg. and yeast; stir in flour. Stir with spoon then let rise and spoon in 3 greased pie tins. Put crumbs on top; let rise and bake at 350° for approx. 30 min. *No need to knead with hands. Crumbs:

⅓ c. brown sugar
⅓ c. flour
3 T. butter
Filling:
2 eggs, whites beaten
2 t. vanilla
1 (8 oz.) cream cheese

1 t. cinnamon
½ c. chopped pecans
  or walnuts

2 c. powdered sugar
¼ t. salt

Cream together and add 1½ c. Crisco and 2 c. powderd sugar. Cut cakes through and fill with filling. *Add 1 small box lemon jello to filling for an added distinctive flavor.*

## Cream-Filled Pineapple/Mandarin Cake

*Mrs. Freeman (Mabel) Yoder*

1 box yellow or white cake mix
1 11 oz. can mandarin oranges
½ c. oil
w2 eggs

20 oz. can crushed pineapple,
  drained
1 small pkg. vanilla pudding
3-4 c. ready-to-whip non-dairy
½ c. chopped pecans  topping

Combine cake mix, oranges, oil and eggs. Blend well. Pour into greased 9 in. round cake pans. Bake at 350° for 30 - 35 min. Cool layers then slice in the middle of each one to make 4 layers. Mix together pineapple, pecans and vanilla pudding. Set aside then whip the topping and fold into the pineapple mixture. Fill between layers then spread over and around the top and the sides. Refrigerate. This cake keeps for quite a while. The longer it sets the better it is.

## Earthquake Cake

*Mrs. Noah (Amanda) Lehman*

1 c. coconut
1 c. pecans, chopped
1 box choc. cake mix
8 oz. cream cheese, softened
1 stick oleo, softened
1 box powdered sugar

Press coconut and pecans in a greased 9 x 13 in. pan. Mix cake according to directions on box. Spread over pecans and coconut. Mix cream cheese, oleo and powdered sugar together and drop by spoonfuls on top of cake mix. Bake at 350° for 30 - 35 min.

## Easy Choc. Frosting

*Mrs. Elmer (Martha) Yoder*

1/3 c. butter
1/4 c. milk
1 t. cocoa
1 t. vanilla
1 c. white sugar

Mix everything together and boil 1 min. Cool and spread.

## German Bundt Cake

*Mrs. Merlin (Mary) Lehman*

yellow or butter cake mix
3/4 c. oil
3/4 c. water
4 eggs, 1 at a time
2 t. butter flavor
1 t. vanilla
1 3 oz. box instant pudding
(vanilla or lemon)

Mix everything together.

1/4 c. white sugar
2 t. cinnamon

Mix and put in between layer of cake before baking. I use a bundt cake pan. Bake for 55 min. at 350°.

**Frosting:**

1 c. powdered sugar
2 T. milk
1 t. butter flavoring
1 t. vanilla

## Golden Chiffon Cake

*Mrs. Freeman (Mabel) Yoder*

7 egg whites
1/2 t. salt
1/2 t. cream of tartar
3/4 c. sugar
1/2 c. flour
1/2 t. vanilla
7 egg yolks
3/4 c. sugar
2 T. hot water
1/2 t. vanilla
3/4 c. flour
1 t. baking powder

Beat egg whites with salt. And when foamy add cream of tartar and beat until stiff. Slowly add sugar. Beat, then fold in flour and vanilla. Set aside. In another bowl, beat egg yolks, add sugar and beat until well mixed. Add flour and baking powder; mix. Add vanilla and pour into an ungreased angel food cake pan. Fold two parts together. Bake at 350° for approx. 50–60 min.

# Good Coffee Cake

Mrs. Daniel (Esther) Yoder

¼ lb. butter or oleo
1 c. sugar
3 eggs, beaten
2 c. flour
¼ t. salt
1 t. baking powder

1 t. baking soda
1 c. sour cream
1 t. vanilla
½ c. chopped walnuts
½ c. sugar
1 t. cinnamon

Cream butter or oleo with 1 c. sugar. Add beaten eggs and mix. Sift together dry ingredients and add to egg mixture alternately with sour cream to which vanilla has been added. Mix just to blend walnuts, ½ c. sugar and cinnamon. Turn ½ of dough into a greased 9" tube pan. Sprinkle ½ of crumb mixture over this. Pour on rest of batter. Top with remaining crumbs. Bake 45 min. at 350°. I always bake it in loaf pan.

# Grandma's Shortcake

Mrs. Harry (Polly) Bontrager
Submitted by Mrs. Sam (Viola) Miller
in memory of Grandma

2 c. flour
1 c. sugar
2 t. baking powder
1 t. soda
½ t. salt

1 egg
2 t. vanilla
½ c. lard
1 c. sour milk

Mix together like a cake and bake at 350° for 30 - 40 min. Serve with fresh fruit.

# Ice Water Cake

Mrs. Reuben (Martha) Yoder

3½ c. cake flour
2 c. sugar
¾ t. salt
3 t. baking powder
½ c. shortening (softened butter)

1½ c. ice water
1 t. vanilla extract
¼ t. almond extract
4 egg whites

Mix dry ingredients; add shortening and egg whites. Blend well. Add the rest of the ingredients, beating well after each ingredient. Yield: 2 - 8 in. layer cake pans. Bake at 350° for 30 min.

If you put it together this way you will have a light and fluffy cake.

*Faith makes all things possible*
*Hope makes all things bright*
*Love makes all things easy.*

## Layered Toffee Cake

*Mrs. Freeman (Mabel) Yoder*

1 angel food cake, baked
3 c. whipping cream or non-
   dairy ready-to-whip topping
1 t. vanilla

½ c. caramel or butterscotch ice
   cream topping
2 - 6 oz. bags Heath toffee bits

In a mixing bowl beat cream until it just begins to thicken. Gradually add the ice cream topping and vanilla, beating until soft peaks form. Cut cake horizontally into 3 layers. Place the bottom layer on a serving plate. Spread with 1 c. cream mixture and sprinkle with a thick layer of toffee bits. Repeat with second layer. Place top layer on cake; frost top and sides with remaining cream mixture and toffee bits. Store in refrigerator.

## Marble Cake

*Mrs. Ora N. (Orpha) Miller*

¾ c. oleo or shortening
1½ c. sugar
1½ t. soda
1½ t. baking powder
½ t. salt

2½ c. flour
1½ c. sour milk
1½ t. vanilla
2 unbeaten eggs

Stir oleo or shortening to soften, then add and mix rest of ingredients, except eggs. After the rest is mixed well, add eggs and mix well. Pour batter in greased cake pan, except keep approx. ¼ of batter in bowl; scrape down sides. Mix the following in a small bowl:

1 T. sugar
¼ t. soda

2 T. cocoa or carob powder
2 T. hot water

Mix and add to batter in bowl; pour over batter in cake pan. Take a knife and zig-zag through batter to give it a marble effect. Bake 30 - 40 min. at 350°. A never-fail cake for me.

## Mocha Oatmeal Cake

*Mrs. Sam (Viola) Miller*

2 T. coffee
1⅓ c. boiling water
1 c. quick oats
¾ c. butter, softened
1 c. white sugar
1 c. brown sugar (packed)

2 eggs
1½ t. vanilla
2 c. flour
1¼ t. soda
¾ t. salt
3 T. cocoa

Combine coffee and water; pour over oatmeal. Cover and let stand for 10 min. Beat together butter, vanilla and eggs. Add oatmeal mixture; blend well. Add dry ingredients. Bake at 350° for 50 - 55 min. Top with your favorite frosting.

## New England Blueberry Coffee Cake   *Mrs. Ezra (Mary) Miller*

3 c. all-purpose flour
1 c. sugar
2 T. baking powder
2 t. cinnamon
1 t. salt

3 c. fresh or frozen blueberries
2 eggs
1 c. milk
½ c. butter or marg., melted

Topping:
½ c. butter or marg., melted
1½ c. packed brown sugar

2 T. all-purpose flour
1 c. chopped walnuts

In a large mixing bowl combine flour, sugar, baking powder, cinnamon and salt. Gently fold in blueberries. In a small bowl, whisk together the eggs, milk and butter. Add to the flour mixture and stir carefully. Spread into a greased 9 x 13 in. pan. Combine all topping ingredients and sprinkle over batter. Bake at 425° for 20 - 25 min. or until top is light golden brown. Serve warm or at room temp.

## Oatmeal Cake   *Mrs. Sam (Martha) Schrock*

Pour 1¼ c. boiling water over 1 c. quick oats and let stand for 20 min.

¼ c. butter
1 c. white sugar
1 t. vanilla
1 t. soda
½ t. cinnamon

1 c. brown sugar
add 2 eggs, beaten
1⅓ c. all-purpose flour
½ t. salt

Bake in a loaf pan at 350° or until done.

Topping:
½ c. melted butter
¼ c. milk
1 c. coconut

½ c. brown sugar
½ t. vanilla
½ c. pecans or walnuts

Mix together and pour over cake. Put in oven and brown for 15 min.

## Orange Coconut Cake   *Mrs. Freeman (Mabel) Yoder*

2½ c. sugar
¼ c. orange juice (scant)
2 c. sour cream
2½ c. flaked coconut
1 pkg. yellow or white cake mix
1 - 3 oz. pkg. orange gelatin
orange sugar crystals

1 c. water
⅓ c. veg. oil
2 eggs
2 c. non-dairy whipped topping
1 small can mandarin oranges,
  drained

Combine sugar, sour cream, and orange juice. Beat in coconut. Refrigerate. In another bowl combine cake mix, gelatin, water, oil, and eggs and mix well. Pour into 2 greased 9 in. round cake pans. Bake at 350° for 30-35 min. Cool. Then split cakes in half. Set aside 1¼ c. coconut filling; spread remaining filling between cake layers; beat topping and mix with reserved filling. Spread top and sides generously with topping. Garnish with orange sugar crystals and orange manderin halves.

## Peanut Butter Flan Cakes
*Mrs. Eli (Martha) Mullet*

Use your favorite choc. cake recipe and divide into 2 flan pans or 9 in. round pans and bake, then cool completely.

8 oz. cream cheese
½ c. peanut butter
1 T. sugar
1 t. vanilla
1¼ c. milk

1 pkg. (4 serving size) instant vanilla pudding
12 oz. whipped topping
2-3 peanut butter cup candies

Cream together cream cheese and peanut butter. Add the sugar and vanilla. Whisk in the pudding and the milk. Mixture will be wonderfully creamy. Fold in about 8 oz. of the whipped topping, saving some for the garnish. Divide filling between the 2 cakes and spread. Put rest of whipped topping on. Drizzle with Hershey's choc. syrup and chopped peanuts. Cut peanut butter cups into wedges and stand up in whipped topping.

## Pecan Wonder Coffee Cake
*Mrs. Lester (Verna) Bontrager*

2 c. flour
1 t. baking powder
½ t. salt
1 c. sugar
1 c. soft marg.

2 eggs
1 t. vanilla
1 t. soda
1 c. buttermilk

Sift dry ingredients; set aside. Cream marg. and sugar. Add eggs and vanilla and beat well. Put soda in buttermilk; add dry ingredients alternately with buttermilk and beat together.

Make a topping in separate bowl of:

⅓ c. brown sugar
⅓ c. white sugar

1 t. cinnamon
1 c. chopped pecans

Spread ½ of batter in a greased 9 x 13 in. cake pan. Sprinkle ½ of topping over batter. Repeat. Bake at 350° for 30 min. or until toothpick inserted in center comes out clean.

## Pineapple Cake
*Mom (Rosa) Bontrager*

2 c. sugar
2 c. flour
2 eggs

1 t. soda
1 #2 can crushed pineapple

Mix together and bake at 350° for 35 min.

**Topping:**

8 oz. cream cheese
1 t. vanilla

½ stick oleo
1 c. powdered sugar

Spread on hot cake. Delicious!

## Pineapple Sheet Cake

*Regina Miller*

2 c. sugar
1 lb. 4 oz. crushed
   pineapple (drained)
2 eggs
1 c. oil

2 c. flour
1 t. soda
1 t. salt
1 t. vanilla

Icing:
1 c. sugar
1 small can evaporated milk
1 stick oleo
½ t. salt

½ c. nuts
1 t. vanilla
1½ c. coconut

Mix all ingredients together. Bake in 9 x 13 in. pan at 350° for 25 min. Ice while still hot. Icing: Boil sugar, milk, and oleo and cook 10 min. Remove from heat. Add nuts, vanilla and coconut. Pour over hot cake.

## Pumpkin Roll Cake

*Grandma (Edna) Yoder*

3 eggs, beaten
1 c. sugar
²/₃ c. pumpkin
salt

¾ c. flour
1 t. soda
2 t. cinnamon

Mix together. Pour into greased and floured jelly roll pan (15 x 10 x 1). Bake at 350° for 15 - 20 min. Sprinkle a clean towel with powdered sugar. Put cake on the towel and roll up (as you would a jelly roll). Let cool half an hour.

**Filling:**

8 oz. cream cheese
5 T. butter

1 c. powdered sugar
½ t. vanilla

Beat cream cheese until smooth. Add powdered sugar, butter and vanilla. Unroll cake. Spread with cream cheese filling and roll up again. Cool before cutting.

*What I kept, I lost,*
*What I spent, I had,*
*What I gave, I have.*

## Rhubarb Bread (Cake)

*Mrs. Clarence T. (Ruby) Yoder*

6 c. whole wheat flour
2 t. baking powder
1 t. soda
1½ t. salt
1 c. brown sugar
1 c. maple syrup
Topping:
2 T. soft butter
1 c. sugar

2 eggs, beaten
¾ c. oil
2 t. vanilla
2 c. sour milk
3 c. rhubarb, finely chopped
1 c. nuts (or sunflower seeds)

1 c. flour
1½ t. nutmeg

Mix together dry ingredients in a bowl then add sugars, eggs, oil, vanilla and milk. Mix well then add rhubarb and nuts. Pour into a greased cake pan. Mix the topping and sprinkle over top of the cake. Bake for 45 min. at 350° (or until done). Yields: 1 big cake 12" x 18" or 2 normal cakes 8" x 13". One of our favorites for supper.

## Rhubarb Coffee Cake

*Mrs. Elmer (Wilma) Beachy*

1½ c. brown sugar
½ c. shortening
1 egg
2 c. all-purpose flour
Topping:
¼ c. sugar
¼ c. brown sugar, packed
½ c. chopped pecans

1 t. soda
½ t. salt
1 - 8 oz. sour cream
1½ c. chopped rhubarb

1 T. butter or oleo
1 t. cinnamon

Cream together sugar and shortening; add egg. Combine flour, soda and salt. Add alternately with sour cream to other mixture. Fold in rhubarb. Put in greased 13 x 9 in. pan. Sprinkle topping over batter. Bake at 350° for 45 to 50 min.

## Royal Apple Cake

*Mrs. Clarence T. (Ruby) Yoder*

Sift together in a bowl:
6 c. flour (½ of this can be
  whole wheat flour)
1 t. salt
2 t. soda
Add to dry ingredients:
4 eggs, beaten
2 c. brown sugar
1 c. oil

2 t. baking powder
2 t. nutmeg
4 t. cinnamon

2 c. water
4 c. diced or sliced apples,
  canned or fresh

Mix together and pour into a greased baking pan. Bake at 350° for 45 min. Yields: 1 big cake 12" x 18" or 2 normal cakes 8" x 13". One of our favorites for supper.

## Sour Cream Coffee Cake

*Mrs. Ivan (Arlene) Bontrager*

1 pkg. Pillsbury hot roll mix
1 c. warm water
3 T. sugar
2 eggs
1 c. sour cream
⅓ c. sugar
1 t. vanilla
¼ c. sugar
½ t. cinnamon

Dissolve yeast from mix in warm water mixed with 3 T. sugar. Add flour mixture from pkg. and the eggs. Mix well then spread in a 9 x 13 in. cake pan. Let rise till double. (Or mix up your favorite sweet roll dough, enough for 1 - 1½ doz. rolls, and spread the dough in the cake pan and let rise.) Combine the sour cream, ⅓ c. sugar and vanilla. Pour ½ of the sour cream mixture evenly over dough in pan. Bake 30 min. at 350°. Mix ¼ c. sugar and cinnamon. Set aside. When cake is done, spread remaining sour cream mixture over top and sprinkle evenly with the sugar cinnamon mixture while still hot.

## Sour Cream Pound Cake

*Mary Miller*

1 c. marg.
2 c. white sugar
6 eggs
1 c. sour cream
¼ t. soda
3 c. flour
1 t. vanilla
1 t. lemon juice
1 t. salt
other flavors may be used
instead of vanilla or lemon

Bake at 300° for 1½ hours in an angel food cake pan.

## Spice Angel Food Cake

*Mrs. Daniel A. (Ida) Miller*

1¼ c. sugar
½ c. water
6 egg whites
¼ t. salt
¾ t. cream of tartar
6 egg yolks
¼ t. cinnamon
¼ t. cloves
¼ t. nutmeg
1 c. cake flour
1 t. vanilla
½ t. lemon extract

Boil together sugar and water until it spins a hair from spoon. Beat egg whites with salt until foamy, add cream of tartar, and beat until stiff. Continue beating while adding hot syrup; cool. Add well beaten egg yolks. Sift together spices with flour, several times to mix thoroughly. Fold into egg mixture and add flavorings. Bake in a tube pan for 1 hour at 275° to 320°. Invert pan to cool cake.

# Sunshine Cake

*Mrs. Elmer (Ida) Yoder*

9 egg whites
1 t. vanilla
¼ t. salt
1¼ c. white sugar

8 egg yolks
¼ t. cream of tartar
1 c. flour

Put egg whites in a large bowl; add vanilla and salt; beat until very stiff. Add sugar slowly and beat thoroughly. In a separate small bowl add cream of tartar to egg yolks. Beat egg yolks and cream of tartar thoroughly. Pour the yolks over the whites and beat lightly, just enough to mix. Sift the flour over the top of the mixture. Fold in lightly. Bake at 350° for 45 min. or until done. Bake in angel food cake pan.

# Very Good Chocolate Cake

*Mrs. Allen (Elsie) Bontrager*

½ c. shortening
2 c. white sugar
2⅔ c. flour
2 t. baking powder
2 c. boiling water

2 eggs
½ c. cocoa
2 t. soda
½ t. salt

Cream shortening and sugar well. Add beaten eggs. Then add flour which is sifted together with soda, salt, baking powder and cocoa alternately with boiling water. Dough is very thin, but do not add more flour. Bake at 350° for approx. 40 min. or until toothpick comes out clean.

# Wacky Cake

*Mrs. Lloyd (Edna) Raber*

1½ c. flour
1 c. white sugar
2 T. cocoa

1 t. soda
½ t. salt

Sift dry ingredients in a mixing bowl. Make three holes in dry mixture. In first hole add 1 T. vinegar. In second hole add 5 T. melted lard (do not use oil). In third hole add 1 c. water. Stir until well blended. Put in ungreased, shallow 8 x 10 in. pan and bake in a 350° oven. Double the recipe makes 16 cupcakes or one double layer cake.

# Wedding Cake Icing

*Mrs. Eli (Martha) Mullet*

4 c. powdered sugar
1 c. Crisco
¼ c. milk (very hot)

¼ t. salt
1 t. clear vanilla (almond or
maple flavoring may be used)

Put 2 c. powdered sugar in large bowl and add shortening. Pour hot milk over shortening. Beat until smooth. Gradually add the rest of powdered sugar, beating after each addition to ensure smoothness. Add salt and vanilla.

# Pies

*There is something better than understanding God. That is trusting Him.*

*But the fruit of the Spirit is love, joy, peace, longsuffering, gentleness, goodness, faith. Meekness, temperance: against such there is no law. Galatians 5:22,23*

# Hints For Pies

- A pie crust will be easier to make if all ingredients are cool.
- A teaspoon of vinegar added to pie dough helps make a flaky crust.
- Add a minimum amount of liquid to the pastry, or it will become tough.
- Pie crust will not be hard or tough when milk is used in place of the water.
- When making pie crust, add a little baking powder to keep the crust light and tender.
- Sprinkle the pastry board with ¾ tablespoon of quick rolled oats before rolling a pie crust. It tastes nutty and provides extra nutrition.
- When baking a single pie crust, place gently in the pan and prick thoroughly. Check after baking 5 minutes and prick again in any puffed areas.
- For a single pie crust, use a scrap of pastry and press the crust against the sides of the pan so that no air can get under the crust.
- Pies should be baked in non-shiny pans to enhance the browining. Glass baking dishes also work well.
- To prevent soggy pie crusts, brush the bottom crust with egg white before pouring in fruit filling, or sprinkle with a light coating of flour and sugar.
- For a quick crust, coat a pie pan with butter and press in crushed cornflake crumbs. This is especially good with pumpkin pie.
- For a shiny pie crust, brush the top of the pie with a mixture of 1 egg, 1 t. sugar, ¼ t. salt, and 1 t. cooking oil. Bake as usual.
- One tablespoon of lemon jello over apple pie before putting on the top crust will prevent runover and add flavor. Try raspberry jello on cherry pie.
- When making pumpkin pie, separate the eggs, reserving the whites. When all ingredients are mixed add the stiffly beaten whites for a fluffier pie.
- Put a layer of marshmallows in the bottom of a pumpkin pie, then add filling. You will have a nice topping as they come to the surface.
- Vanilla adds flavor to fruit pies.
- The meringue on pie will be higher if you add a pinch of cream of tartar to the beaten whites.
- Mix 1 t. cornstarch for each egg white with the sugar, then add it to the whites for a nice meringue.
- If the juice from your apple pies runs over in the oven, shake some salt on it, which causes the juice to burn to a crisp so it can be removed.
- To prevent crust from becoming soggy with cream pie, sprinkle crust with powdered sugar.

## Apple Pie
*Mrs. Edwin (Annie) Ropp*

3 c. sliced apples
1 c. sugar
3 T. flour

½ t. cinnamon
2 T. butter
3 T. rich milk

Mix apples, sugar, flour, milk and cinnamon together. Blend well. Place mixture in a 9 in. unbaked pie shell. Add dots of butter on top. Put crust on top. Bake at 375° for 45 min. Also very good with crumb topping.

**Crumbs:**
½ c. sugar
⅓ c. butter

1 c. flour

Mix together.

## Apple Pie
*Mrs. Elmer (Ida) Yoder*

3 c. sliced apples
½ t. cinnamon
1¼ c. white sugar
pinch of salt

2 T. oleo
3 drops vinegar
2 T. clear jel

Combine all ingredients in a saucepan except clear jel; bring to a boiling point. Mix clear jel with small amount of water; add to apples and pour in crust when thickened and bake at 350° to 400° until crust is browned. 1 double crust pie.

## Apple Pie
*Grandma (Mary) Bontrager*

2 c. shoestring apples
¾ c. brown sugar
2 eggs, beaten
5 T. hot water

2 T. flour
¾ c. white sugar
1 T. butter
cinnamon on top

Mix together. Bake at 400°. Makes 1 pie.

## Apple Cream Pie
*Mrs. Ivan (Arlene) Bontrager*

2 c. peeled, chopped apples put into an unbaked pie shell.
**Mix:**

¾ c. brown sugar
¾ c. granulated sugar
2 beaten eggs

1 T. flour
½ c. cream
1 t. vanilla

Pour over apples. Cover with the top crust or crumb topping and bake at approx. 400° till golden brown.

**Crumb Topping:**
Mix with fork in bowl **1 c. quick oats,** ⅓ **c. brown sugar,** ½ **c. melted butter or marg.** After putting on pie, sprinkle generously with **cinnamon.**

## Apple Crumb Pie
*Mrs. Christy (Anna) Bontrager*

**Mix:**

2½ T. minute tapioca
¾ c. sugar

¼ t. salt
4 c. sliced apples

Let set 5 min. Put into an unbaked 9 in. pie shell and top with the following.

**Crumb Topping:**

⅓ c. brown sugar, packed
¼ c. flour
½ t. cinnamon

2½ t. soft butter,
mix and spread
over apples

Bake at 425° for 45 - 50 min.

## Berry Pie
*Mrs. Daniel A. (Ida) Miller*

1 can Eagle Brand milk
1 pt. any kind berry juice,
grape juice is good

2 T. lemon juice
16 oz. Cool Whip

Mix in order given. Pour into 3 baked pie shells. Ready to eat when set.

## Blueberry Cream Pie
*Mrs. David (Rachel) Plank*

1½ c. graham cracker crumbs
¼ c. sugar
⅓ c. melted oleo or butter
1 can blueberry pie filling

8 oz. cream cheese
2 eggs
½ c. sugar
1½ T. lemon juice

For crust: Mix well first 3 ingredients. Press into pie pan and bake 8-10 min. at 350°. Second layer: Put softened cream cheese in bowl and beat in eggs one at a time with egg beater. Add sugar and lemon juice; beat well. Pour into crust and bake at 350° 15 to 20 min. till slightly set. Cool and top with fruit filling (of your choice) and whipped cream. Delicious! I sometimes just put the crust in a cake pan as it's easier. . . tastes the same! This can also be used for fruit pizza.

## Bob Andy Pie
*Mrs. Elmer (Martha) Yoder*

1 c. sugar
1 c. brown sugar
1 T. flour
1 t. cinnamon

½ t. cloves
1 T. butter
3 eggs, separated
2 c. milk

Mix dry ingredients; add butter, beaten egg yolks and milk. Then fold in stiffly beaten egg whites and pour into 2 unbaked pie shells. Bake at 400° for 10 min. Reduce heat to 350° until done. 3 c. milk may be used.

## Caramel Pie

*Mom (Elsie) Yoder*

1 c. brown sugar
3 eggs, separated
1 T. flour
1 T. butter, melted

1½ c. milk, scalded
1 c. cream
1 t. vanilla (maple flv. is
  good too)

Beat egg yolks; add sugar and other ingredients; last add beaten egg whites and add to above mixture. Pour into an unbaked pie shell. Makes 1 large pie. Bake at 400° for 10 min. Reduce heat to 325° for 30 - 35 min.

## Chocolate Pie

*Mrs. Elmer (Ida) Yoder*

1 c. white sugar
1 t. cocoa
1½ c. boiling water
1 t. vanilla

2 heaping T. flour
¼ t. salt
½ c. milk
1 T. butter

Put boiling water in a saucepan. Combine sugar, flour, cocoa, salt and milk. Pour into water and bring to a boil. Remove from heat; add butter and vanilla. When butter is melted pour in an 8 in. baked pie crust and top with whipped topping.

## Chocolate Cheese Pie

*Mrs. Toby (Martha) Yoder*

1 c. choc. chips
1 - 8 oz. cream cheese,
  softened
¾ c. brown sugar
⅛ t. salt

1 t. vanilla
2 eggs, separated
2 c. Cool Whip
1 baked pie crust

Melt choc. and set aside. Blend cream cheese and ½ c. sugar, salt and vanilla. Beat in egg yolks one at a time. Beat in choc.; blend well. Beat egg whites until stiff; gradually beat in remaining ¼ c. brown sugar and beat till stiff. Fold choc. mixture into egg whites. Fold into Cool Whip and put into pie crust. Reserve ¼ of mixture for decorating. Chill until filling sets slightly. With spoon, drop reserved mixture in mounds over top of pie and chill overnight. This will make a full pie and is rich. Cut into 8 pieces.

## Chocolate Chip Pecan Pie

*Mrs. Alvin (Katie Mae) Yoder*

¼ c. oleo
1 c. white sugar
3 eggs
¾ c. light Karo

a pinch of salt
1 t. vanilla
½ c. choc. chips
¾ c. pecans

Pour into unbaked pie shell. Bake at 375° for 40 - 50 min.

# Chocolate Cream Cheese Pie

*Mrs. Elmer (Wilma) Beachy*
*Mrs. Herman (Elsie) Mullett*

6 oz. choc. chips
8 oz. cream cheese
¾ c. brown sugar
½ t. salt

1 t. vanilla
2 eggs, separated
16 oz. Cool Whip

Melt choc. chips over hot, not boiling, water. Cool 10 min. Blend cream cheese, ½ c. brown sugar, salt, vanilla and beaten egg yolks. Beat egg whites until stiff, not dry. Slowly beat in ¼ c. brown sugar. Beat until very stiff. Fold choc. mixture into beaten egg whites and fold in topping. Pour in baked crust and chill. Put no topping on. Garnish with choc. curls if you wish. Makes 2 or 3 pies.

# Chocolate Pie Filling

*Mrs. Sam (Martha) Schrock*

2 c. milk
2 rounded T. flour (pastry)
¾ sq. unsweetened choc. or
   1 T. cocoa

¾ c. sugar
¼ t. salt
1 t. vanilla

Mix together in saucepan. Heat over med. heat until it boils. Stir constantly - cool - stirring occasionally. Pour in a 9 in. pie crust. Cool. Top with whipping cream.

# Chocolate Mousse Pie

*Mrs. Alvin (Katie Mae) Yoder*

1 milk choc. candy bar
   with almonds (7 oz.)
16 large marshmallows or
   1½ c. mini marshmallows

2 c. whipping cream, whipped
1 pastry shell, baked, or graham
   cracker or choc. crumb crust
½ c. milk

Place the candy bar, marshmallows and milk in a heavy saucepan; cook over low heat, stirring constantly, until choc. is melted and mixture is smooth. Cool. Fold in whipped cream; pour into crust. Refrigerate for at least 3 hours. Yield: 6-8 servings.

# Cream Pie

*Mrs. Daniel A. (Ida) Miller*

2¼ c. rich milk
½ stick marg.
¾ c. sugar

¼ c. cornstarch
pinch of salt

Heat milk with sugar, marg. and salt. Mix cornstarch with a little cold milk. Add to hot milk and stir until thick. Pour into baked pie shell and sprinkle with nutmeg.

## Cream Pie

*Mrs. Marvin L. (Erma) Miller*

2 eggs, separated
1/3 c. brown sugar
2/3 c. white sugar
1 T. flour

1 t. vanilla
1 c. cream
pinch salt
1 c. milk, scalded

Mix first 7 ingredients together; add milk and beaten egg whites last. Bake at 425° for 10 min.; reduce heat to 350° for approx. 20 - 25 min. Makes 1 pie.

## Cream Pie or Pudding

*Mrs. Ezra (Mary) Miller*

Heat **16 c. milk** and **1 stick oleo**
Mix the following and stir into boiling milk:

8 eggs
1 c. flour, rounding for pie
1 c. clear jel, rounding for pie
2 T. vanilla
1 t. salt

2 c. white sugar
1 c. brown sugar
2 c. milk
2 t. maple flavoring

I use this for cream pies, such as banana cream. I add some banana flavor and also put a layer of sliced bananas on top and bottom when fixing the pies. For peanut butter pie I use the original filling and add the peanut butter crumbs when fixing the pie. For coconut cream pie I add some coconut flavoring and also coconut on top and bottom when fixing pies. It can also be used for choc. pies if you add cocoa when you make the filling.

## Creamy Banana Pecan Pie

*Mrs. Vernon (Polly) Beechy*

1 c. all-purpose flour
1/2 c. butter or marg.
1 c. finely chopped pecans
1 - 8 oz. cream cheese, softened
1 c. powdered sugar
1 1/3 c. milk

1 8 oz. carton frozen whipped
  topping, thawed, divided
1 large banana, sliced
1 - 3.4 oz. instant vanilla
  pudding mix

Combine flour, butter and pecans. Press into the bottom and up the sides of a greased 9 in. pie plate. Bake at 350° for 25 min. Cool completely. In a 3 qt. mixing bowl beat cream cheese and sugar. Fold in 1 c. of the whipped topping. Spread over the crust. Arrange bananas on top. In a bowl whisk pudding mix and milk. Immediately pour over bananas. Top with remaining whipped topping. Garnish with pecans. Refrigerate until serving. Yield: 6-8 servings. You can use a reg. pie crust instead of the above crust.

*It is better to become bent from hard
work than to become crooked from avoiding it.*

# Cream Cheese Pecan Pie

*Mrs. Lonnie (Norma Mae) Bontrager*
*Mrs. Ora (Susie) Miller*

1- 8 oz. cream cheese, softened
½ c. sugar
1 egg, beaten

½ t. salt
1 t. vanilla
1 c. chopped pecans

Mix and spread into bottom of 10" unbaked pie shell.

**Topping:**

3 eggs
¼ c. sugar

1 c. light corn syrup
1 t. vanilla

Beat until smooth. Pour over pecan layer. Bake 35 - 45 min. at 375° until golden brown. Serve warm!

# Custard Pie

*Mrs. Leroy (Sarah) Yoder*

4 eggs
1½ c. sugar

2 heaping t. cornstarch
5 c. milk

Separate eggs, beating whites until stiff, then add yolks and beat some more. Mix sugar and cornstarch and add scalding milk. Pour this mixture into eggs and pour into 2 pie shells. Sprinkle with nutmeg. Bake at 350° until set.

# Custard Pie

*Mrs. Mervin (Gertie) Eash*

3 eggs, beaten
1 c. sugar

½ t. salt
1 t. vanilla

Stir together, then add 2½ c. hot milk. Pour into unbaked 9 in. pie crust. Bake 10 min. at 425°, then 20 to 30 min. at 325°. Take out when filling sets.

# False Mince Pie

*Submitted by Mabel Yoder in memory of Grandma (Polly) Bontrager*

Pastry for 2 - 9 in. double crusts

¾ c. shortening
2 c. sugar
1 t. cinnamon
1 t. allspice
1 t. nutmeg
¼ t. salt
½ c. vinegar

2 eggs
1 c. cooking molasses
2 c. water
½ c. raisins
1 c. bread crumbs,
    cut into very fine pieces
2 c. peeled and chopped apples

Mix spices with sugar, then add shortening and eggs and blend well. Add remaining ingredients, mixing well. This is a golden oldie Grandmother used to make in bygone years. Bake in a hot 400° oven.

*Even if you are on track,*
*you will get run over if you just sit there.*

## Favorite Pumpkin Pie

*Mrs. Ora N. (Orpha) Miller*

1½ c. sugar, half brown
3 beaten egg yolks
2½ c. milk
1½ c. pumpkin
few drops of lemon flavoring
1 heaping T. butter or marg.,
    melted

3 heaping T. flour
1 t. cinnamon
½ t. cloves
½ t. nutmeg
½ t. allspice
beaten egg whites,
    added last

Mix together all dry ingredients first. Add egg yolks, butter, pumpkin and flavoring; mix well. Then add milk and egg whites last; mix well. Fill pie shells and bake in oven at 375° for 10 min. or so, then turn down to 325° to 350°. They need to bake slow so they won't cook which will cause them to curdle. Remove when filling is set. This is for 2 small pies. Double this recipe for 3 large pies.

## Fresh Strawberry Pie

*Mrs. Orva (Marietta) Yoder*

1 c. berries, crushed
1 c. water
½ c. sugar

2½ t. Perma-flo
water
2 c. sliced strawberries

Bring berries and 1 c. water to a boil and cook for 2 min. Strain; save the juice only. Add sugar and Perma-flo. Mix sugar and Perma-flo and moisten with a small amount of water before adding to juice. Bring to a boil. Set aside to cool. When cool, add sliced strawberries; set aside.

**Cheese Mixture**

1 (3 oz.) cream cheese
½ c. sugar

½ t. vanilla
½ c. whipped cream

Spread cheese mixture in bottom of baked pie shell and spoon glaze mixture on top.

## Hershey Bar Pie

*Mrs. Eli (Martha) Mullet*

22 large marshmallows
5 Hershey candy bars

½ c. milk

Melt over low heat, just so marshmallows are melted; do not let boil. Cool. Beat ½ pt. whipping cream and fold into mixture. Put into baked pie shell. Put a dab of whipped cream on each piece. Break apart a Hershey bar and put a piece on each dab of whipped cream.

## Ice Cream Pie
*Mrs. Harry (Edna Mae) Bontrager*

**miniature marshmallows**      **Rice Krispies**

Mix together as you would for candy.* Then take regular pie pans and press into pans for crust, just like pie crust. When ready to serve fill with ice cream and top with strawberry topping.

**Strawberry Topping:**
**1 box Danish dessert**, prepared as directed. Cool. Then add **2 c. strawberries, fresh or frozen.** Very easy and delicious! ***Recipe for this is in candy section of this cookbook.**

## Japanese Fruit Pie
*Mrs. Freeman (Mabel) Yoder*

**Beat 2 eggs.** Add ½ **c. melted marg.** and **1 c. sugar;** stir well. **Dash salt.**

**Add:**
| | |
|---|---|
| **2 T. vinegar** | **1 t. vanilla** |
| **2 t. water** | |

**Then add:**
| | |
|---|---|
| ½ **c. coconut** | ½ **c. raisins** |
| ½ **c. coarsely chopped pecans** | |

Pour into an unbaked pie shell and bake at 350° until brown and set. My all-time favorite pie!

## Katie's Custard Pie
*Mary Miller*

| | |
|---|---|
| **1 c. brown sugar** | **pinch of salt** |
| ¾ **c. white sugar** | **drop of maple flavoring** |
| **1 T. flour** | **1 c. cream or canned milk** |
| **3 egg yolks** | **2½ c. milk** |

Stir above together with 1 c. cream or canned milk. In the meantime heat 2½ c. of milk. When hot, but not boiling, add to above mixture. Last add 3 beaten egg whites and fold in. Bake in 325° - 350° oven for approx. 30 min. This makes 2 pies.

## Lazy Day Grasshopper Pie
*Mrs. Freeman (Mabel) Yoder*

| | |
|---|---|
| **1 jar (7 oz.) marshmallow creme** | **1½ c. non-dairy ready-to-whip** |
| ¼ **c. milk** | **topping, whipped** |
| **7 drops peppermint extract** | **1 c. choc. Oreo cookies, crushed** |
| **8 drops green cake coloring** | |

In a mixing bowl beat the marshmallow creme, milk, flavoring and coloring until smooth. Fold in whipped cream. Pour crushed cookies into 9 in. pie pan; pour batter onto crust. Cover and freeze overnight until firm. Remove from freezer 20 min. before serving. Garnish with shaved choc. and dabs of whipped cream if desired. I always swirl mine with Hershey's choc. syrup.

## Mock Pecan Pie (Oatmeal)

*Mrs. Freeman (Mabel) Yoder*

¼ c. oleo or butter
½ c. sugar
1 c. dark or light corn syrup
¼ t. salt
½ c. coconut
½ c. quick oats
3 eggs, well beaten
1 9" pie shell, unbaked

Cream butter, syrup, and sugar till fluffy. Add salt and beaten eggs. Beat well. Last stir in coconut and oatmeal. Pour into pie shell. Bake in moderate oven (350°) for 50 min. or until set. Cool before serving.

## Never-Fail Pie Crust

*Mrs. Harry (Edna Mae) Bontrager*

3 c. flour
½ t. salt
1 c. lard
1 egg, beaten well
1 t. vinegar
⅓ c. cold water

Mix flour, salt and lard till crumbly. Beat egg, water and vinegar; add to flour mixture just till it holds together. Makes 3 double crust pies.

## Never-Fail Pie Crust

*Mrs. Freeman (Mabel) Yoder*

4 c. flour
1½ t. salt
1 T. baking powder
1¾ c. lard

Mix together with a pastry cutter or fork until it is mealy and crumbly. If you are using a home rendered lard use as directed, but if you use precreamed shortening use 2 c. Beat 1 egg, 1 T. vinegar and ½ c. cold water. Then add all at once to flour mixture. Fold together gently, then press to form a ball. Handle as little as possible. Let set 15 - 20 min. then roll and use. A good glaze for your pie tops; 1 egg beaten and ¼ c. milk stirred together. Brush or spoon over the top and sprinkle with sugar. Makes them golden brown and slightly shiny; these will not get soggy. *Helpful Hint: Pie dough does not like to be handled a lot, the less it is worked after the liquid has been added the flakier the crust.

## No-Bake Cream Pie

*Regina Miller*

2¼ c. milk
1 c. white sugar
¼ c. brown sugar
¼ c. cornstarch
¼ t. salt
1 T. vanilla
1 stick butter or oleo

Use ¼ c. of the milk to make thickening with cornstarch. Cook together and pour into hot baked shell. Sprinkle with nutmeg or cinnamon. Makes 1 pie.

## No-Bake Cream Pie

*Mrs. Merlin (Mary) Lehman*

2¼ c. milk
¾ c. white sugar
¼ c. cornstarch
1 egg, beaten
1 t. vanilla

Cook until thick, remove from heat, add 1 stick oleo or butter, stir until melted and pour into baked pie crust; top with nutmeg.

## No-Roll Pie Crust
*Mrs. Ivan (Arlene) Bontrager*

**Put into 9 in. pie pan:**
1½ c. all-purpose flour                1 t. salt
1½ t. sugar

Mix with fork. In a small bowl mix ½ c. vegetable oil and 2 T. milk. Mix into flour mixture. Press evenly into a pie pan, bottom and sides. A time-saver when in a hurry.

## Peach Pie
*Sister Elvesta*

1 8 oz. cream cheese                **1 large Cool Whip**
1 can Eagle Brand milk              **2 qt. drained peaches, cut up**

Mix cream cheese and milk together. Then add Cool Whip and peaches. Pour into a baked pie shell.

## Peach Pie
*Mom (Elsie) Yoder*

2 c. water                         ½ c. sugar
pinch of salt
**Bring to a boil. In the meantime make a paste of:**
3 heaping T. clear jel             ¼ c. peach jello
3 t. apricot jello                 ¾ c. water

Add to first mixture; heat till thickens. Cool. Then add 2 c. fresh chunked peaches. Pour in a baked pie shell. Makes one pie. Top with ½ c. whipped topping.

## Pecan Pie
*Mrs. Elmer (Martha) Yoder*

3 eggs, beaten                     1 c. pecans
1 c. Karo                          ¼ t. salt
¼ c. brown sugar                   ½ c. water
¼ c. butter or oleo

Mix everything together except pecans then pour into unbaked pie shell. Add pecans to the top. Bake at 400° for 10 min., then at 350° for approx. 45 min. until set.

## Pecan Pie
*Mom (Elsie) Yoder*

1 c. brown sugar                   2 T. butter
2 c. Karo (white)                  1 c. water
2 T. flour                         1 t. vanilla
4 eggs                             1 c. pecans
pinch of salt

Mix all ingredients together. Pour into 2 unbaked pie shells. Bake at 375° for 10 min., then at 325° for 30 to 35 min.

## Pecan Pie
*Mrs. Melvin (Mary Esther) Shrock*

4 eggs, beaten
1 c. sugar
4 T. flour
4 T. water
4 T. oleo, melted
1 t. vanilla
2 c. Karo

Beat 4 eggs (in med. bowl) until fluffy. Mix together flour and sugar and add to eggs. Add water, oleo, and vanilla and mix well. Add Karo and stir till smooth. Put 1 c. pecans in pie shell (unbaked) and add mixture. Bake at 325° till firm in center. Don't let it cook in oven. 2 small pies. Very good!

## Pumpkin Pie
*Mom (Rosa) Bontrager*

1½ c. cooked pumpkin
1¼ c. pancake syrup
3 T. flour
1 t. cinnamon
2 pt. milk
1¼ c. sugar
½ t. cloves
¼ t. salt
4 egg yolks

Stir together. Beat egg whites and fold into mixture. Pour into unbaked pie shells and bake at 350° for 1 hour or until firm.

## Pumpkin Pie
*Mrs. Emmon (Edna) Schmucker*

2 c. cooked pumpkin
2 c. brown sugar
¾ c. white sugar
6 T. flour
1 t. allspice
1 t. cinnamon
½ t. salt
5 c. milk
6 eggs, separated

Beat egg yolks in large bowl. Add cooked pumpkin. Add sugars mixed with flour, spices and salt. Add milk and last of all beaten egg whites. Pour into 3 unbaked pie shells. Bake at 350° until set.

## Quick Hawaiian Pie
*Mrs. Simon (Martha) Schmucker*

16 oz. crushed pineapple
8 oz. sour cream
1 box instant vanilla pudding

Mix together; pour into baked crust. Chill and top with Cool Whip.

## Best-Ever Chocolate Pie
*Mrs. Freeman (Mabel) Yoder*

16 oz. Cool Whip
1 (8 oz.) pkg. cream cheese
1 c. sugar
¾ c. chocolate syrup

Cream sugar and cream cheese together. Fold in Cool Whip and chocolate syrup; blend well. Pour into 2 baked 9-in. pie shells. Swirl with chocolate syrup. Chill before serving.

## Raisin Cream Pie
*Mrs. Lester (Mary) Lehman*

Heat:
8 c. milk and 3 c. sugar
Add:
6 rounded T. cornstarch, pinch of salt mixed with 12 egg yolks, beaten, and 1 c. sugar.
Add:
1 c. milk and bring to a boil.
Last add:
3 c. raisins (cooked and drained)       ½ stick butter or oleo
1 T. vanilla

Yield: 4 pies. Pour into baked pie shells and top with whipped cream.

## Rhubarb Cream Pie
*Grandma (Mary) Bontrager*

| | |
|---|---|
| 2½ c. cut rhubarb | 1 T. melted butter |
| 1¼ c. white sugar | 2 eggs |
| 2 T. flour | 3 T. water |

Beat egg yolks with water. Add 1 c. sugar, flour and butter. Stir until smooth. Add rhubarb and put in unbaked pie crust. Bake in 450° oven for 15 min. Then reduce heat to 350° to finish baking. Add meringue made of well beaten egg whites and remaining sugar and bake till meringue is lightly brown. Yield: 2 small pies.

## Rhubarb Delight Pie
*Regina Miller*

| | |
|---|---|
| 1½ c. diced rhubarb | 3 oz. jello (strawberry) |
| 4 T. water | 1 c. whipped cream |
| ¾ c. sugar | |

Cook first 3 ingredients till rhubarb is soft; add jello. When partially set, add whipped cream and pour into pie crust.

## Ritz Cracker Pie
*Mrs. David (Rachel) Plank*

| | |
|---|---|
| beat 3 egg whites stiff | 1 c. pecans |
| add 1 c. sugar, gradually | 24 Ritz cracker crumbs |
| fold in 1 t. baking powder | 1 t. vanilla |

Pour into buttered pie pan. Bake at 350° for 25 min. (or golden brown). Cool and top with whipped topping.

## Shoofly Pie

*Mrs. Freeman (Mabel) Yoder*

1 c. sugar
1 c. molasses or maple flavored syrup
2 c. water
¼ t. salt
Crumbs:
2 c. flour
¾ c. brown sugar
½ c. butter or margarine

2 eggs (well beaten)
2 T. flour
1 t. vanilla

1 t. cream of tartar
1 t. soda

Mix crumbs with a fork until crumbly; set aside. Mix flour and sugar. Add syrup and salt. Gradually add water, then beaten eggs. Bring to a boil until thickened; cool slightly, then add vanilla; divide into 2 unbaked pie shells. Cover with the crumbs and bake at 375° for 10 min., then approx. 30 min. longer at 350°.

## Sour Cream Rhubarb Custard Pie

*Mrs. Ivan (Arlene) Bontrager*

2 c. finely diced fresh rhubarb
1½ c. sugar
3 T. flour (slightly rounded)

2 eggs, beaten
½ c. sour cream

Put rhubarb into unbaked pie shell. Mix sugar and flour. In another bowl, beat eggs, then add sugar and flour mixture and sour cream to eggs and mix well. Pour over rhubarb. Bake at 400° for 5 min. or so. Then reduce heat to 325° - 350° and bake till set. Middle should not be too hard set. Note: If you like a browned meringue-like top, beat egg yolks and whites separately and fold egg whites in last. We prefer a thin sprinkling of cinnamon on top before baking. No top crust is needed.

## Sweet Cream Rhubarb Pie

*Mom (Rosa) Bontrager*

2 c. cut up rhubarb
1¼ c. sugar
1 T. flour

1 egg (save white)
1 c. cream
⅛ t. salt

Blend together sugar and flour; add salt, cream and egg yolk. Stir well. Beat egg white separately and fold into the mixture. Spread rhubarb into a 9 in. unbaked pie shell. Pour mixture over rhubarb and bake at 350° until golden brown.

*God never puts anybody in a place to small too grow in.*

## Tassies

*Mrs. Andy (Dorothy) Miller*

**Pastry:**

1 pkg. (3 oz.) cream cheese,
  softened

½ c. butter
1 c. flour

Filling:

¾ c. packed brown sugar
1 T. butter or oleo, softened
1 egg
1 t. vanilla

dash of salt
1⅓ c. finely chopped pecans,
  divided

Blend cream cheese and butter until smooth, then stir in flour and mix well. Chill about 1 hour. Divide into 12 balls and place into ungreased muffin tins. Press the dough against bottom and sides of tin cups.

For filling, mix all ingredients together except the pecans and stir well. Mix in ⅓ c. pecans and divide into the pastry cups. Top with remaining pecans and bake at 375° for 20 min. or until pastry is golden brown. Cool before removing from pans and put into an airtight Tupperware container. Yield: 12 tarts.


## Vanilla Tart Pie

*Mrs. Daniel A. (Ida) Miller*
*Mrs. Ora N. (Orpha) Miller*

1 egg, beat well
1½ c. sugar
1½ c. molasses
  This is the bottom part.

1½ pt. cold water
1 t. vanilla

1 egg, beat well
1½ c. sugar
½ c. lard or oil
  This is the top part.

1 scant c. sour milk
1 t. soda
2 c. flour

Make the top part first. Beat together the first 3 ingredients. Add the sour milk, then the last 2 ingredients. Divide it in 4 unbaked pie shells.

Bottom part - Mix it in order given and pour over the top part. Bake at 350° for 30 min. or until golden brown. Makes 4 pies.


*The yoke of God does not fit a stiff neck.*

# Desserts

—◆—

*O weary mothers, mixing dough,*
*Don't you wish that food would grow?*
*Your lips would smile, I know, to see*
*A cookie bush or a doughnut tree!*

*O taste and see that the Lord is good:*
*blessed is the man that trusteth in him.*
*The young lions do lack and suffer hunger:*
*but they that seek the Lord shall not*
*want any good thing.*
*Psalm 34:8, 10*

# As The Life Of A Flower

As the life of a flower, as a breath or a sigh.
So the years that we live as a dream hasten by.
True today we are here, but tomorrow may be
Just a grave in a vale and a mem'ry of me.

Cho.  As the life ................. of a flower .................
(As the life of a flower, as the life of a flower)
As a breath ................. or a sigh .................
(As a breath or a sigh, as a breath or a sigh)
So the years ................. glide away .................
(So the years glide away, so the years glide away)
And alas ................. we must die .................
(And alas we must die, and alas we must die).

As the life of a flower, be our lives pure and sweet,
May we brighten the way for the friends that we greet,
And sweet incense arise from our hearts as we live
Close to Him who doth teach us to love and forgive.

While we tarry below let us trust and adore
Him who leads us each day towards the radiant shore.
Where the sun never sets and the flowers never fade;
Where no sorrow or death may its borders invade.

## 4-Layer Torte
*Mrs. Leland (Orpha) Yoder*

*Layer 1:*
Crust - Melt ½ **c. oleo;** mix with **1 c. flour and some chopped nuts.** Bake this for 15 min. at 375°.

*Layer 2:*
Blend **1 (8 oz.) pkg. cream cheese, 1 c. powdered sugar, & 1 c. Cool Whip.** Put this on layer 1 after it has been cooled.

*Layer 3:*
Mix **2 pkgs. of instant pudding with 3 c. milk.** Pour on layer 2. I use vanilla pudding but you can use other flavors too.

*Layer 4:*
Spread the rest of the Cool Whip on layer 3. A 16 oz. container of Cool Whip is needed to start with.

## Apple Crunch
*Mrs. Toby (Martha) Yoder*

**1 c. flour**

**¾ c. oatmeal**

**1 c. brown sugar**

Filling:

**1 c. sugar**

**2 T. cornstarch**

**½ c. melted butter**

**1 t. cinnamon**

**4 c. diced apples**

**1½ c. water**

**1 t. vanilla**

Mix first 6 ingredients until crumbly; press half into a 9 x 9" baking pan. Cover with apples. Cook filling until clear and thick. Pour over apples; top with remaining crumbs. Bake at 350° for 1 hour.

## Apple Dumplings
*Mom (Elsie) Yoder*

**12 half apples**

**1 egg**

**3 c. flour**

Sauce:

**1 stick butter**

**1 c. white sugar**

**1¼ c. Crisco**

**1 t. salt**

**⅓ c. water**

**1 c. water**

Make a dough similar to a pie dough and set aside. Heat the sauce ingredients together in a kettle until it's heated. Pour into a 9 x 13" cake pan. Roll out dough as for pie; cut in 4ths. Take the apples; cover with dough. Set each one separately in sauce. Bake at 350° for 30 - 35 min. *This is a recipe Freeman's grandmother used to make.*

## Apple Nut Ring

*Mrs. Daniel A. (Ida) Miller*

2 pkg. refrigerated buttermilk
  biscuits
¾ c. sugar
1 T. cinnamon
¼ c. margarine
2 med. apples
⅓ c. nuts
¼ c. raisins

Separate biscuits into 20 pieces in a 9 x 13" pan. Combine sugar and cinnamon. Pour melted margarine over biscuits, then sprinkle ⅓ of the sugar mixture over the biscuits. Place sliced apples over that. Mix raisins and nuts with the rest of the mixture. Then spread evenly over all. Bake at 400° till apples are soft. *This is good warm with ice cream or cold with whipped cream.*

## Baked Apples

*Mrs. Clarence (Ruby) Yoder*

Wash, peel, and slice **12 apples** into a large baking dish. Mix in a saucepan the following and cook until clear.

2 c. boiling water
1 c. sugar
1 t. cinnamon
½ t. salt
3 T. cornstarch or clear jel (dissolved with a little cold water)

Pour over apple slices and bake until apples are soft. Let cool and serve with whipped cream.

## Baked Fudge Pudding

*Mrs. Sam (Martha) Schrock*

1 c. flour (pastry)
2 T. cocoa
¼ t. salt
¾ c. white sugar
2 t. baking powder
½ c. milk
1 t. vanilla
2 T. butter
¾ c. chopped nuts

Mix all this and put in a 9 x 13" baking pan. Mix 1 c. firmly packed brown sugar, ¼ c. cocoa, and 1¾ c. hot water and pour over the batter. Bake 45 min. at 350°. *This is very good to serve with ice cream.*

## Baked Oatmeal

*Mrs. Eldon (Katie) Nisley*

½ c. melted butter or margarine
⅓ c. brown sugar
1 egg, beaten
1 c. milk
2 c. quick oatmeal
1 c. coconut
½ t. salt
½ t. baking powder
½ c. raisins
¼ c. chopped nuts, opt.

Mix egg with milk and add remaining ingredients. Spread into a well greased 9 x 9" pan. Sprinkle with cinnamon and bake in 350° oven for 30 min. Serve with milk and fruit.

## Blueberry Cheesecake
*Mrs. Ray (LeEtta) Yoder*

Mix **16 brown crackers, crushed, ¾ c. white sugar, and ½ stick oleo.** Press into a 9 x 13" pan. (Mix **2 eggs, beaten, 2 (8 oz.) pkg. cream cheese, 1 c. sugar, and 1 t. vanilla.**) Spread over crackers. Bake 15 min. at 375°. When cool, pour blueberry pie filling over it. Serve with whipped cream on top.

## "Broken Glass"
*Mom (Rosa) Bontrager*

| | |
|---|---|
| **1 box green jello** | **1 c. boiling water** |
| **1 box red jello** | **1 c. crushed pineapple** |
| **1 box orange jello** | **1 pt. whipping cream** |
| **2 env. plain gelatin** | **½ c. sugar** |
| **½ c. cold water** | **⅛ t. salt** |

Dissolve jello in 1½ c. hot water each and pour into separate cake pans. Dissolve plain gelatin in cold water; add boiling water & pineapple; cool. Whip the cream with sugar & salt; mix into pineapple mixture. Cut the jello into cubes and fold into mixture. Pour in pans lined with:

**24 graham crackers, crushed**     **½ c. melted oleo**
**½ c. brown sugar**

Save crumbs for the top.

## Buster Bar Dessert
*Mrs. Freeman (Mabel) Yoder*

| | |
|---|---|
| **1 pkg. (15 oz.) Oreo cookies** | **2 c. salted peanuts** |
| **½ c. margarine** | **1 (8 oz.) jar caramel topping** |
| **½ gal. vanilla ice cream** | **3 c. non-dairy ready-to-whip** |
| **1 bottle (8 oz.) chocolate syrup** | **topping** |

Crush cookies; melt margarine and pour over cookies. Press into a 9 x 13" pan. Bake at 350° for 3 min.; let cool then slice ice cream and layer on top. Then freeze until hard; spread chocolate over the top and cover with the peanuts. Spread with caramel topping. Whip the cream and spread over all; sprinkle a few reserved cookies on top. Serve at once or return to the freezer until ready to serve.

## Butter Pecan Delight
*Mrs. Eli (Martha) Mullet*

| | |
|---|---|
| **3 (3 oz.) boxes butter pecan pie filling** | **1 qt. butter pecan ice cream** |
| **2 c. milk** | **8 oz. Cool Whip** |

Mix all together and pour onto crust:

**2½ c. graham cracker crumbs**     **3 - 4 crushed Heath candy bars**
**½ stick melted butter**

Save some crumbs for top. Serve immediately or freeze.

## Butterscotch Ice Cream
*Mrs. Christie (Anna) Yoder*

2 qt. milk
3 pkg. Knox gelatin
½ c. milk
4 eggs, beaten
½ t. maple flavoring

1½ c. brown sugar
1 pkg. butterscotch instant
 pudding
½ can Carnation milk
dash of salt

Heat milk; dissolve 3 pkgs. Knox gelatin in ½ c. milk. Beat eggs; add brown sugar; mix pudding as directed on pkg. Add Carnation milk, salt, and maple flavor. Mix all together. Makes 1 gallon.

## Butterscotch Nut Torte
*Mom (Elsie) Yoder*

6 eggs, separated
1½ c. white sugar
1 t. baking powder
2 c. graham cracker crumbs
Sauce:
½ c. water

½ c. nutmeats
2 t. vanilla
2 c. whipped topping

¼ c. melted butter

Blend in **1 c. brown sugar**. Make a paste of **1 T. flour, 1 egg, a little water, and ½ t. vanilla.** Mix well and bring to a boil until thick.

Beat egg yolks well; add sugar, baking powder, and vanilla. Mix well. Beat egg whites until stiff peaks form. Fold into yolk mixture; add crumbs and nuts. Bake at 350° for 30 min. When cake and sauce are cooled, cut cake in cubes and fix layers with sauce and whipped topping. Sauce can be doubled as is almost too small amount.

## Butterscotch Pudding
*Mrs. Clarence (Anna Marie) Miller*

1 c. water
1 can Eagle Brand milk
1 box instant butterscotch pudding

1 pkg. graham crackers,
 crushed fine
2 c. whipped topping

Mix together water, milk, and pudding. Put in fridge for 10 min.; stir whipped topping into pudding mix. Press ¾ c. of cracker crumbs into a 9 x 13" pan. Pour in pudding and rest of crackers on top. Refrigerate.

## Butterscotch Tapioca
*Miriam Yoder (in memory of Katie)*

12 c. water
4½ c. tapioca
2½ c. brown sugar
2 c. milk
4 eggs

1 cube oleo
2 t. vanilla
Cool Whip
Snickers candy bars or choc.
 chips
1 c. white sugar

Bring water to a boil; add tapioca and boil until clear. Add brown sugar and boil again. Add milk, eggs, and sugar. Bring to a boil. Add oleo and vanilla. Cool. Before serving, add desired amount of Cool Whip and candy bars or choc. chips.

## Butterscotch Sauce

*Mrs. Owen (Verna) Hershberger*

¾ c. sugar
½ c. light corn syrup
¼ t. salt
¼ c. butter
½ c. cream

Cook over low heat; cook to soft ball stage (234°). Cook to a thick smooth consistency. Remove from heat and stir in ½ **t. vanilla**. Serve over ice cream.

## Cake Dessert

*Mrs. Merlin (Mary) Lehman*

1 box white or yellow cake mix
1 sm. box jello
1 c. hot water
1 sm. box instant pudding
1 c. Rich's topping

Bake cake as directed on box. Prick with fork when baked. Mix jello with hot water and spoon over cake while it is still hot. Set in refrigerator until cold. Mix pudding and put on cake; chill. Then whip Rich's topping and put on top of pudding.

## Caramel Tapioca

*Mrs. Harry (Edna Mae) Bontrager*

7 c. boiling water
½ t. salt
1½ c. baby pearl tapioca
4 beaten egg yolks
1 c. cream
3 c. brown sugar
1 stick butter or oleo
¼ t. soda
⅓ c. hot water
candy bars
whipped cream

Boil water, salt, and tapioca until soft. Take off stove and add: egg yolks and cream beaten together. Put on stove and stir until it boils again. Take off stove. Boil together brown sugar, butter, soda, and hot water. Add this to tapioca mixture. Cool. Add bananas and candy bars and whipped cream.

## "Cherry Berries on a Cloud"

*Mrs. Eli (Martha) Mullet*

Shell:

Heat oven to 275°. Cover baking sheet with a brown grocery bag. Beat **3 egg whites and ¼ t. cream of tartar** until foamy. Beat in ¾ **c. sugar** (1 T. at a time). Continue beating until stiff and glossy. On paper bag, shape meringue, building up sides.

Bake 1½ hours at 275°. Turn off oven; leave meringue in oven with door closed for 1 hour. Remove from oven; finish cooling away from draft.

Filling:

1 (3 oz.) pkg. cream cheese
½ c. sugar
1 t. vanilla
1 c. whipped topping

Blend cream cheese, sugar, and vanilla. Gently fold in topping. Pile into shell. Chill. Before serving top with pie filling. (Cherry, strawberry, blueberry, or peach.) *A delicious summer dessert with fresh fruit. Melts in your mouth!*

## Cherry Bread Pudding

*Mrs. Lester (Verna) Bontrager*

1 (21 oz.) cherry pie filling
4 - 5 slices bread, cubed
¼ c. butter or margarine
1 T. lemon juice
1 c. milk
3 eggs, beaten
½ c. sugar
½ t. almond extract
cinnamon

Spread pie filling evenly in bottom of square glass baking dish. Cover with cubed bread. Drizzle melted butter over bread. Mix other liquid ingredients; pour over bread, then press bread down lightly so it absorbs the liquid. Sprinkle with cinnamon. Bake at 350° until set in center.

## Cherry Cheesecake

*Mrs. Lloyd (Edna) Raber*

Bottom Layer:
½ c. sugar
1 t. vanilla
12 oz. cream cheese
1 egg
1 can cherry pie filling

Top Layer:
1 white cake mix
1 c. water
2 eggs
12 oz. cream cheese

Mix all bottom layer ingredients together and pour into a well greased and floured 13 x 9 x 2" cake pan. Separately mix all ingredients together for top layer. Then pour evenly over top of ingredients in pan. Bake at 375° for 25 min. Cool for 1 hour.

## Chocolate Cream Cheese Pudding

*Mrs. Ora (Susie) Miller*

1 (6 oz.) choc. chips
1 (8 oz.) cream cheese
¾ c. brown sugar
½ t. salt
1 t. vanilla
2 eggs, separated
2 c. heavy cream, whipped
graham cracker crust

Melt chocolate over hot, not boiling, water. Cool 10 minutes. Blend cheese, sugar, salt, and vanilla. Add beaten egg yolks. Beat egg whites until stiff, not dry. Slowly beat in ¼ c. sugar. Beat until very stiff. Fold chocolate mixture into beaten egg whites and fold in whipped cream. Pour into crust and chill overnight. Very good.

## Chocolate Truffles

*Mrs. Ervin (Clara) Yoder*

1 chocolate cake, baked
2 sm. boxes instant choc. pudding
½ c. cold brewed coffee
1 c. chocolate chips
1 (12 oz.) container whipped topping

Mix pudding according to directions on box. Thin with coffee. Set aside. Cut cake into small squares about 1½". Put layer of cake into bowl. Pour about ⅓ of pudding over it. Put ⅓ of whipped topping on pudding and sprinkle with ⅓ of chips. Repeat for 2 more layers. You will probably not use an entire 13 x 9" cake. Maybe ⅔ of it. Use the rest as you wish.

## Chocolate Truffle Torte
*Mrs. Freeman (Mabel) Yoder*

4 c. semisweet choc. chips (or milk choc. chips work best)
3 c. whipping cream or non-dairy ready-to-whip cream
½ c. powdered sugar
1 T. vanilla
4 c. Oreo cookies, crushed
2 (1.6 oz.) boxes Junior mints, found by the candy bar and gum section in a grocery store (usually by the cash register)

In a heavy skillet, melt choc. chips and 1 c. whipping cream. Stir until smooth. Remove from heat, and cool to room temperature. Stir in powdered sugar and vanilla; set aside. In a mixing bowl, whip the rest of the cream and fold into chocolate mixture. In a 13 x 9" cake pan, put 4 c. crushed Oreo cookies then spoon choc. mixture onto cookies. Add dollops of whipped cream on top. Sprinkle with Junior mints. Can be fixed in pie plates and garnished with wholew Oreos stuck into top of pudding.

## Cornflake Pudding
*Mrs. Ora (Susie) Miller*

4 c. crushed cornflakes          ½ c. sugar
1 stick oleo

Mix like pie dough. Pat into pan, reserving some for the top. Then cream together:

8 oz. cream cheese          ½ c. sugar

Add **2 eggs, well beaten.** Fold in **8 oz. or 12 oz. Cool Whip.** Pour into cornflake crust. Garnish with reserved cornflakes. Chill.

## Country Ice Cream
*Mrs. Ervin (Clara) Yoder*

4 eggs                    4½ t. vanilla
2 c. sugar                ½ t. salt
5 c. milk                 2 sm. pkg. instant vanilla pudding
4 c. cream

Beat eggs for 5 min. Beat in 2 c. sugar and 1 c. milk until thick. Add rest of milk and cream, vanilla and salt. Sprinkle pudding on top and beat in. This will fill a 6 qt. ice cream freezer. Other flavors pudding may be used instead of vanilla if preferred.

*Gather crumbs of happiness and they will make you a loaf of contentment.*

## Cracker Fluff

*Mrs. Edwin (Annie) Ropp*

Soak **1 pkg. unflavored gelatin in** ⅓ **c. cold water**. Then bring to a boil the following:

½ c. sugar                          2 egg yolks, beaten
1½ c. milk

Boil 1 minute and add the gelatin and 1 t. vanilla. Cool. When set add:
2 stiffly beaten egg whites
1 c. cream, whipped (I use Rich's topping)

Mix well. Then mix cracker crumbs as follows:

2 pkgs. graham crackers, finely crumbled
¼ c. brown sugar                    ¼ lb. oleo or butter

Melt and brown butter in skillet; add crackers and sugar. Put buttered graham cracker crumbs in bottom of glass dish. Fill with fluff mixture. Sprinkle a few cracker crumbs over the top. Fills 1 glass bowl.

## Creamy Mocha Frozen Dessert

*Mrs. Lester (Verna) Bontrager*

1 T. hot water
2 t. instant coffee granules
1 c. cream–filled chocolate cookie crumbs
¾ c. chopped pecans, divided
¼ c. margarine, melted

2 (8 oz.) pkgs. cream cheese, softened
1 (14 oz.) can sweetened condensed milk
½ c. chocolate flavored syrup
1 (8 oz.) carton whipped topping

In a small bowl, dissolve coffee granules in hot water; set aside. In another bowl, combine cookie crumbs, ½ c. pecans and margarine. Pat into the bottom of a 9 x 13" cake pan. In a mixing bowl, beat cream cheese until fluffy. Blend in coffee mixture, milk, and chocolate syrup. Fold in whipped topping and spread over crust. Garnish with remaining pecans and additional cookie crumbs. Freeze.

*When you feel dog tired at night -
it may be because you growled all day.*

## Delicious Chocolate Dessert

*Mrs. Freeman (Mabel) Yoder*

½ c. shortening (room temp.)
4 T. cocoa
¾ c. sugar
2 eggs
3 T. milk
1 t. vanilla
½ t. baking powder
⅔ c. flour
½ t. salt
½ c. chopped pecans or nuts
chocolate sauce
4 c. ready-to-whip non-dairy
topping
2 (6 oz.) bags Heath Toffee Bits

Mix shortening, sugar, eggs, milk, and vanilla. Gradually add the cocoa, flour, baking powder, salt and nuts; stir well. Bake at 350° for approx. 20 min. or until done.

Chocolate Sauce:

6 - 8 c. *water
5 c. sugar
2 t. vanilla
4 T. cocoa
3 T. clear jel, Perma-flo or
cornstarch

*Milk may be used instead of water for a richer pudding. (Instead of this sauce 2 lg. boxes instant chocolate pudding may be used, but milk should be heated and cooled before using.) In a 4 qt. kettle, mix water and sugar; bring to a boil. Mix cocoa with thickener you will use, then add enough water to make a thick sauce. Then add carefully and slowly to boiling sugar water. Stir until thick. Remove from heat and cool well. Add vanilla.

Cut cake into 1 inch squares and put half in bottom of a 6 qt. bowl; pour half of sauce over cake. Then whip 2 c. of topping and pour over sauce. Cover with one bag Heath Toffee Bits. Repeat layers.

## Delicious Cottage Cheese Jello

*Mrs. Orva (Marietta) Yoder*

16 oz. Cool Whip
24 oz. small curd cottage cheese
1 can crushed pineapple
1 sm. can mandarin oranges
1 sm. box orange jello

Mix the dry jello with the cottage cheese; stir together well. Add the rest of the ingredients and whip together. A simple and easy dessert.

## Delicious Rhubarb Dessert

*Mrs. Mervin (Gertie) Eash*

4 c. diced rhubarb
1 c. sugar
½ c. strawberry jello
1 box yellow cake mix
2 c. water

Place rhubarb evenly in a 13 x 9" cake pan. Sprinkle sugar and jello over rhubarb, then the cake mix; last pour the water over all. Do not stir. Bake in 350° oven for 45 minutes.

## Dessert Pizza

*Mrs. Ivan (Arlene) Bontrager*

Crust:

Mix ¾ c. powdered sugar & ½ c. soft butter. Add 1 sm. egg & ½ t. vanilla. Mix. Then mix in 1¼ c. flour, ¼ t. soda, ¼ t. cream of tartar. Put dough onto a 12" pizza pan or into 2 nine inch pie pans and press evenly to edges. Bake at 375° about 20 min. or until golden. Cool.

Cheese:

Mix 3 or 4 oz. cream cheese with 4 oz. whipped topping. Spread over cooled crust.

Sauce:

Blend 1 c. sugar and 2 T. cornstarch, rounded. Add 2 egg yolks, 1 T. vinegar, 1 T. butter, and the juice drained from a 20 oz. can of pineapple chunks. (Reserve pineapple.) Cook until thick, stirring constantly. Cool. Spread sauce over top of cheese mixture. Cut into individual serving sizes and then add toppings to pizza.

Toppings:

Any combination that suits your taste of pineapple chunks, fresh blueberries, fresh sliced strawberries, fresh peach slices, banana slices, green and red seedless grapes, cantaloupe chunks, unpeeled Red Delicious apple slices, chocolate or butterscotch morsels, chopped nuts, maraschino cherries ...... (4 toppings are sufficient.) Serves 12.

## Easy, Delicious Fruit Dessert

*Mrs. Sam (Viola) Miller*

1 (6 oz.) pkg. orange jello
1 c. boiling water
1 pint vanilla ice cream
1 c. cream, whipped
1 can crushed pineapple
1 sm. can mandarin oranges, drained (opt.)

Dissolve jello with boiling water. Stir in ice cream. When partially set, fold in whipped cream and pineapple with their juice. Arrange orange slices on top.

## Fruit Pizza

*Mrs. Daniel A. (Ida) Miller*

½ c. oleo
¾ c. sugar
1 egg
1½ c. flour
½ t. baking powder
1 t. salt
½ c. milk
8 oz. cream cheese
½ c. sugar
2 t. pineapple juice
2 c. fruit juice
2 T. clear jel (rounded)

Beat the egg, oleo, and sugar. Add salt and baking powder then the milk and flour. Put in a greased 14" pizza pan. Bake at 350° for 12 min. Mix cream cheese, ½ c. sugar, and pineapple juice and put on crust. Let set. Arrange any kind of fruit on it, then put the glaze on top made with fruit juice and clear jel cooked together. *You can also use a 9 x 13" cake pan instead of a pizza pan.*

## Gelatin Ice Cream
*Mrs. Leland (Orpha) Yoder*

Soak **2 env. Knox gelatin in ½ c. cold water;** heat **4 c. milk**, hot but not boiling. Remove from heat; add gelatin, **2 c. sugar, 2 T. vanilla, & 1 t. salt.** Cool and add **3 c. heavy cream.** Put in 1 gal. freezer and freeze. You may have to add a little milk yet. Ingredients may be varied to suit taste, like maple flavoring or chocolate. A family favorite!

## Honey Fruit Cups
*Mrs. Freeman (Mabel) Yoder*

**8 c. cut-up fruit, red & green grapes, pears, apples, bananas, & oranges**
**2 (6 oz.) cartons vanilla or lemon yogurt, or homemade yogurt**
**2 T. honey**                    **¼ t. almond flavoring**
**1 t. grated orange peel**

Mix fruit together gently, then transfer to a colander, and drain excess juice. In another bowl combine yogurt, honey, orange peel and flavoring, then mix with fruit. This is a good not so rich fruit mixture.

## Ice Cream Sandwiches
*Mrs. Clarence (Ruby) Yoder*

**3 eggs**                        **⅓ c. sugar**
**1 c. cream**                    **2 T. jello or 2 t. flavoring**

Separate the eggs. In a med. size bowl, beat the egg whites until very stiff. Add sugar and jello (or flavoring). Rinse the beater. Next beat the cream until fairly stiff in a larger bowl then beat the yolks in a small bowl. Mix whipped cream and yolks together in a large bowl; add the first mixture (whites) and beat all together. Put graham crackers in cake pan - then filling and crackers on top. Put out to freeze at 10° or lower. We also like it frozen without the crackers.

*The man who says it can't be done is likely*
*to be interrupted by someone doing it.*

## Jelly Roll

*Mrs. Christie (Anna) Yoder*

4 eggs, well beaten
¾ c. sugar
¾ c. flour
¾ t. baking powder
1 t. vanilla
½ t. salt

Beat eggs about 5 min. Gradually add sugar. Mix flour and rest of ingredients. Pour in 10 x 15" jelly roll pan, with greased waxed paper on it. Bake 12 - 15 min. or until toothpick comes out clean at 375°. Invert onto a clean towel sprinkled with powdered sugar. Roll up in towel. Remove and fill with one of the following fillings.

Filling for Jelly Roll #1:

½ t. salt
½ c. flour
1⅓ c. hot water
½ c. brown or white sugar

Combine and heat until very thick; remove. Stir in **6 T. butter** and let cool. Add flavoring. Spread on cake and roll quickly.

Filling for Jelly Roll #2:

3 T. white sugar
1½ T. flour
1 egg yolk, beaten
1 c. milk
1 T. butter
vanilla

Stir together first 4 ingredients. Cook until thick. Add butter and vanilla. Let cool. Spread on cake and roll quickly.

## Layered Chiffon Cake

*Mrs. Freeman (Mabel) Yoder*

1 golden chiffon cake *(recipe found elsewhere in the cake section of this cookbook)*
4 c. whipping cream, or non-dairy cream ready-to-whip
¾ c. caramel ice cream topping
½ t. vanilla
8 Butterfinger candy bars, crushed

In a lg. mixing bowl, whip the cream; gradually add caramel topping until soft peaks form. Set aside. Cut cake in 3 layers horizontally. Place bottom layer on serving platter. Spread with a thick layer of cream mixture (divide it up so you have enough for all 3 layers). Then sprinkle with approx. ½ c. candy bars. Repeat with second layer; place the third layer on top. Frost top and sides with remaining cream mixture. Sprinkle candy bar bits on top and all sides, until completely covered. A large sheet of wax paper may be placed under cake platter before starting to catch the candy bar pieces when sprinkling them on the cake. An angel food cake may also be used. Refrigerate a few hours before serving.

# Lemon Dessert

*Mrs. Edwin (Annie) Ropp*

Mix:

| | |
|---|---|
| 1 c. flour | ½ c. chopped nuts |
| ½ c. oleo | |

Mix as for pie dough. Press in a 9 x 13" cake pan. Bake 12 min. at 350°. Cool. Then mix:

| | |
|---|---|
| 8 oz. cream cheese | 1 c. whipped topping, whipped |
| 1 c. powdered sugar | 2 c. small marshmallows |

Spread over cooled crust **2 pkgs. instant lemon pudding** or any flavor you like, and **3 c. milk** (boil milk and cool off before you add instant pudding). Mix well until thickened and spread on top of cheese mixture. Spread whipped topping on top and sprinkle with nuts. Refrigerate until ready to serve.

# Lime Jello Dessert

*Mrs. Vernon (Polly) Beechy*

**5 sm. boxes lime jello**

Mix as directions on box. Let thicken a little. Then take:

| | |
|---|---|
| 1 (8 oz.) pkg. cream cheese | ¼ c. white sugar |

Stir until soft and creamy. Add:

| | |
|---|---|
| 4 c. whipped topping, whipped | 1½ c. marshmallows |

Stir into softened jello and mix together. Pour in desired bowls.

# Milk Tapioca

*Grandma (Edna) Yoder*

| | |
|---|---|
| 1 qt. milk | pinch of salt |
| ½ c. small pearl tapioca | vanilla |
| 2 eggs, beaten | sm. can crushed pineapple, or |
| 1¼ c. sugar | bananas |
| 1 T. cornstarch | 1 c. whipping cream |

Bring milk and tapioca to a slow boil, stirring often. When tapioca is clear add beaten eggs, sugar, cornstarch, and salt. Let thicken; add vanilla. Cool and add pineapple and whipped cream.

# Mini Cherry Cheesecakes

*Regina Miller*

| | |
|---|---|
| vanilla wafers | 1 T. lemon juice |
| 2 (8 oz.) cream cheese | 1 t. vanilla |
| 2 eggs | cherry pie filling |
| ¾ c. sugar | |

Place one vanilla wafer in the bottom of a cupcake paper in muffin tin pan. Beat remaining ingredients until fluffy. Fill muffin cup ½ to ¾ full. Bake in a 375° oven for 15 - 20 min. Top with cherry pie filling when cool. Chill and serve.

# Mint Brownie Pie

*Mrs. Freeman (Mabel) Yoder*

1 c. sugar
2 sq. unsweetened chocolate
  (1 oz. each)
6 T. butter, no substitutes

1 t. vanilla
2 eggs, beaten
½ c. flour
dash of salt

Filling:
1 pkg. (8 oz.) cream cheese, softened
¾ c. sugar
½ t. peppermint extract
6 - 8 drops green cake coloring
8 oz. frozen whipped topping, whipped
chocolate syrup (ice cream topping)

In saucepan over low heat, melt butter and chocolate. Add beaten eggs, sugar, vanilla, salt, and flour. Stir well. Pour into 9" springform pan or 10" pie plate. Bake at 350° for 18 - 20 min. Stir together filling ingredients, adding whipped topping last; mix gently. Cool cake well; spread filling over the top. Swirl chocolate syrup over all and garnish with dollops of whipped cream and chocolate chips if desired.

# Old-Fashioned Apple Dumplings

*Mrs. LaVern (Martha) Yoder*

6 apples
2 c. flour
2½ t. baking powder
½ t. salt
⅔ c. margarine
½ c. milk

Sauce:
2 c. brown sugar
2 c. water
¼ t. cinnamon
¼ c. butter

Pare and core apples; leave whole. Mix flour, baking powder, and salt together. Cut in margarine until crumbly. Add milk and mix together lightly, working dough together. Roll dough into 6" sq. Place an apple on each. Fill cavity in apple with sugar and cinnamon. Wrap dough around apple. Place dumplings in baking dish. Combine all sauce ingredients except butter. Cook 5 min. Add butter and pour over dumplings. Bake at 375° for 35 to 40 min.

# Orange Tapioca Pudding

*Mrs. Marvin (Ruby) Shrock*

1 (3 oz.) box orange jello
1 box instant vanilla pudding
1 (3 oz.) box vanilla tapioca pudding
2½ c. cold water

1 can (11 oz.) mandarin
  oranges
1 c. whipped topping

Put water and juice from oranges in saucepan. Add jello and puddings. Bring to a boil; cool; fold in topping and oranges into pudding mixture. Refrigerate.

## Oreo Crunch Pudding

*Mrs. Andy (Dorothy) Miller*

1 pkg. Oreo cookies
1 c. M & M's
½ gal. vanilla ice cream or ice cream of your choice
8 oz. whipped topping
½ c. butter

Set ice cream out to soften. Crumble cookies and pat half of them into a 13 x 9" cake pan or a Tupperware of about that size. Melt butter and pour over cookie crumbs in pan then top with ice cream. Spread whipped topping over ice cream then sprinkle the other half of cookie crumbs all over whipped topping. Sprinkle M & M's on top and freeze for 6 hours or overnight.

## Party Dessert

*Mrs. Lloyd (Edna) Raber*

2½ c. Rice Krispies
½ c. melted oleo
½ c. brown sugar
¾ c. chopped nuts
½ c. coconut
½ gal. ice cream
1 jar butterscotch topping

Mix together, except for ice cream and topping. Spread half of Rice Krispies mixture in an 8 x 8" cake pan, and put ¼ of butterscotch topping over it. Next put ice cream on top of mixture and cover with remaining mixture. Put rest of butterscotch topping over all and freeze.

## Peanut Butter Dessert

*Mrs. Orva (Marietta) Yoder*

Put in bottom of pan:
1 pkg. graham crackers, crushed
¼ lb. butter
½ c. sugar

2nd Layer, cream together:
1½ c. powdered sugar
1 c. peanut butter
1 pkg. cream cheese

3rd Layer, mix together:
2 boxes choc. instant pudding
1 box vanilla instant pudding
4 c. milk

Top with whipped cream, and garnish with choc. chips.

*The recipe for a good
speech includes shortening.*

# Peanut Delight Dessert

*Mrs. Lester (Verna) Bontrager*

First Layer:

²/₃ c. chopped peanuts          ½ c. butter or margarine
1 c. flour

Blend flour and butter together with a fork until crumbly; add nuts. Press in a 9 x 13" pan. Bake at 350° for 20 min. Cool.

Second Layer:

¹/₃ c. peanut butter          1 c. powdered sugar
1 (8 oz.) pkg. cream cheese   2 c. whipped topping

Cream peanut butter and cream cheese; add powdered sugar and mix well. Blend in whipped topping. Spread over cooled first layer.

Third Layer:

1 (3¾ oz.) pkg. vanilla instant pudding
1 (3¾ oz.) pkg. chocolate instant pudding
3 c. cold milk

Mix well; spread over second layer. Cool a few min. to set.

Fourth Layer:

Top with **1 or 2 c. whipped topping.** Sprinkle with **½ c. peanuts and a chopped candy bar (Hershey's or Snickers etc.).**


# Pineapple Tapioca

*Mrs. Ezra (Mary) Miller*

1 qt. milk                    pinch of salt
½ c. baby pearl tapioca       1 t. vanilla
2 eggs, beaten                1 c. whipping cream
1¼ c. sugar                   1 sm. can crushed pineapple
1 T. cornstarch

Heat milk, then add tapioca. Stir until boiling. Turn burner real low and cook until clear. Add beaten eggs with sugar and cornstarch; cook until it boils again. Add salt and vanilla, then cool and add pineapple and whipped cream.


# Prune Pudding

*Grandma (Edna) Yoder*

¹/₃ c. sugar                  Syrup:
2 T. butter                   1 c. brown sugar
½ c. milk                     2 T. butter
1½ c. flour                   1 t. vanilla
3 t. baking powder            2 c. water
1 t. vanilla
1 c. pulp from boiled prunes, cut up
(½ c. nuts if desired)

Heat ingredients for syrup. Mix all of first part and drop by spoonsful into hot syrup. Bake 20 to 30 min. in moderate oven. Cool and serve with whipped cream.

## Pumpkin Pudding

*Mrs. Clarence T. (Ruby) Yoder*

4 eggs
1½ c. sugar
pinch of salt
1 T. cinnamon
1 c. clear jel
½ c. flour
4 c. mashed pumpkin (or squash)
8 c. milk
vanilla & maple flavoring (opt.)

Beat the eggs; add sugar, salt, and cinnamon. Mix in clear jel, flour, and pumpkin; stir well. Add milk and flavoring; stir and pour into 2 cake pans. Sprinkle with cinnamon and bake in 350° oven for an hour or more. After it has cooled, top with whipped cream and serve.

## Rhubarb Torte

*Mrs. Ezra (Mary) Miller*

1 c. butter
2 c. flour
4 T. sugar

Mix until crumbly and put into cake pan. Bake at 350° for 10 min.

5 c. rhubarb, fine
6 egg yolks
2 c. sugar
7 T. flour
1 c. cream
1 t. vanilla
¼ t. salt

Pour over crust and bake at 350° for 45 min. or until custard is set.

## Spicy Apple Pudding

*Mrs. Ora (Susie) Miller*

1½ c. sugar
1 c. flour
1 c. dry bread crumbs
1 t. soda
1 t. cinnamon
1 t. cloves
1 t. salt
½ c. melted shortening
2 eggs
6 chopped apples

Mix all together. Spread in pan and bake at 325° for 45 min. I omit the bread crumbs and use rolled oats instead. Just as good.

## Strawberry Ice Cream

*Mrs. Vern (Irene) Schlabach*

4 eggs
4 c. milk
2 c. sugar
2 c. miniature marshmallows
2 t. vanilla extract
4 c. pureed unsweetened strawberries
2 c. half and half cream
1 c. whipping cream

In a heavy saucepan, combine eggs and milk. Stir in sugar; cook and stir over medium - low heat until mixture is thick enough to coat a metal spoon and until thermometer reads 160°, approx. 14 min. Remove from the heat. Stir in the marshmallows until melted. Set saucepan in ice and stir the mixture for 5 - 10 min. or until cool. Stir in the remaining ingredients. Cover and refrigerate overnight. When ready to freeze, pour into cylinder of an ice cream freezer and freeze according to manufacturers' directions. Yields: 1 gal.

## Strawberry Pretzel Dessert

*Mrs. Harry (Edna Mae) Bontrager*
*Mrs. Daniel (Ida) Miller*

3 T. sugar
2 c. crushed pretzels, not fine
¾ c. oleo or butter, melted
½ c. powdered sugar
8 oz. cream cheese
2 c. miniature marshmallows

6 oz. strawberry jello
2½ c. boiling water
10 oz. frozen strawberries
1 pkg. frozen whipped topping
or 2 c. ready-to-whip topping,
whipped

Mix first 3 ingredients together and bake 15 min. at 350° in a 9 x 13" pan. Set aside. Soften cream cheese and add powdered sugar. Fold in whipped topping and marshmallows. Spread over crust in pan. Dissolve jello in hot water and cool until partly set. Stir in strawberries and spread over other layer. Serves 16 - 20. Can be made a day ahead.

## Sweetheart Pudding

*Mrs. Freeman (Mabel) Yoder*
*Mrs. Vernon (Polly) Beechy*

½ c. sugar
½ c. brown sugar
3 heaping T. cornstarch
3 egg yolks
4 c. milk
pinch of salt
3 egg whites

1 t. vanilla
2½ c. graham crackers,
crushed fine
½ c. sugar
⅔ c. melted butter

Mix last 3 ingredients together and line a 9 x 13" pan with all but 1 c. crumbs. In a bowl combine 1 c. milk and egg yolks; gradually add cornstarch and sugars. Beat well. In a 3 qt. saucepan, heat the rest of the milk until almost boiling, then add egg mixture and cook until thick. Add vanilla; cool. Pour into crumb-lined pan. Beat egg whites and layer on top of filling, then add reserved crumbs. Bake in broiler a few minutes until golden on top. *Variations: Flour can be used instead of cornstarch. Filling can be fixed in layers with graham crackers and bananas, also nuts.*

## Tapioca Dessert

*Mrs. Leroy (Sara) Yoder*

1 qt. water
1 c. tapioca

Cook 5 min., add **1 c. brown sugar** and cook until done. Mix **1 c. milk, 2 eggs, beaten, ½ c. sugar, and pinch of salt** to cooked tapioca. Bring to a boil again. Cool. When cold, add **1 c. cream, whipped.** Snickers candy bars go good with it.

## Tapioca Pudding

*Grandma (Mary) Bontrager*

½ c. baby pearl tapioca
1 qt. milk
1¼ c. white sugar
2 eggs
1 T. cornstarch

pinch of salt
1 t. vanilla
1 c. crushed pineapple
1 c. whipped topping

Bring tapioca and milk to a boil. Keep stirring until it cooks, then cook until clear (over low heat), then add white sugar, eggs, cornstarch, salt, and vanilla. Stir until it thickens. When cold, add crushed pineapple and whipped topping.

## Tin Roof Sundae Pie

*Mrs. Freeman (Mabel) Yoder*

2 ozs. semisweet choc. chips
1 T. butter, no substitutes
Peanut Layer:
20 caramels
⅓ c. whipping cream
Chocolate Layer:
8 oz. chocolate chips
2 T. butter, no substitutes
1 c. whipping cream or non-dairy
  ready-to-whip topping

1 pastry shell (9"), baked

1½ c. salted peanuts

2 t. vanilla
caramel ice cream topping
peanuts & whipped cream for
  garnish

In double boiler, melt butter and chocolate. Spread onto the bottom of crust. In a saucepan over low heat, melt caramels and cream, stirring frequently, until smooth. Remove from heat; stir in peanuts. Spoon into pie shell. <u>Refrigerate.</u> In a saucepan over low heat, melt chocolate and butter. Remove from heat; let stand 15 min. Meanwhile in a mixing bowl, beat cream and vanilla until soft peaks form. Carefully fold whipped cream into chocolate mixture. Spread over peanut layer. Garnish with whipped cream around the edges then sprinkle with peanuts and drizzle with caramel topping over all. Refrigerate a few hours before serving.

*We can't take it with us - but how we got it
may help determine where we will go.*

## Toll House Cookie Torte
*Mrs. Toby (Martha) Yoder*

⅔ c. shortening, softened
(part butter)
½ c. white sugar
½ c. brown sugar
1 egg
1½ c. flour
½ t. soda
1 t. vanilla
½ t. salt
½ c. chopped nuts, opt.
1 c. chocolate chips
½ c. light corn syrup
1½ c. ready-to-whip non-dairy
topping

Preheat oven to 350°. Line 3 baking sheets with foil. Mix shortening, egg, sugars, and vanilla thoroughly. Blend in flour, soda, & salt. Mix in nuts if desired. Divide dough into 3 equal parts. With floured hands, pat each part into 8" circles on prepared baking sheet. Bake 12 - 15 min. until lightly browned. Cool. In a saucepan over low heat, stir chocolate chips & corn syrup until melted. (It may be necessary to thin it with evaporated or reg. milk.) Set aside.

Whip topping until stiff. Spread ⅓ of the whipped topping on baked cookie circle; drizzle ¼ of chocolate mixture over whipped cream. Place cookie circle on top and repeat with whipped topping and chocolate syrup. Place third cookie circle on top and repeat with whipped topping. Wait to put on the chocolate until ready to serve. Cover and chill 8 hours. Remove from fridge 15 min. before serving. Yield: 10 - 12 servings. It needs to be refrigerated for that long so you can cut it. Drizzle caramel ice cream topping over the top (optional). *I very seldom use all the chocolate syrup as I think it's too much and too rich. The rest is good on ice cream.*

## Upside-Down Date Pudding
*Mom (Rosa) Bontrager*

1 c. cut up dates
1 c. boiling water
½ c. brown sugar
½ c. white sugar
1 egg
2 T. melted butter
1⅓ c. flour
1 t. soda
½ t. baking powder
½ t. salt
1 c. chopped nuts

Combine dates and boiling water. Let set until cool. Cream sugars, egg, and butter until light. Add flour and rest of ingredients; stir in nuts and cooled date mixture. Mix well.

Combine 1½ c. brown sugar, 2 t. butter & 1½ c. boiling water. Pour this in your cake pan first, then add your other mixture. Bake at 375° for 40 - 45 min.

*Let the words I speak today be soft and tender - for tomorrow I may have to eat them.*

# Soups, Salads, & Sandwiches

# The Garden Argument

The tomato said, with a face rosy red,
"I'm the queen of the whole garden bed.
So tart and delicious, most everyone wishes
On my juicy meat to be fed."
Said the onion so strong, "You couldn't go wrong
To partake of my elements rare.
With such a sweet savor I give a rich flavor
So all who might wish me may share."
Said the carrot so yellow, "I'm a popular fellow.
At present I'm having my day!
My elements mild are so good for a child;
They make him grow rosy and gay."
The cabbage head from the same garden bed
Said, "I'm bursting to have my say:
So crisp and so white, with flavor just right,
I'm fit for a king any day!"
The corn pricked his ears and said, "Listen, my dears!
I have heard every word you have said,
For I am so tall, I look down on you all -
I'm the king of the whole garden bed!"
The celery said, "Look! Here comes the cook.
We'll let her wise judgment decide
Which one she may choose - the rest of us lose."
"Fair enough! We agree!" they all cried.
The cook came along with a smile and a song.
The vegetables she viewed as a group.
She cut and she sliced with her sharp paring knife,
And they all went into the soup.

-Leona Duggan

## Bacon - Potato Soup

*Mrs. Eli (Martha) Mullet*

2 lbs. bacon
2 c. potatoes
1 c. carrots
½ c. celery
1 med. onion
1½ c. frozen peas, thawed
1 c. bacon drippings

1½ c. flour
2 qt. milk
1 t. salt
2 t. seasoning salt
½ t. pepper
1 t. liquid smoke

Cut and fry bacon and drain. Cook potatoes, carrots, celery, & onion with 1 t. salt. Mix bacon drippings and flour; add milk and bring to a boil, stirring constantly. Add salt, seasoning, pepper & liquid smoke. Pour over drained vegetables; add bacon and peas. Stir all together; serve and enjoy! *Handy Hint: Make a big batch for supper; for a quick dinner the next day, cook macaroni and put in baking dish; pour leftover soup over macaronis. Top with cheese and french fried onions. Bake at 350° for 20 - 30 min.*

## Beef and Sausage Soup

*Mrs. Freeman (Mabel) Yoder*

1 lb. beef stew meat, cut into bite size pcs.
1 lb. bulk pork sausage, shaped into balls
3 c. tomato juice - 2 whole chopped tomatoes may be added
3 c. water
1 c. chopped onion
1 t. salt
1 t. Italian seasoning
1 T. Worcestershire sauce

2½ c. potatoes
1 c. diced celery
2 T. vegetable oil
½ t. pepper

In a lg. skillet, heat oil over medium heat. Brown beef on all sides. Remove with a slotted spoon and set aside. Brown sausage and drain fat. Put all ingredients in a large kettle and bring to a boil; reduce heat and simmer, covered, until beef is tender, about 1½ hours. This soup can be made into double batches and put into jars and cold packed 2½ hours or pressured at 10 lbs. pressure for approx. 1 hour.

## Broccoli Noodle Cheese Soup

*Mrs. Ora (Susie) Miller*

¾ c. diced onion
6 c. water
6 chicken bouillon cubes
2 (10 oz.) pkg. frozen broccoli

2 - 3 T. oil
6 c. milk
1 (8 oz.) pkg. noodles
8 - 16 oz. cheese

Brown onion in oil. Add water and bouillon cubes. Bring to a boil. Add noodles; cook until noodles are soft - 10 min. Add broccoli and cook for 5 min. more. After mixture is heated through, add cheese. Stir gently until cheese is melted. Add milk and heat until hot.

## Cheddar Chowder

*Mrs. Mervin (Gertie) Eash*
*Mrs. Marvin (Erma) Miller*

2 c. water
2 c. diced potatoes
½ c. diced carrots
½ c. diced celery
¼ c. chopped onion
1 t. salt
¼ t. pepper

White Sauce:
¼ c. butter
¼ c. flour
2 c. milk
2 c. cheddar cheese, grated
1 c. cubed ham, bacon or bologna

Combine all ingredients, except the white sauce, in a lg. kettle. Boil 10 to 12 min. Meanwhile in another saucepan make white sauce by melting butter. Add flour and stir until smooth. Fry about 1 minute. Slowly add milk; cook until thickened. Add cheese and stir until melted. Add this cheese sauce and cubed ham to the vegetables that have not been drained. Serve hot. 6 servings.

## Cheeseburger Soup

*Mrs. Daniel A. (Ida) Miller*

½ lb. hamburger
¾ c. onions
¾ c. shredded carrots
1 c. diced celery
1 t. dried basil
1 t. parsley flakes
4 T. margarine
3 c. chicken broth

4 c. diced potatoes
¼ c. flour
8 oz. cheese, 2 c.
1½ c. milk
¾ t. salt
pepper to taste
¼ c. sour cream

In a 3 qt. saucepan, brown hamburger; drain and set aside. In same saucepan, saute onions, carrots, basil, parsley, and potatoes in margarine until vegetables are tender. Add broth and hamburger; bring to a boil. Reduce heat; cover and simmer 10 - 12 min. Meanwhile make thick with flour and milk. Boil and stir 2 min. Reduce heat; add cheese, salt, and pepper. Blend in sour cream. Makes 8 servings. (2¼ qts.)

*When you flee temptation make sure you*
*don't leave a forwarding address.*

## Chili Soup

*Mrs. Freeman (Mabel) Yoder*

2 qts. tomato juice
1 can dark red kidney beans
1 can light red kidney beans
1 can pork-n-beans
1 can chili beans
1 can refried beans
½ c. macaroni
2 - 3 T. mustard
¼ c. ketchup
1½ c. brown sugar
6 - 9 t. chili powder, level
1 lb. hamburger or ground turkey
1 lb. pork sausage
1 sm. onion

In a frying pan, brown sausage and hamburger with onion and refried beans. Drain fat. In lg. 8 qt. kettle combine the rest of the ingredients and bring to boiling point, then simmer and add hamburger mixture. Simmer a half hour for the flavors to blend well. Some beans may be omitted. May be doubled or tripled and put in jars; pressure can a half hour at 10 lbs. pressure.

## Cream of Broccoli Soup

*Mrs. Orva (Marietta) Yoder*

6 T. butter
5 T. flour
2 c. milk
dash of pepper
½ c. cut up ham
1 t. chicken base
1 T. finely chopped onion
1 c. chicken broth
¾ t. salt
1 (10 oz.) box broccoli, thawed

Saute butter and onion; blend in flour. Gradually add broth, milk, salt, and pepper, stirring until smooth. Cook until thickened. Puree broccoli in blender. Add to mixture and heat 3 or 4 min.

## Cream of Celery Soup

*Mrs. Daniel (Esther) Yoder*

3 T. butter
2 T. flour
1 t. salt
⅛ t. pepper
4 c. milk or water
1 c. cooked celery
1 T. chicken base

Melt butter in saucepan. Add flour, salt, and pepper. Blend until smooth. Stir in liquid. Bring to a boil, stirring constantly. Boil 1 min. Add soup base and celery. If you want to can it, use only ½ of liquid. Cold pack for 2 hours. Add rest of liquid when ready to use. *I like to use some cream for liquid.*

*Think all you speak,*
*but speak not all you think.*

## Cream of Tomato Soup

*Mrs. Ivan (Arlene) Bontrager*

2 T. margarine
2 T. onion, chopped
3 T. flour
2 t. sugar
1 t. salt
1/8 t. black pepper

dash each of garlic salt, basil,
oregano, thyme, and rosemary
(according to your taste)
2 c. tomato juice
2 c. cold milk

Heat margarine in large skillet; sauté onion. Blend in flour, sugar, salt, and seasonings. Remove from heat. Gradually stir in tomato juice. Bring to a boil, stirring constantly. Boil 1 min. Stir hot tomato mixture into cold milk. Heat, but do not boil. Serve.

## Hearty Hamburger Soup

*Mrs. Reuben (Martha) Yoder*

2 T. butter or margarine
1 c. chopped onion
1 c. sliced carrot
1/2 c. chopped green pepper
1 lb. ground beef
1 c. tomato juice

1 c. diced potatoes
1 1/2 t. salt
1 t. seasoning salt
1/8 t. pepper
1/3 c. flour
5 c. milk

Melt butter in a saucepan or 10" skillet. Add onion, carrots, & green pepper. Cook until onion is tender. Add beef and cook until crumbly. Stir in tomato juice, potatoes, & seasonings. Cover; cook over low heat until vegetables are tender. About 20 - 25 min. Combine flour with 1 c. of the milk and beat until free of lumps. Stir into soup mixture. Add remaining milk and heat, stirring frequently. DO NOT ALLOW TO BOIL. Yield: 10 servings.

## Hearty Potato - Sauerkraut Soup

*Mrs. Lester (Verna) Bontrager*

1 can cream of mushroom soup
1 (16 oz.) can sauerkraut, drained
4 c. chicken broth
2 (4 oz.) cans mushrooms, drained
1 med. potato, cubed
2 med. carrots, chopped
1 med. onion, chopped
2 stalks celery, chopped

3/4 lb. Polish sausage, cubed
1/2 c. cooked chicken
2 T. vinegar
2 t. dried dillweed
1/2 t. pepper
2 slices bacon, cooked &
crumbled (opt.)
2 hard-cooked eggs, (opt.)

In a 4 qt. kettle stir together all ingredients except bacon and eggs. Cover and cook on low heat until vegetables are tender. Sprinkle each serving with bacon and chopped eggs, if desired.

## Potato Soup
*Mrs. Ervin (Clara) Yoder*

¼ c. butter
¼ c. flour
¼ c. chopped onion
2 stalks celery, chopped
1 lb. cubed ham
4 c. shredded potatoes
5 - 6 c. milk
1 c. American or Velveeta cheese

Cook vegetables together with water to cover until tender. In separate kettle melt butter then add 5 c. milk. While milk heats, make a thickening with flour and remaining milk. Add to hot milk and when it comes to a boil, add vegetables. Add ham and cheese and salt & pepper to taste. Stir until cheese is melted. Serve with crackers or toast. (Do not drain veg. before adding white sauce.) *Our favorite.*

## Potato Soup
*Ola Bontrager*

3 - 4 potatoes, peeled & diced
¼ c. celery, chopped
1½ c. water
2 T. butter
1 qt. milk
1 T. parsley
salt & pepper to taste
2 hard-boiled eggs, diced

Cook the potatoes and celery in the water and butter until tender. Then add the milk, seasonings, and eggs. Beat thoroughly. Makes 6 servings.

## Sausage Chowder Soup
*Mrs. Freeman (Mabel) Yoder*

2 c. cubed potatoes
½ c. shredded carrots
¼ c. diced celery
1 lb. sausage
½ t. salt
¼ t. pepper
½ t. Italian seasoning
2 c. cut up American cheese
   slices, or cheddar cheese
4 c. milk
2 T. flour
1 c. milk

In a medium saucepan, put potatoes, carrots, celery, and seasonings. Cover with water and cook until soft. Meanwhile, cook sausage until well done in frying pan. Pour into kettle with vegetables; add milk (less milk may be used for a thicker soup). Make a sauce of flour and 1 c. milk. When vegetable mixture starts to boil, add sauce and stir until thick. Add cheese and stir well. Remove from heat to avoid scorching.

## Split Pea Soup
*Mrs. Christy (Anna) Bontrager*

Bring **1 ham bone or shank end of ham and 3 qt. water** to a boil. Then add:

1 lg. minced onion
2 finely cut carrots
3 stalks celery
potatoes, opt.
sprig of parsley
2 c. split peas

Season to taste with salt and pepper. Simmer another 1 - 2 hours.

## Taco Soup

Mrs. Merlin (Mary) Lehman
Mrs. Simon (Martha) Schmucker

**1 lb. hamburger, browned with onions**
Drain then put in **½ pkg. or ⅛ c. taco seasoning**. Add **1 qt. tomato juice and 1 pt. pizza sauce and 1 pt. kidney beans**. Simmer 15 min. When serving have cheddar cheese, Dorito chips, and sour cream to put on top.

## Turkey or Chicken Chowder

Mrs. Ervin (Clara) Yoder

To every 4 c. broth and meat add:

**1 med. onion, chopped**
**1 c. carrots, chopped or shredded**
**1 c. potatoes, or may substitute
   noodles**
**salt to taste**

**6 T. flour**
**2 c. milk**
**1 c. Velveeta cheese**
**¼ c. butter**

Simmer vegetables in broth 20 min. or until tender. Shake flour and milk together in shaker or jar and add to broth. Bring to a boil then add cheese and butter. Stir until melted. Season to taste. *Variation: 1 c. celery may be added.*

## 3-Layer Salad

Mrs. Vern (Irene) Schlabach

Bottom Layer:
**2 boxes or ¾ c. orange jello**
**3¾ c. water**
**1 can crushed pineapple, drained**
**½ c. nuts, (opt.)**
   Chill until set.
Third Layer:
**3 eggs**
**3 T. flour**

Second Layer:
**1 (8 oz.) cream cheese**
**1 c. whipped cream, whipped**
   Mix together, put on top of first layer. Chill until set.

**1 c. sugar**
**1 c. pineapple juice**

Cook until it thickens. Cool well. Then spread on top of second layer.

## 7-Up Salad

Mrs. Ora (Susie) Miller

**14 oz. 7-Up**
Heat and melt: **30 lg. marshmallows in the 7-Up.**
**1 (8 oz.) pkg. cream cheese**          **1 lg. jello (6 oz.)**
   Also add **1 can crushed pineapple and nuts** if desired. When cool add **2 c. cream, whipped,** and add **sugar, vanilla, or 2 c. topping.**

*You can't expect to sail with the eagles
during the day, if you hoot with the owls during the night.*

# Autumn Fruit Salad

*Mrs. Freeman (Mabel) Yoder*

1½ c. sugar
½ c. flour or clear jel or Perma-flo
1½ c. water
1 t. butter
1 t. vanilla

6 c. cubed, unpeeled apples
2 c. halved red seedless grapes
1 c. green seedless grapes
1 c. diced celery
1 c. walnut halves

In a saucepan, combine sugar and thickener. Stir in water; bring to a boil. Cook and stir until mixture thickens. Remove from heat; stir in butter and vanilla. Cool. In a large bowl, combine apples, grapes, celery, and walnuts. Add the dressing and toss gently. Refrigerate until serving. 10 to 12 servings.

# Broccoli Salad

*Mrs. Ora N. (Orpha) Miller*
*Rosa (Mom) Bontrager*

1 bundle broccoli - (usually about 3 sm. heads in a bundle)
1 head cauliflower
a little chopped onion
2 c. grated cheese
8 pieces bacon, fried & cut up

Dressing:
¾ c. sour cream
¾ c. Miracle Whip - s. dressing
⅓ c. sugar
dash of salt

Cut up broccoli and cauliflower quite fine. Bacon has to be cooled before mixed in. Do not add cheese until ready to serve; save with dressing. Is good leftover, but will get watery or thinner the second day. *I used this recipe for 3 of our weddings. Taking the recipe 18 times fills enough bowls for approx. 250 people.*

# Cinnamon Apple Salad

*Mrs. Milo (Lorene) Yoder*

½ c. red hot candies
1 pkg. (3 oz.) lemon gelatin
1 pkg. (8 oz.) cream cheese, softened
½ c. chopped pecans

1 c. boiling water
1 c. applesauce
½ c. mayonnaise
¼ c. chopped celery

In a bowl dissolve candies in water (reheat if necessary). Add gelatin; stir to dissolve. Pour half into 8" square pan that has been lightly coated with cooking spray. Refrigerate until firm. Cover and set remaining gelatin at room temp. Meanwhile combine the cream cheese, mayonnaise, pecans, & celery. Spread over chilled mixture. Carefully pour remaining gelatin mixture over cream cheese layer. Chill overnight.

*A candle loses nothing of its
light by lighting another candle.*

# Cool Whip Cabbage Salad

*Mrs. Ivan (Arlene) Bontrager*

Prepare Dressing:

**4 oz. (1½ c.) non-dairy whipped topping, thawed**
**1 c. salad dressing or mayonnaise     3 T. vinegar**
**½ c. sugar                            2 T. sour cream & onion powder**

Blend well with wire whip. Set aside. Prepare salad ingredients:

**3 c. crushed snack crackers (such as Town House or Ritz)**
**2½ c. cabbage, grated              2 c. broccoli, cut up**
**1½ c. carrots, grated              3 c. cheddar cheese, grated**
**2 c. tomatoes, cubed**

Put half of the cracker crumbs in the bottom of an 8 x 12" cake pan or plastic container. Then put the vegetables in layers on top of the crackers, saving about ½ c. each of the broccoli and tomatoes. Cover with 2 c. of the cheese. Pour the dressing over top. Poke holes in with a spoon at intervals to let the dressing run down among the vegetables. Cover with remaining cracker crumbs. Garnish with the remaining cheese, broccoli, and tomatoes.

# Coleslaw for Canning

*Grandma (Edna) Yoder*
*Mrs. Melvin (Mary Esther) Schrock*

**4½ qts. shredded cabbage      3 t. salt**
**6 med. carrots, fine          2¼ c. oil**
**3 onions, fine                1 t. mustard seed**
**3 green or red peppers**

Then boil the following:

**1 c. vinegar                   1 c. water**
**3 c. sugar**

And mix with 1 lg. pkg. lemon jello (6 oz.).

Mix all of 1st ingredients and let set 1 hour. Bring to a boil vinegar, sugar, and water. Add lemon jello; cool and add to cabbage mixture. For canning, put in pint jars and put in water bath in canner. Bring to a boil. Then turn off heat, and let cool in water. Or put in containers and freeze.

# Cottage Cheese Salad

*Mrs. Mervin (Gertie) Eash*

**1 c. lime jello                1 c. crushed pineapple**
**1 c. cottage cheese           ½ c. diced celery**

Mix jello in 2 c. hot water. Add 1½ c. cold water. Let set until it starts to thicken. Blend in cottage cheese, pineapple, and celery. Chill until firm.

## Cottage Cheese Salad

*Mrs. Eli (Martha) Mullet*

1 (24 oz.) container cottage cheese
¾ c. orange jello powder
½ c. sugar

2 (11 oz.) cans mandarin
  oranges
1¼ c. whipped topping

Stir jello powder and sugar into cottage cheese. Whip the topping and fold in. Add oranges. *Variation: May use grape or lime jello and use 1 (20 oz.) can crushed pineapple instead of oranges.*

## Crab N Cracker Salad

*Mrs. Ivan (Arlene) Bontrager*

4 c. crisp salad greens, bite size
  (lettuce & spinach are ideal)
2 tomatoes, cut into chunks
1 pkg. (6 oz.) frozen crab meat,
  thawed and cut up
6 radishes, sliced

1 c. snack crackers, broken up
  (Ritz or other brand)
⅓ c. Italian salad dressing
additional salt and pepper
  (if desired)

Combine salad ingredients. Toss with dressing.

## Cranberry Salad

*Mary Miller*

2 sm. boxes cherry jello
3 c. hot water

2 c. sugar

Mix and let cool off, then add: **2 c. ground cranberries**. Let stand for 4 hours. Cut **2 c. celery** really fine and chop **walnuts to make 2 c.** Add to above mixture.

juice of 2 lemons & oranges
1 c. sugar

pinch of salt
4 eggs, beaten well

Cook in double boiler until it thickens. Takes only a few minutes. Add to rest of salad with **4 c. whipped cream**. Make a nice bowl full.

## Creamy Fruit Salad

*Mom (Rosa) Bontrager*

1 pkg. (3 oz.) lemon jello
1 c. fruit juice, brought to a boil
1 c. cottage cheese
2 c. mixed fruit
  (grapes, oranges, pineapple)

½ c. sliced apples
½ c. chopped nuts
¼ c. ReaLemon juice
¾ c. cream or evaporated milk

Dissolve jello in hot fruit juice & let cool. Mix other ingredients and pour cooled jello over it, mixing well. Pour into bowl to set.

*If you would not be forgotten as soon as you were dead, either write things worth reading, or do things worth writing. –Ben Franklin*

## Crunchy Lettuce Salad with Potato Sticks

*Mrs. Freeman (Mabel) Yoder*

1 c. celery, diced
½ c. shredded carrots
3½ c. cooked, cubed chicken
¼ c. chopped onions
1 c. spiral macaroni, cooked
1 c. fresh chopped mushrooms, opt.
1 c. mayonnaise

½ c. sour cream or ¼ c. milk
4 T. red or white wine vinegar
4 t. prepared mustard
½ t. pepper
4 c. shoestring potato sticks
1 lg. head lettuce, torn

In a large bowl, combine celery, carrots, onions, macaroni, mushrooms, and lettuce; toss well. Fold in chicken. In separate bowl combine mayonnaise, sour cream, mustard, pepper and vinegar. Just before serving, pour dressing over salad; toss until lightly coated. Then gently mix in potato sticks and serve at once.

## Crunch Salad

*Mrs. Ivan (Arlene) Bontrager*

4 c. fresh broccoli florets
   (about ¾ lb.)
4 c. fresh cauliflower florets (about ¾ lb.)
Dressing:
1 c. mayonnaise or salad dressing
½ c. sour cream
1 to 2 T. sugar

1 med. onion, chopped
2 c. cherry tomatoes, halved

1 T. vinegar
dash of salt & pepper

In a large bowl, combine vegetables. In a smaller bowl, whisk the dressing ingredients until smooth. Pour over vegetables and toss to coat. Cover and chill for at least 2 hours. 16 - 18 servings.

## Egg Salad for Church

*Mrs. Lester (Mary) Lehman*

Makes 4 gallons:
14 doz. eggs, cooked and shredded
4 lbs. wieners, ground
3¼ lb. Colby cheese, shredded
3 c. celery, cut up fine
1 c. onions, cut up fine
Dressing:
6 c. sugar
2 qts. salad dressing

Makes 5 gallons:
18 doz. eggs, cooked and shredded
5 lbs. wieners, ground
4¼ lbs. Colby cheese, shredded
3 c. celery, cut up fine
1 c. onions, cut up fine

1 T. Worcestershire sauce
mustard and salt to taste

## Favorite French Dressing

*Mrs. Freeman (Mabel) Yoder*

1 c. vinegar
¾ c. sugar
¼ c. chopped onion
1½ t. salt

1½ t. dry mustard
1½ t. paprika
1 (12 oz.) bottle chili sauce
1 c. vegetable oil

In a quart jar with tight-fitting lid, mix vinegar, sugar, and onions. Combine salt, mustard, and paprika. Put in mix and shake well. Add chili sauce and oil; shake well. Store in refrigerator upside down to help oil blend better. Let set 24 hours before using. This is good on all sorts of salads. Especially taco salads. Makes 3½ cups.

## Fruit Salad Ring

*Mrs. Freeman (Mabel) Yoder*

First Layer:
1 pkg. (3 oz.) cherry gelatin
¾ c. boiling water

3 c. pear halves

Second Layer:
1 pkg. (3 oz.) lemon gelatin
¾ c. boiling water
½ c. cold water

1 pkg. (8 oz.) cream cheese
1 c. whipping cream, whipped

Third Layer:
1 pkg. (3 oz.) lime gelatin
¾ c. boiling water

1 can (20 oz.) pineapple, crushed

Drain pears, reserving ¾ c. juice. Put pears in a glass bowl. Dissolve cherry gelatin in boiling water; add reserved juice. Pour over pears; chill until firm. In the meantime, beat cream cheese until smooth and creamy. Dissolve lemon jello in boiling water; gradually add to cream cheese. Beat until smooth. Stir in cold water. Add whipped cream and with wire whip blend until smooth. Pour over first layer. Chill until firm. For third layer, drain pineapple; reserve ¾ c. juice. Dissolve lime gelatin in boiling water; add pineapple and juice. Pour over second layer. Chill until firm. This salad takes time to fix, but it is worth the effort in taste and how pretty it looks.

## Hellman's Salad

*Mrs. Christie (Anna) Yoder*

Prepare and mix:
1 c. carrots
1 c. nuts
1 box Cool Whip

1 c. Hellman's mayonnaise
1 c. celery
1 box cottage cheese

Heat:
1 can crushed pineapple

1 c. sugar

Then add:
6 T. water

2 pkgs. gelatin (plain)

Mix all together.

## Lemon Salad

*Mrs. Daniel (Esther) Yoder*

1 lg. box lemon jello

Dissolve in **2 c. hot water**. Then add **1 med. sized can crushed pineapple.** Let set then add:

2 c. grated cheddar cheese

1 pt. cream, whipped

½ c. walnuts

## Lettuce & Chicken Salad

*Mrs. Freeman (Mabel) Yoder*

1 head lettuce, torn
1 small head broccoli
1 c. shredded carrots
1 c. sliced radishes
½ c. chopped celery
½ c. cut-up onion
1 c. chunked tomatoes, fresh

1 c. french fried onions
1 c. colored spiral macaroni,
   cooked, drained, & cooled
2 c. shredded cheese
   (mozzarella, cheddar, or
   bacon flavored cheese)
3 c. fried till tender chicken
   breasts, cut up

Dressing:
1 c. mayonnaise
1 c. sour cream
¼ c. sweet cream

½ c. sugar
6 T. red wine vinegar

In a large bowl, combine all salad ingredients; set aside. In a small bowl, combine dressing, mixing well after each addition. Just before serving, mix with salad and toss gently. Hint: The secret to scrumptious salads is using red wine vinegar. It adds a distinctive flavor.

## Lime Sherbet

*Mrs. Milo (Lorene) Yoder*

1 pkg. lime jello
1 c. hot water
½ c. sugar
2 c. milk

1 c. top milk or light cream
¼ c. lemon juice
1 t. grated lemon peel

Dissolve gelatin in hot water; add remaining ingredients. Mix thoroughly. Freeze in cake pan or refrigerator tray. Break into chunks with wooden spoon. Turn into chilled bowl; beat until fluffy. Return to freezer until firm. Makes 6 to 8 servings. *Other gelatin flavors may be substituted.*

## Orange Salad

*Mrs. Lester (Mary) Lehman*

1 sm. pkg. vanilla pudding
   (cook type)
1 (3 oz.) pkg. orange jello
1 (3 oz.) pkg. instant vanilla pudding

2 c. hot water
½ c. whipped topping
1 can mandarin oranges

Combine puddings and jello with hot water. Cook until thick and clear. Stir constantly. Let cool completely. Fold in topping and oranges. Chill until set.

## Potato Salad

*Mrs. Owen (Verna) Hershberger*
*Mrs. Mervin (Gertie) Eash*

12 c. potatoes
12 eggs, hard-boiled
Dressing:
3 c. mayonnaise
3 T. vinegar
3 T. prepared mustard

1½ c. chopped onions
1½ c. diced celery

4 t. salt
2 c. sugar
½ c. milk

Cook potatoes and eggs. Let cool and shred. Put potatoes, eggs, onions, and celery into a bowl. Mix your dressing and pour over the potato mixture. It is important to shred the potatoes and eggs instead of cubing (shoestring). This can be eaten right away, but it seems by fixing it and refrigerating overnight, it has an even better taste. (This recipe times 3 makes a 13 qt. bowl full.) Very delicious! Best we ever tried.

## Potato Salad

*Mrs. Edwin (Anna) Ropp*
*Mrs. Daniel (Esther) Yoder*

14 c. potatoes, shredded & cooked
10 eggs, cooked & chopped
½ onion
2 c. chopped celery
3 c. salad dressing

3 T. mustard
¼ c. vinegar
½ c. milk
1½ c. white sugar
4 t. salt

Mix salad dressing, mustard, vinegar, milk, white sugar, and salt together. Stir real good before you toss it with potatoes, etc. 1 batch makes 5 qts. *Variations: ½ c. more sugar may be added, ½ c. more onions and milk omitted. A few more eggs added and a few cups less potatoes.*

## Ribbon Salad

*Grandma (Mary) Bontrager*

First Layer:
2 pkg. lime jello (large)
Let stand. Second Layer:
1 box lemon jello - 1 c. hot water
1 pkg. marshmallows
1 (8 oz.) cream cheese

4 c. water

1 No. 2 can crushed pineapple
1 c. whipped topping

Dissolve cream cheese and marshmallows in hot gelatin. Add pineapple. When starting to set, add whipped topping; pour on set lime jello.
Third Layer:

2 lg. pkg. strawberry jello                    4 c. water

## Spaghetti Chicken Salad     *Mrs. Ivan (Arlene) Bontrager*
1 c. mayonnaise or salad dressing    2 c. cooked elbow spaghetti
1 T. lemon juice                     2 med. stalks celery, diced
¼ t. salt                              (about 1 cup)
¼ t. black pepper                    ½ c. frozen green peas, thawed
2 c. cut-up cooked chicken           ½ c. cashew pieces, opt.
   Mix first 4 ingredients until blended. Toss with remaining ingredients. Cover
and refrigerate about 2 hours before serving.

## Spinach Salad with Honey     *Mrs. Freeman (Mabel) Yoder*
4 qts. spinach, cut up               1 c. salted sunflower seeds
2 c. peas, blanched                  ¾ c. mayonnaise
6 eggs, cooked and diced             ¼ c. honey or sugar
2 lg. tomatoes, cut up               ½ c. sour cream
1 c. sliced green onions             dash of salt
1 c. shredded Parmesan cheese        1 t. lemon juice
1 lb. bacon, fried & crumbled        5 T. red or white wine vinegar
½ c. chopped celery                  1 t. prepared mustard
   Combine salad ingredients in a large bowl. Then in another bowl, combine
dressing ingredients. Chill well. Pour over salad just before serving. Toss well.
I like to add green peppers and kohlrabi when it is in season.

## Summer Pasta & Fruit Salad     *Mrs. Ivan (Arlene) Bontrager*
2½ c. elbow macaroni                 4 c. water
   In a 3 qt. kettle, heat water to boiling. Cook pasta about 12 min. or until
tender. Drain; immerse in cold water. Drain when chilled.
⅓ c. mayonnaise                      2 T. chopped green onions
¼ c. milk                            1 can (11 oz.) mandarin orange
1 pkg. (3 oz.) cream cheese, softened   segments, drained
1½ c. cut up cooked chicken          1 can (8 oz.) pineapple chunks,
                                        drained
   Stir cream cheese into mayonnaise. Blend well. Mix milk with cream cheese
and mayonnaise. Put pasta, chicken, onions, oranges, and pineapple in bowl.
Pour dressing over all and toss until mixed; chill.

*A house is built by human hands,*
*but a home is built by human hearts.*

## Taco Salad

*Mrs. Freeman (Mabel) Yoder*

2 heads lettuce, chopped
5 med. tomatoes
1 can kidney beans
1 lb. shredded cheddar cheese
2 lbs. hamburger
1 pkg. taco flavored chips
1 pkg. taco seasoning
1 green pepper, chopped
1 sm. onion, chopped

¼ c. red wine vinegar or reg. vinegar
¾ c. sugar
¼ c. ketchup
½ t. celery seed
½ t. paprika
⅛ t. pepper
1 bottle (16 oz.) bacon flavored Western dressing
¾ c. vegetable oil

Fry hamburger with taco seasoning. Drain fat and cool well. Mix salad ingredients together in a large bowl; add chips last. Mix dressing together and mix gently with salad. Add crushed chips just before serving.

## Tuna Salad

*Mrs. Eli (Martha) Mullet*

2 c. shell or screw macaroni
1½ c. frozen peas, thawed

3 (6 oz.) cans tuna, drained

Cook macaroni with 1 t. salt. Drain and cool thoroughly. Mix in peas and tuna. Dressing:

1½ c. salad dressing
½ c. sugar

½ t. salt

A good salad for the tuna lover!

## Tuna Salad

*Ola Bontrager*

1 lb. tuna in water, drained well
¾ c. celery, sliced thin

8 hard-boiled eggs, chopped
¾ c. mayonnaise, approx.

Mix well; serve on toast, bun, or bread. Real good. Refrigerate.

## Under the Sea Salad

*Mrs. Christie (Anna) Yoder*

Bottom Layer:
1 lg. pkg. lime jello
1 can crushed pineapple
½ c. nuts, crushed

Center:
1 lg. pkg. lemon jello
1 pkg. cream cheese
¾ c. whipped cream or 1 pkg. Dream Whip

Top Layer:
1 lg. pkg. red jello (any flavor)

Let each layer set before adding the next. Chill well before serving.

## Waldorf Salad
*Mrs. Martin (Katie) Wickey*

2 c. pineapple tidbits
½ c. chopped celery
2 c. seeded grapes, red & green
6 diced apples
nuts & marshmallows may be added if desired

Bring to a boil **1 c. pineapple juice.** Combine ⅔ **c. sugar, 1 T. cornstarch, ½ t. salt, and 1 egg.** Add to pineapple juice over low heat until thoroughly cooked. Do not overcook. Cool dressing and add to salad. Chill well.

## BLT Pizza
*Mrs. Eli (Martha) Mullet*

Prepare your favorite pizza dough and line pan. Spoon on a layer of **pizza sauce.** Sprinkle with **mozzarella or provolone cheese** and plenty of **fried and crumbled bacon.** Bake until crust is done. Remove from oven & spread with **mayonnaise.** Layer on **shredded lettuce and diced tomatoes.** Enjoy! *Is also good spread with dip instead of pizza sauce.*

## Vegetable Pizza
*Mrs. Eli (Martha) Mullet*

Crust:

2 c. flour
4 t. baking powder
1 t. salt
2 T. sugar
½ c. shortening
1 egg
⅔ c. milk

Mix all dry ingredients and shortening until crumbly. Stir in egg and milk. Spread evenly on large cookie sheet and bake at 400° for 10 - 12 min.

Dressing:

1 (8 oz.) pkg. cream cheese
¾ c. mayonnaise
1 pkg. Hidden Valley Ranch dressing mix

Mix and spread onto cooled crust. Spread in layers:

shredded lettuce
broccoli
tomatoes
shredded cheese
radishes
frozen peas, thawed
fried & crumbled bacon

About 1 - 1½ c. of each.

## Chicken & Sunflower Sandwiches
*Mrs. Freeman (Mabel) Yoder*

1 c. mayonnaise
2 T. lemon juice
¼ t. salt
4 c. cooked, cubed chicken
2 t. mustard
1 c. chopped celery
½ c. salted sunflower seeds
2 t. tarragon
lettuce leaves
8 double buns or bread slices

In a bowl, combine all ingredients except lettuce and sunflower seeds; mix well. Just before serving, add rest of the things except take lettuce leaves and line each bun with several of them and fill with filling. A quick filling sandwich. Is great served with hot chocolate or cappuccino.

# Runza Rolls

*Mrs. David (Rachel) Plank*

2 c. warm water
2 T. yeast
½ c. sugar
1 ½ t. salt
cheese slices
¼ c. oil

2 eggs, beaten
5 - 6 c. flour
1 ½ lbs. ground beef, browned
   with onions
salt & pepper to taste

Mix water, yeast, sugar, and salt. Add eggs and oil. Stir in flour as needed. Dough shouldn't be too stiff or buns will be more dry. Let rise then roll dough into two oblong rectangles. Cut each into eight squares. Put beef on dough (a lg. handful to each square). Put a dab of ketchup and a slice of cheese on top of meat. Pull up corners of dough and press together so all edges are closed. Place edges down on greased cookie sheet. Let rise for 15 to 20 min. Bake 20 min. or until light brown (325°). These take practice so don't despair if they don't turn out right the first time! Different kinds of meat and cheese may be used. When taken out of the oven, brush oleo over top and cover lightly for a few min. This helps to soften crust. Good Luck!

*Even though the tongue weighs practically nothing, it's surprising how few persons are able to hold it.*

# Meats &
# Main Dishes

*The happiest people are those who are
too busy to notice whether they are or not.*

*If ye then be risen with Christ, seek
those things which are above, where Christ sitteth
on the right hand of God.
Colossians 3:1*

# A Farmer's Love Letter

My "sweet potato," do you "carrot" all for me? You are the "apple" of my eye... With your "radish" hair and "turnip" nose, my heart "beets" for you. My love for you is strong as "onions." If we "cantaloupe," "lettuce" marry and we will make a happy "pear."

# WHICH ARE YOU???

A lot of people are like "wheelbarrows" .... Not very good unless pushed.

Some are like canoes .... They have to be paddled.

Some are like footballs .... Not knowing which way they'll bounce next.

Some are like kites ... If you don't keep them on a string, they'll fly away.

Some are like balloons .... Full of air and ready to blow up.

Some are like trailers .... They have to be pulled.

Some are like a good watch .... Open-faced, pure gold, quickly busy and full of good works.

*The trouble with the average farmer is too much month left at the end of the money ....*

## Apple Sausage Bake

*Mrs. Freeman (Mabel) Yoder*

2 lbs. pork sausage
½ c. milk
2 eggs
1½ c. finely chopped,
  peeled apples
1½ c. white crackers,
  crushed
1 small onion, chopped
2 T. ketchup

In a large bowl, beat eggs; add milk, sausage, crackers, apples and onion. Mix well. Press into a casserole dish and bake uncovered at 350° for approx. 1 hour or until done.

## Amish Dressing/Stuffing

*Mrs. Freeman (Mabel) Yoder*

8-9 eggs, beaten
½ c. margarine
1 qt. potatoes, cooked
2 c. carrots
2 c. celery or 2 t.
  celery seed
¾ c. chopped onion
2½ qt. toasted bread cubes
1 qt. chicken broth
4 c. chicken bits, cooked
1 t. salt
½ t. pepper
1 t. poultry seasoning
½ T. chicken base

Seasonings may be adjusted to taste. Preheat oven to 325° and place margarine in a cake pan (13 x 9") and melt in oven. Meanwhile, combine eggs, potatoes, carrots, celery and onions. Stir well then add broth and chicken bits. Fold in toasted bread; add seasonings. Take pan from oven; add margarine then pour all into cake pan and bake approx. 45-60 min. until set and golden brown. Do not stir more than once. *Potatoes, carrots, celery and onions must be cooked to just crisp tender so they have a bit of crunch yet.

## Baked Chicken Delight

*Mrs. Simon (Martha) Schmucker*

12 slices bread, butter
  on both sides
3 c. cooked and cut up chicken
1 small can mushroom pieces, drained
¼ c. chopped onion
2 hard-boiled eggs, chopped
2 cans cream of chicken soup,
  not diluted
1 c. crushed cornflakes
½ c. melted oleo

Layer 6 slices of bread in a 9 x 13 in. pan. Butter both sides. Mix chicken, eggs, onions, mushrooms and one can of soup. Spread over bread slices; layer 6 slices of bread over chicken mixture; spread with one can soup. Sprinkle crushed cornflakes over soup. Drizzle oleo over cornflakes. Make day before and refrigerate overnight. Bake 35 min. at 375°. Serves 12.

## Baked B-B-Q Chicken

*Mrs. Ora (Susie) Miller*

2 c. ketchup
1 c. vinegar
1 c. brown sugar
1 T. Worcestershire sauce
1 t. garlic or onion salt

Fry chicken pieces in hot oil. Dip pieces in mixture of ingredients and arrange in roaster. Cover and bake for 1 to 2 hours at 350° - 400°.

## Baked Beans

*Mrs. Clarence T. (Ruby) Yoder*

4 c. cooked, dried beans
1 c. cream
½ c. ketchup
½ t. salt and a little
  pepper

2 t. prepared mustard
onion
5 slices cheese
3 dabs butter (optional)
Add bits of ham, wieners or
  bacon if desired

Bake in covered dish at 350° for 45 min. to one hour.

## Baked Beans

*Mom (Rosa) Bontrager*

4-5 c. cooked beans (navy)
1 cup cream
½ cup ketchup
2 T. oleo
½ c. brown sugar

2 t. mustard
4-5 slices cheese
some chopped onions
salt and pepper to taste

Meat can be ham pieces, wieners, bacon, browned hamburger or sausage. Mix all together and heat till boiling or bake awhile.

## Ballard Biscuits

*Mrs. Lonnie (Norma Mae) Bontrager*

½ lb. hamburger
1 c. chopped onions
1 can mushroom soup
1 can chicken soup
1 (8 oz.) pkg. cream cheese

¼ c. milk
1 t. salt
¼ c. ketchup
biscuits

Fry the onions, hamburger and salt together until done. Add the two kinds of soups, cream cheese, milk and ketchup. Pour in loaf pan and put in oven till bubbly. Remove from oven and top with your favorite biscuits. Bake at 375° for 15-20 min.

## Baked Oatmeal

*Mrs. Christy (Anna) Bontrager*

½ c. margarine
3 c. oatmeal
½ t. salt
½ c. brown sugar

2 t. baking powder
2 eggs
1 c. milk

Mix together in order. Bake at 350° for 45 min. Serve with milk and Dutch Honey (recipe below). Makes one 8 x 8" pan.

## Dutch Honey

1 c. brown sugar
½ c. butter

½ c. evaporated or reg. milk
½ t. vanilla

Heat until almost boiling. If it boils it will curdle.

## Baked Pizza Sandwich

*Mrs. Marvin L. (Erma) Miller*

2 lbs. hamburger
1 pt. pizza sauce
1 t. oregano
1 (8 oz.) pkg. cream cheese
¼ c. Parmesan cheese (optional)
2 c. Bisquick
1 egg
²/₃ c. milk
1 can mushroom soup

Cook and drain meat. Stir half of pizza sauce and the oregano into the meat. Heat to boiling. Mix Bisquick, egg, and milk. Measure ¾ of batter into 9 x13 in. pan. Pour remaining sauce over batter, spreading evenly. Put 4 slices cream cheese, the meat mixture, mushroom soup and remaining cream cheese and batter on top. Sprinkle with remaining Parmesan cheese. Bake uncovered until brown in a 400° oven for 20-25 min.

## B-B-Q Chicken Sauce

*Mrs. Ora (Orpha) Miller*

1 c. butter or margarine
½ c. prepared mustard
1 c. brown sugar
2 T. paprika
2 c. ketchup
1 T. Tabasco or to suit
    taste (very hot!)
4 T. salt
2 t. black pepper
1 T. Worcestershire sauce
1 cup or less lemon juice
    or ReaLemon (optional)

Melt butter or margarine; mix brown sugar and paprika together dry, then add to butter and melt, stirring occasionally, over low heat. Mix mustard with some ketchup so it will blend together better. Add to mixture then add rest of ingredients; stir well till boiling point. This mixture keeps well refrigerated. Can be canned; boil 2 hours in cans. This is if you make a large batch and have left-overs. Enough for 12 - 14 chickens, quartered. Use this mixture hot on chicken; also good on cooked meat baked in oven for awhile. Our method for chicken to grill is to partially cook chicken first, covered with water and a dash of vinegar; cook 5 -10 min., but not too soft to come off of the bones.

## B-B-Q'd Beef Patties

*Mrs. Elmer (Wilma) Beechy*

1½ lb. hamburger
¼ t. pepper
1 c. milk
1 egg
B-B-Q Sauce:
¾ cup oatmeal
1 t. salt
small onion

2 T. Worcestershire sauce
2 T. vinegar
¼ c. water
4 T. sugar
1 c. ketchup
onion to taste

Shape hamburger into patties and fry on both sides; mix and pour sauce over patties and cook slowly for 20 min.

## B-B-Q Meatballs

*Mrs. Vernon (Polly) Beechy*

3 lbs. hamburger
2 c. quick oats
2 eggs
¾ c. chopped onion
½ t. garlic salt
2 t. salt
1 t. pepper

2 t. chili powder
1 c. evaporated milk
2 c. ketchup
1 T. liquid smoke
½ t. garlic salt
1½ c. brown sugar

Mix the first 9 ingredients together using ice cream dipper to make balls. Put in 9 x 13" cake pan. Mix last 4 ingredients and pour over balls. Makes 24 balls. Bake at 350° for 1 hour.

## B-B-Q Meatballs

*Mrs. Freeman (Mabel) Yoder*
*Mrs. Sam (Viola) Miller*

1 can evaporated milk
3 lbs. hamburger
2 c. quick oats
2 eggs
1 c. chopped onion

½ t. garlic
2 t. salt
½ t. pepper
2 t. chili powder

Mix and shape into balls; place in cake pan and pour sauce over them.

Sauce: 2 c. ketchup
2 T. liquid smoke
1½ c. brown sugar

1 t. garlic powder
½ c. chopped onion

Stir sauce well until dissolved and pour over meatballs. Bake at 350° for 1 hour, covered.

## B-B-Q Sausage Bake

*Mrs. Freeman (Mabel) Yoder*

1 lb. ground beef
1 lb. pork sausage
1 pint pizza sauce
½ c. chopped onion
½ t. salt
¼ t. pepper
½ c. ketchup

½ c. brown sugar
2 T. mustard
1½ c. Bisquick
1 c. milk
2 eggs
2 c. shredded cheese
(cheddar or mozzarella)

Preheat oven to 375°. In frying pan fry hamburger and sausage together with onion until well done. Then add salt, pepper, ketchup, mustard, pizza sauce, and sugar. Let simmer on low. In the meantime, in a small bowl combine Bisquick, eggs, and milk. Stir briskly. Pour meat into a casserole dish or cake pan. Cover with shredded cheese and carefully spoon Bisquick mixture over all and bake for 25 - 30 min.

## Beef and Potato Loaf
*Mrs. Vern (Irene) Schlabach*

4 c. thin sliced raw potatoes
1 can cream of mushroom soup

1 T. cut up onions or more to suit taste

Arrange in greased 2 qt. casserole. Mix soup, ⅛ t. **pepper, 1 t. salt,** and **1 t. parsley** and pour over potatoes.
In another bowl mix:

1 lb. lean ground beef
½ c. cracker crumbs or oatmeal
¼ c. cut up onions
1 t. salt

⅛ t. pepper
¾ c. milk
¼ c. ketchup

Spread evenly over potatoes. Garnish top with more ketchup if desired. Bake at 350° for 1 hour or until potatoes are done.

## Beef Log
*Mrs. Marvin L. (Erma) Miller*

3 lbs. hamburger
3 T. Tenderquick
½ t. onion
½ t. garlic salt

1 T. mustard seed
1½ T. liquid smoke
⅛ t. pepper
1c. water

Mix thoroughly. Form into long thin rolls and wrap in tinfoil. Punch holes in bottom. Let set in refrigerator for 24 hours. Bake at 300° for 1½ hours.

## Blueberry French Toast
*Mary Miller*

12 pieces bread
2 (8 oz.) boxes cream cheese
1 c. blueberries

12 eggs, beaten
2 c. milk
⅓ c. maple syrup

In bottom of a greased pan put 6 slices of bread cut into 1" cubes. Next cut cream cheese into small cubes. Over this sprinkle blueberries. Cut 6 more pieces of bread into cubes and spread over top evenly. Beat 12 eggs well and add 2 c. milk and ⅓ c. maple syrup. Pour this mixture over all. Use a T. to smooth contents. Bake in a 9 x 13" cake pan at 350° for 1 hour. Serve with blueberry sauce or maple syrup. Yield: 1 pan.

## Baker Chop Suey
*Mrs. Ora (Orpha) Miller*
*Mrs. Ray (LeEtta) Yoder*

1 lb. hamburger
1 small onion
1 (10½ oz.) can cream of
  chicken soup
1 (10½ oz.) can cream of
  mushroom soup

1 c. celery
1 can Chinese noodles
1½ c. warm water
¼ t. soy sauce
½ c. uncooked rice
salt and pepper to taste

Brown hamburger with onion. Mix together all ingredients except noodles. Bake at 350° for one hour. Add noodles. Mix ¾ in casserole and spread the rest evenly over top. Bake 15 min. longer.

## Breakfast Burritos

*Mrs. Freeman (Mabel) Yoder*

12 eggs
½ c. chopped onion
1 med. green pepper,
  chopped
1 lb. pork sausage, browned
  and drained
4 c. cooked and shredded potatoes
3 c. shredded cheddar or
  processed cheese slices,
  cut up
12 flour totillas (10"), warmed
1 t. salt
salsa (optional)

In a large skillet fry potatoes till golden brown. Remove and set aside. In a large bowl beat eggs, onion and green pepper; pour into the same skillet; cook and stir until eggs are set. Remove from heat; add potatoes and sausage; mix gently. Place about ¾ c. of filling on each tortilla and top with about ¼ c. cheese. Roll up and place on a greased baking sheet. Bake at 350° for 15-20 min. or until heated through. Serve with salsa if desired.

## Breakfast Casserole

*Mrs. Daniel A. (Ida) Miller*

12 pieces of bread
6 eggs
3 c. milk
2½ c. ham
salt and pepper to taste
16 oz. mozzarella cheese
16 oz. cheddar cheese

Grease pan. Put 6 pieces of bread in bottom of pan. Mix eggs, milk, ham, salt and pepper and put half of this in pan. Put the other 6 pieces of bread in and the other half of the mixture. Put the cheeses on top. Put in fridge overnight. Before putting in oven put 3 c. cornflakes and ½ c. oleo on top. Makes 1 pan. Bake 45 min. - 1 hour.

## Breakfast Pizza

*Mrs. Orva (Marietta) Yoder*

biscuit dough
¾ lb. hamburger or
  sausage, browned
5 or 6 med. potatoes, fried
1 lb. ham, diced
½ package bacon, fried
  and crumbled
6 beaten eggs
cheese sauce

Mix together your favorite biscuit dough and spread evenly in pizza or cake pan and bake until half done. Then put in layers in order given on top of dough. Last of all add cheese sauce. Bake at 350° for 1 hour or until dough is done.

## "Brot & Wurst" Casserole

*Mrs. Ivan (Arlene) Bontrager*

1 lb. sausage
1 T. veg. oil
1 c. pizza sauce
½ c. cheese cubes
  (or grated cheese)

12 slices bread
4 eggs, beaten
2 c. milk
½ t. salt
½ c. grated cheese

Brown sausage in oil. Drain off fat. Mix sausage, pizza sauce and cheese cubes. In an 8" greased square baking dish, line bottom with 4 slices of bread. Spread ½ of sausage mixture over bread. Put 4 more slices of bread on top of meat; spread remaining meat mixture onto second layer and top with last 4 slices of bread. Mix eggs, milk and salt; pour over all. Top with grated cheese. Bake at 350° for approx. 30 min. or until heated through. Note: Cheddar, Colby, mozzarella or processed American cheese could be used.

## Calico Beans

*Edna Raber*

½ lb. bacon
1 lb. hamburger
1 c. chopped onions
1 pint pork & beans
1 pint navy beans

1 pint lima beans
2 t. vinegar
1 t. mustard
¾ c. brown sugar

Fry bacon; drain and crumble. Brown hamburger and onions and drain. Mix sugar, mustard and vinegar and add to meat. Mix beans and add to meat mixture. Bake in 7 x 11" baking dish at 350° for 40 min.

## Cheese Souffle

*Mrs. Emmon (Edna) Schmucker*

8 slices bread
1 lb. grated cheese
6 eggs, beaten
¼ c. margarine
2 c. milk

1 t. onion salt
salt and pepper
cubed ham, bacon
  or mushrooms

Cube bread and put in bottom of casserole. Combine cheese, margarine, and meat. Sprinkle over bread cubes. Mix eggs, milk and seasoning. Add over top of the other ingredients. Refrigerate overnight. Bake at 325° for 45 min.

## Chicken and Dumplings

*Mrs. Eldon (Katie) Nisley*

Use a large kettle with a tight-fitting lid. Remove a qt. of chicken meat from bones, add broth and make gravy as usual. **Dumplings: Beat 1 egg; add 2 T. milk, ½ t. salt, 3 t. baking powder and enough flour to make a good stiff dough.** Drop by t. full into boiling gravy. Place lid on and let covered for 5-8 min. It is important that the lid is not removed until the time is up. Remove from heat, take off lid and serve at once.

# Chicken Coating

Mrs. Freeman (Mabel) Yoder
Mrs. Harry (Edna Mae) Bontrager

2½ lb. white soda crackers
2 (15 oz.) boxes Rice Krispies
2 (18 oz.) boxes corn flakes

Crush very fine and mix well. Measure crumbs then add 1 T. salt for each qt. of crumbs. Add 1 T. garlic powder, 2 T. onion salt, and 3 T. paprika to one batch; may add 2 boxes frying magic (optional). Mix thoroughly. Makes a 13 qt. mixing bowl full. Store in an air-tight container in a cool place. To use melt butter; dip chicken pieces in it then roll in cracker mixture. Place on greased cookie sheet and bake at 350°-375° for 45 min. Then transfer to a roaster or casserole dish and bake till tender.

# Chicken Casserole

Mrs. Marvin L. (Erma) Miller

6-8 med. potatoes (shoestring)
16 oz. mixed vegetables
3 c. chopped chicken
salt and pepper
1 pint chicken broth
1 can cream of chicken soup
1 t. minced onion
1 cup shredded cheese

Put first 5 ingredients in layers in a baking dish. Heat the broth, soup and onion. Pour over veg. mixture. Bake 1 hour at 350° or until potatoes are done. Add the cheese when almost done. Also add crushed potato chips if desired.

# Chicken Croquettes

Mrs. Mervin (Emma) Yoder

2 c. ground chicken
⅛ t. pepper
½ t. celery salt
White Sauce:
2 T. butter
1 c. milk
½ t. salt
¼ t. onion salt
cracker crumbs

2½ T. flour

Make the white sauce by bringing the 3 ingredients to a boil. Cool sauce, then add to chicken and seasonings. Mix well. Shape into patties and roll into beaten eggs and then coat with crushed cracker crumbs. Fry in ¼" oil to a golden brown or bake at 350°, turning patties once.

# Chinese Casserole

Mrs. Daniel (Esther) Yoder

1½ lb. hamburger fried
½ c. rice (uncooked)
1½ c. celery
½ c. onions
1 can cream of chicken soup
1 can cream of mushroom soup
3 c. water
3 T. soy sauce

Bake at 350° for 1½ hour, then add chow mein noodles and bake longer if you wish or serve immediately. Small casserole. *I substitute homemade cream of celery soup for the chicken and mushroom soup as it's very fitting for this one.*

## Chicken Dressing
*Mrs. Lonnie (Norma Mae) Bontrager*

6 qt. toasted bread cubes
2 qt. chicken broth
12 eggs
3½ c. milk
3½ c. warm water
¾ c. carrots, diced
2 c. potatoes, diced
½ c. onion, chopped
1¼ c. celery, diced
2 t. salt
½ t. pepper

Beat eggs and mix all together. Add chicken base, spike and parsley flakes to suit taste. Brown butter (¼ c.) and drizzle over top. Sprinkle with paprika. Bake at 350° for 1 hour or until done.

## Chicken Enchiladas
*Mrs. Allen (Elsie) Bontrager*

1 can deboned chicken
1 can cream of chicken soup
1 can cream of mushroom soup
1 can chopped green chilies
1 small onion, chopped
¾ bag of Doritos
shredded cheddar cheese
1 soup can of milk

Combine chicken, soups, milk, green chilies and onion. Layer mixture with chips. Bake at 350° for 30 min. or until soup mixture is heated through. Top with cheese and bake until cheese is melted, approx. 15 min.

## Chicken Fajitas
*Mrs. Simon (Martha) Schmucker*

4 boneless chicken breasts
1 small jar Italian dressing
2 green peppers, sliced
2 red peppers, sliced
½ lb. fresh mushrooms, sliced
1 pkg. flour tortillas, warmed
shredded cheese
cooking oil

Cut breasts into ½ in. strips. Place strips in bowl, then add dressing. Cover and refrigerate for 6 hours or longer, stirring occasionally. In a large skillet heat oil, just enough to cover bottom. Add chicken and stir every 2-3 min. until almost done, about 7-8 min. Add mushrooms and peppers; cook 3-4 min. or until done. Spoon ¾ c. mixture onto warmed shells, top with a handful of cheese, fold in sides and serve immediately with sour cream or salsa.

## Chicken Gravy
*Mrs. Ivan (Arlene) Bontrager*

Fill 6 qt. kettle ¾ full of chicken broth. If you have reserved water from boiling potatoes you can add it to make the desired amount and heat to boiling.

1½ c. clear jel (a thickening agent similar to cornstarch which turns clear when cooked), 1 c. cold water, 5 egg yolks, 3 T. chicken base, salt and pepper to taste (chicken base has salt in it and broth may also have), 6-10 drops yellow food coloring, optional. Mix clear jel and water to form a paste. Add egg yolks and mix well. Blend into hot broth over low heat. When smooth, turn heat to med. Keep stirring, scraping bottom of kettle to keep gravy from getting lumpy. Reheat to boiling. Boil on low heat until thickened. Add seasonings and coloring if desired.

## Chicken Parmesan

*Mrs. Ivan (Arlene) Bontrager*

6 large chicken thighs
  (about 1½ lb.)
⅓ c. flour
¼ t. salt
⅛ t. black pepper
½ c. milk
1 egg, beaten slightly
½ c. fine dry bread crumbs
2 T. veg. oil
1 c. mozzarella cheese
  (4 oz.), shredded
2½ c. spaghetti or pizza
  sauce
¼ c. grated Parmesan
  cheese

Peel skin off of chicken and cut out bone. Pound chicken pieces to ¼ in. thickness. Mix flour, salt, and pepper and coat chicken with it. Mix milk and egg. Dip chicken into milk and egg mixture and coat with bread crumbs. Heat oven to 375°. Heat oil in 10 in. skillet over med. heat. Fry chicken in oil, turning till golden brown on both sides. (Add oil to skillet if needed.) Place chicken in ungreased 13 x 9 in. pan. Sprinkle with mozzarella cheese. Cover with sauce. Spinkle with Parmesan cheese. Bake uncovered approx. 20 min.

## Chicken - Potato Casserole

*Mrs. Daniel (Esther) Yoder*

enough potatoes for 13 x 9" pan
2 c. cooked chicken
1 can cream of mushroom or
  chicken soup
1 c. chicken broth
1 (8 oz.) sour cream
bread crumbs
1 stick butter

Mix first 5 ingredients together. (This is best if potatoes are cooked first.) Cover with bread crumbs then drizzle melted butter over everything. Bake at 350° for 45 min. or until it is browned and hot. Could also use beef or sausage instead of chicken. Cottage cheese is also a good substitute for the sour cream. Add onions if desired.

## Chicken Shake and Bake

*Mrs. Milo (Lorene) Yoder*

4 c. flour
4 c. cracker meal
4 T. salt
¼ c. cooking oil
2 T. sugar
2 T. poultry seasoning
2 t. garlic powder
2 t. onion powder
3 T. paprika

Dip chicken in melted butter. Shake in bag with mixture and bake 1½ hour. Store in container for later use.

## Chicken Tetrazzini
*Mrs. Harry (Edna Mae) Bontrager*

1 med. onion, chopped
¾ c. green peppers, chopped
½ c. margarine
1 T. flour
1 c. cheese, grated
1 can mushroom soup
2 cans chicken broth
1 t. salt
½ t. celery salt
3 c. cooked chicken pieces
1 small can mushrooms
1 sm. jar pimento, chopped
1 sm. pkg. spaghetti, cooked

Sauté onion, pepper and celery salt in margarine. Add flour, cheese and soup. Stir to blend well. Add broth. Blend until smooth. Stir in remainder of ingredients. Pour into large casserole or flat baking dish. Sprinkle top with cracker crumbs. Bake at 400° for 15-20 min. Serves 8.

## Chicken Wrap with Mushroom Sauce
*Ola Bontrager*

4-6 chicken breasts,
    skinless, boneless
1 pkg. dried beef
1 pkg. bacon
4-6 servings of instant rice
1 (12 oz.) can cream of
    mushroom soup
1 (12 oz.) sour cream
1½ c. fresh mushrooms

Using a kitchen mallet, pound chicken breasts flat to ¼" thickness. Wrap the chicken breasts with the dried beef and then the bacon. Put toothpicks in to hold together. Bake at 375° to 400° for 45 min. Drain chicken. Mix the mushroom soup and the sour cream in a separate bowl. Add fresh mushrooms and pour sauce over drained breasts and bake an additional 30 min. Serve with rice. Very good.

*If any lift of mine can ease
The burden of another,
God give me love and care and strength
To help my ailing brother.*

## Chop Suey
*Mrs. Ezra (Mary) Miller*

2 lb. beef hamburger
3 c. celery, cut fine
2½ qt. water
¾ c. beef gravy mix
¾ c. flour and clear jel
(half & half)

⅔ c. sugar
⅓ c. soy sauce
salt and pepper
(chow mein noodles)

Fry the hamburger. Cook the celery. Now add these two together plus the water. Bring to a boil. Mix flour, clear jel, sugar and gravy mix with some water and add to your hamburger and celery. Now add your soy sauce, then salt and pepper to taste. To eat put chow mein noodles on plate and put chop suey on top.

## Cornflake Potatoes
*Mrs. Orva (Marietta) Yoder*

Peel and slice potatoes (like french fries); put on paper towel to dry. Dip in melted butter then in crushed cornflakes seasoned with Lawry's seasoning salt and pepper. Bake at 350° for 1 hour.

## Cornmeal Mush
*Mrs. Lester (Mary) Lehman*

1 gal. water
6 c. cornmeal
1 c. milk

1 c. flour
2 T. salt

Mix dry ingredients. Heat 2½ qts. water to boiling. In the meantime use 1½ qts. lukewarm water (be sure it's not hot); mix gradually with dry ingredients mixture. Then mix with the boiling water. Cook slowly for 60 min. Pour in cake pan and let set overnight. Cut in pieces and deep fat fry in veg. oil. Very good.

## Cornmeal Mush (to eat right away)
*Mrs. Freeman (Mabel) Yoder*

1¾ c. cornmeal
¼ c. flour
3 t. salt

1 c. milk
1 c. cold water
2½ c. boiling water

Stir the first 5 ingredients together. Pour into 2½ cups boiling water in heavy saucepan. Cook 15-20 min., stirring almost constantly with a potato masher to avoid lumps. Meanwhile in large skillet heat ¼" oil till very hot, sprinkle liberally with flour then drop hot mush by spoonfuls into oil and fry each side till golden brown. Sprinkle flour on the other side too. We like this method better than molding the mush and slicing. Faster when in a hurry.

## Cornmeal Patties

*Mrs. Freeman (Mabel) Yoder*

1½ c. yellow cornmeal
1 c. milk
1 t. sugar
1 t. salt
1 lb. pork sausage, cooked,
  drained and crumbled

2¾ c. boiling water
flour
4 T. butter
maple syrup, optional

In a saucepan combine cornmeal, milk, sugar, and salt. Gradually stir in water. Cook and stir until bubbly. Reduce heat and cook covered 10 min. longer or until very thick, stirring occasionally. Remove from heat and stir in sausage. Pour in a greased loaf pan and cover with wrap and refrigerate. To serve, unmold and cut into ⅓" slices. Dip both sides in flour. In skillet melt butter over med. heat; brown on each side until golden. Serve with maple syrup if desired. Instead of refrigerating, this may be dropped by T. into hot melted butter right away and fried with flour. A quick meal.

## Creamed Eggs and Ham

*Mrs. Mervin (Emma) Yoder*

3 T. butter or margarine
½ t. dry mustard
⅛ t. pepper
1 c. cooked ham or sausage
4 hard-boiled eggs (cut up)

3 T. flour (level)
¼ t. salt
2¼ c. milk
2 T. chopped onion

Melt butter in saucepan over low heat. Blend in flour, onion and seasonings. Cook over low heat; stir till mixture is smooth and bubbly. Remove from heat and stir in milk. Heat to boiling, stirring constantly. Boil and stir 1 min. Gently stir in meat and eggs. Heat through. Serve over toast or your favorite biscuits, like Melt-In-Your-Mouth Biscuits found elsewhere in this cookbook. May also be served over rice.

## Cream of Chicken Soup

*Mrs. Lester (Mary) Lehman*

¼ c. oleo
5 T. flour
2 t. chicken base

3 c. boiling water
½ c. cut up chicken
1 c. milk

Melt oleo in saucepan over low heat. Blend in flour. Dissolve soup base in boiling water. Gently add to flour and oleo mixture; stir until smooth. Add milk and chicken and bring to a boil. Additional seasonings may be added if desired.

## Creamy Bacon -N- Broccoli Dish

*Mrs. Eli (Martha) Mullet*

2 qt. potatoes

2 bunches broccoli

2 lbs. bacon

1 c. carrots

Cook potatoes and carrots together; steam broccoli; fry bacon and drain. Combine 1 c. bacon drippings and 1½ c. flour. Cook over low heat and gradually add enough milk till the thickness of gravy.

Add: 1½ t. salt

1 t. seasoning salt

¼ t. pepper

Melt in: **1 pint sour cream**

**1 lb. Velveeta cheese**

Pour over potatoes, broccoli and bacon mixture. Stir all together. Put in oven long enough to heat all the way through. May top with french fried onions or crushed B-B-Q chips.

## Crumb–Coated Potato Halves

*Mrs. Ezra (Mary) Miller*

1 c. Italian seasoned
   bread crumbs

2 t. paprika

2 t. salt

¼ t. pepper

8 large potatoes, peeled and
   halved

2 T. butter, melted

In a shallow bowl, combine the bread crumbs, paprika, salt and pepper. Roll potato halves in crumb mixture. Place in greased 13 x 9 x 2" pan. Bake for ½ hour uncovered at 375°, then cover and bake another ½ hour at 350° or until tender. Potatoes should only be ½ to ¾" thick.

## Croutons

*Mrs. Ivan (Arlene) Bontrager*

½ c. salad oil, or ¼ lb.
   butter or margarine

1½ t. dried sage

1 t. dried thyme

½ t. black pepper

8 c. soft bread cubes

Heat oil or butter with the seasonings. Add bread cubes and mix to coat cubes. Spread on cookie sheet and toast in 300° oven till golden brown (thoroughly dry). Cool and store in tight container. Use in salads or casserole and stuffing recipes. You may wish to experiment with other seasonings.

## Crouton Sausage Casserole

1 pkg. (6 oz.) prepared stuffing mix*

½ lb. mozzarella cheese, sliced

1 lb. fresh sausage

Follow directions on stuffing mix package. Brown sausage. Drain and mix with stuffing. Spoon half into 8" baking dish. Cover with cheese slices. Put remaining meat mixture on top of cheese and top it with another layer of cheese slices. Bake at 325° for approx. 20-30 min.

*If using homemade croutons (recipe above) add 1 small onion, chopped into sausage when browning it. Mix 1½ c. boiling water, 2½ c. croutons, ¼ c. margarine, ½ c. carrots, diced and cooked, ½ c. celery, diced and cooked. Then mix with onion and sausage and layer in baking dish with cheese. Bake as above.

## Crumb-Topped French Toast

*Mrs. Freeman (Mabel) Yoder*

4 eggs, well beaten
½ t. vanilla
1 c. milk
1¼ t. salt

10 slices homemade bread or
other thick-sliced bread
3 c. cornflakes, crushed fine
½ c. butter, melted

Combine eggs, milk, salt and vanilla; mix well. Dip bread into egg mixture and coat both sides with cornflake crumbs. Preheat oven to 400° and melt butter in a 10 x 15" pan. Place each piece of bread on cookie sheet as soon as it is coated. Bake 15 min. on one side then flip toast and bake approx. another 20 min. Serve with your favorite syrup. This toast does not get soggy easily and is our all-time favorite.

## Crunchy Cheese Potatoes

*Mrs. Andy (Dorothy) Miller*

1½ c. milk
1 T. onion, chopped
½ t. salt
¼ t. pepper
6 med. potatoes, peeled and sliced about ¼" thick

1 c. American cheese, cut
in small squares
½ c. finely crushed cornflakes

Combine milk, onion, salt and pepper. Add potatoes and mix well. Spread into 13 x 9" pan and bake at 350° for 30 min. Sprinkle cornflakes over all and cheese on top of cornflakes. Put back in oven and bake for another 20-30 min. or until poatoes are tender. Yield: 6-8 servings.

## Deep-Dish Taco Squares

*Mrs. LaVern (Martha) Yoder*

½ lb. ground beef
½ c. sour cream
½ c. mayonnaise
1 or 2 med. tomatoes
½ c. chopped green peppers

1 T. chopped onion
1 c. Bisquick
½ c. shredded cheddar cheese
¼ c. cold water

Heat oven to 375°. Grease baking dish; a square cake pan works well. Cook and stir ground beef till browned. Mix sour cream, mayonnaise, cheese and onion; reserve. Mix Bisquick with water and put dough in pan. Press dough ½" up on sides. Layer beef and green peppers in pan; spoon sour cream mixture over top. Sprinkle with paprika if desired. Bake until edges are light brown, 25-30 min.

## Dressing

*Grandma (Mary) Bontrager*

3 carrots
2 potatoes, diced
1 c. celery
½ c. diced onions
½ t. chicken base
1 t. salt
dash of pepper
1 c. diced chicken and broth
1 loaf bread, toasted & cubed
1 c. milk
4 eggs
2 T. butter (browned)

Boil carrots, potatoes, and celery together and also add the water. Mix together all ingredients. Bake 1 hour at 325°. Serves 25 people.

## Dressing for a Wedding

*Mrs. Ivan (Arlene) Bontrager*

| For 7 roasters full: | For a single batch: |
|---|---|
| 16 loaves bread (20 oz. ea.), cut in cubes and toasted | 1 loaf bread |
| 4 qt. celery, finely diced | 1 cup |
| 7 qt. potatoes, cooked and diced | 2 cups |
| 5 cups carrots, shredded | ¾ cup |
| ½ c. parsley | ½ T. |
| 4 c. finely chopped onions | ¼ cup |
| 1 c. seasoning salt | 1 T. |
| 2 c. chicken base | 2 T. |
| 5½ doz. eggs, beaten | 4 eggs |
| 3 gal. milk | 3 cups |
| 16 qt. chicken with broth | 1 qt. |
| 4 lbs. margarine | ¼ lb. (1 stick) |
| approx. 1 T. black pepper | dash |

Heat broth and add seasonings to broth to dissolve. Mix all ingredients, except margarine, in large tubs, adding liquids last. (For single batch mix in large bowl.) Grease roasters with margarine. Divide into 7 roasters and bake approx. ½ hr. at 350°. Brown rest of margarine in skillets and pour over partially baked dressing. Finish baking (till well set and nicely browned). Stir as little as possible during baking-no stirring after margarine is poured over top.

## Easy Chicken Pot Pie

*Mrs. Freeman (Mabel) Yoder*

2 c. potatoes, diced and cooked
½ c. peas
¼ c. carrots, cooked
1 c. cut-up cooked chicken
½ c. chicken broth
1 can (10 ¾ oz.) condensed
cream of chicken soup
1 c. Bisquick mix
¾ c. milk
2 eggs

Heat oven to 400°. Mix veg., chicken, broth and soup. Pour into a greased 13 x 9" pan or small casserole dish. Then mix Bisquick mix, eggs and milk and spread evenly over veg. mixture and bake until golden brown. Approx. 40 min.

## Easy Taco Bake

*Mrs. Milo (Lorene) Yoder*

1 lb. ground beef
½ c. chopped green pepper
½ c. chopped onion
1 pkg. (1 ¼ oz.) taco seasoning
¾ c. water
½ c. Miracle Whip salad
dressing
8 (6") corn tortillas
1 jar (8 oz.) salsa
1 c. (4 oz.) shredded cheese

Brown meat and drain. Add green pepper and onion. Cook until tender. Stir in seasoning mix, water and dressing. Cook 5 min. over med. heat. Arrange tortillas overlapping on bottom of 9" pie plate or cake pan. Top with meat mixture and salsa. Bake 30 min. at 350°. Sprinkle with cheese; continue baking 5 min. Let stand 15 min. Top with shredded lettuce. Tomatoes and sour cream, optional.

## Egg - Meat Souffle

*Mrs. Marvin (Ruby) Shrock*

1 lb. meat-ham, sausage or bacon
6 slices bread, cubed
6 eggs
2 c. milk
1 t. salt
1 t. dry mustard
1 c. shredded cheese

Brown meat and beat eggs. Add milk, salt, mustard, cheese, bread and meat. Mix well. Place in buttered 8 x 12" dish. Let set overnight. Bake at 350° for 45 min. or until brown.

*There is something better than understanding
God and that is trusting Him.*

# Enchiladas

*Mrs. Ivan (Arlene) Bontrager*

1 T. salad oil
1 lb. fresh ground beef
½ c. onions, chopped fine
½ c. pizza sauce

½ c. margarine or oil
8 flour tortillas
1 c. pizza sauce
1 c. shredded cheddar cheese

Heat salad oil in skillet. Fry ground beef and onions till beef is browned. Mix the ½ cup pizza sauce with meat and onions. In another skillet heat margarine or oil. Fry each tortilla about 2 or 3 seconds on each side. Drain on paper towels. (Frying tortillas too long will cause them to become crisp and they will break when you want to roll them up.) Spoon about ⅓ c. meat mixture onto a tortilla, roll it up, and place in an 8 x 12" baking dish. Repeat till all tortillas are distributed evenly in baking dish. Spoon pizza sauce over enchiladas in dish. Top with shredded cheese. Cover with foil and bake 25 min. at 350°. Uncover and bake 5 min. more.

# Famous Meatballs

*Mrs. Mervin (Gertie) Eash*

1 lb. chopped ham or wieners
1½ lb. sausage
2 c. bread crumbs
2 eggs, well beaten
1 c. milk

Sauce:
½ c. water
½ c. vinegar
1 c. brown sugar
1 t. dry mustard

Mix ham, sausage, crumbs, eggs and milk. Shape into balls, and place in 9 x 13" pan. Combine water, vinegar, brown sugar and dry mustard in a saucepan and bring to a boil. Pour over meatballs. Bake for 45 min. at 325°. Serves 10-12.

# Farmhouse Spoon Bread

*Mrs. Freeman (Mabel) Yoder*

1½ c. boiling water
1 c. cornmeal
1 T. butter or margarine
3 large egg yolks
1 c. buttermilk or sour milk

1 T. sugar
1 t. salt
1 t. baking powder
¼ t. soda
3 large egg whites

In med. bowl, using a wire whisk, stir boiling water into cornmeal until smooth and thickened. Whisk in butter until melted. Cool for 5 min. Whisk in egg yolks. Add buttermilk, sugar, salt, baking powder and soda. Blend well. Beat egg whites until soft peaks form. Mix batter into beaten egg whites. Pour into greased baking dish. Bake at 325° for 45-50 min. or until knife inserted in center comes out clean. Serve at once as this has a tendency to become soggy if it sets too long. Serve with sausage gravy.

## French Toast Deluxe

*Mrs. Freeman (Mabel) Yoder*

6 large pcs. french toast
   (keep warm)
6 pcs. shaved ham
9 pcs. turkey ham
8 eggs

¼ c. milk
½ t. salt
⅛ t. pepper
6 American cheese slices
syrup, heated

Make your favorite french toast. Meanwhile, heat both hams; keep warm. Beat eggs, milk, salt and pepper. Bake over med. heat, omelette style, cutting eggs into 4 x 4 inch squares. Layer hams, cheese and eggs on 3 pcs. of french toast; top with remaining 3 pcs. Cut diagonally and serve with your favorite syrup. Serves 6.

## Frosted Meat Loaf

*Mrs. Andy (Dorothy) Miller*

2 lbs. ground hamburger
¾ c. quick oats
¼ c. chopped onion
¾ c. milk

1½ t. salt
¼ t. pepper
1 egg

Mix meat loaf thoroughly and spread into a jelly roll pan. Bake at 350° for one hour. Frost with 6 cups mashed potatoes, top with cheese of your choice and return to oven for 5-10 min. or long enough to melt cheese. Cut into squares to serve. Yield: 20 squares.

## Golden Potato Surprise

*Mrs. Freeman (Mabel) Yoder*

8 med. white potatoes,
   peeled and diced
2 T. butter or margarine
1 med. onion, chopped
2 T. all-purpose flour
½ t. dried thyme
½ t. salt
½ t. black pepper

1 c. half and half or
   evaporated milk
1 t. Dijon mustard
¼ c. mayonnaise
¼ c. sour cream
½ lb. bacon, cooked and
   crumbled

Cook potatoes in boiling salted water until tender; drain and set aside. In saucepan, melt butter. Sauté onion until tender. Stir in flour, thyme, salt and pepper. Gradually add cream or evaporated milk, stirring constantly until sauce thickens. Remove from heat. Let cool slightly. Add mayonnaise, mustard and sour cream; stir until well mixed and smooth. Place potatoes in a 13 x 9" cake pan. Cover with sauce. Bake at 350° for 30 min. Before serving sprinkle with crumbled bacon.

## Gold Rush Brunch
*Mom (Elsie) Yoder*

16 oz. hash browns
2 onions, chopped
2 lb. Canadian ham or bacon

2 T. parsley
8 hard-boiled eggs
2 c. toasted bread cubes

Put in roaster in order given. Add white sauce.

White Sauce: ¼ c. butter
       ¼ t. salt
      ¼ c. flour

1½ c. sour cream
1 c. Velveeta cheese

Bake at 375° for 30-40 min. Serve with sausage gravy.

**Sausage Gravy: 1 pint beef broth or beef base**
      **1 pint water**
      ½ t. salt - Bring to a boil then add a paste of **2 round T.
flour and 1 c. water.** When thick, add **1 pint fried and crumbled sausage meat.** Makes a good breakfast brunch for Christmas gatherings.

## Gold Rush Brunch
*Mrs. LaVern (Martha) Yoder*

16 oz. hash browns
2 onions, chopped
2 T. parsley
White Sauce:
¼ c. butter
¼ c. flour
¼ t. salt

1 lb. bacon or ham
8 hard-boiled eggs

1½ c. sour cream
enough cheese to cover
top of dish

In a greased pan put in layers in order given. Pour white sauce over all and top with cheese. Bake at 375° for 30-40 min.

## Grandma's Chicken - Rice Dish
*Mrs. Lester (Verna) Bontrager*
*Mary Miller*

3 c. cooked, diced chicken
1 c. diced celery
2 c. cooked rice
¾ c. melted butter
1 t. onion salt
1 t. salt
Topping:
1 stick butter or margarine, melted
1 c. crushed cornflakes
½ c. almonds or pecans

1 t. lemon juice
1 can cream of chicken soup
3 hard-boiled eggs, chopped
¾ c. mayonnaise
1 can (4 oz.) mushrooms,
drained

In small saucepan, sauté celery in ¾ cup butter until crisp tender, then combine all ingredients in a baking dish. Mix topping ingredients and sprinkle on top. Bake uncovered at 350° - 375° until casserole starts to bubble, about 30 min.

# Ham Balls

*Mrs. Freeman (Mabel) Yoder*

1 lb. ground pork sausage
1 lb. fully cooked ham (ground)
2 eggs
¾ c. milk
1 c. crushed shredded wheat

Sauce:
1½ c. brown sugar
⅔ c. water
⅓ c. vinegar
¾ t. mustard

In a bowl combine pork, ham, eggs, milk and cereal. Mix well. In saucepan combine brown sugar, water, vinegar and mustard. Bring to a boil then reduce heat and simmer uncovered 4 min. Shape meat into 1 inch balls and put into a casserole dish, single layer. Then cover with sauce and bake uncovered at 350° for approx. 1½ hours or until well browned. DO NOT ADD ANY SALT TO THIS RECIPE, AS PORK AND HAM ARE SALTY.

# Hamburger Helper

*Mrs. Herman (Elsie) Mullett*

1 lb. ground beef
3 cups hot water
1½ c. macaroni
1 t. salt
pepper

1 t. chili powder
¼ t. celery seed
Velveeta cheese
chopped onions (optional)

Brown ground beef and onions in pan. Add hot water and seasonings. When water boils, stir in uncooked macaronis. Simmer until macaronis are soft. Add slices of cheese on top. Serve when cheese is melted. Yield - 8 servings.

# Harvard Beets

*Ola Bontrager*

6 cups red beets

Cover red beets in saucepan with water and simmer 20 min. Then add: ½ c. sugar, ½ c. vinegar and ¼ t. salt. Let this simmer till beets are soft then thicken with ¼ cup clear jel mixed with a little water and bring to a boil again.

# Hamburger Potato Bake

*Mrs. Freeman (Mabel) Yoder*

4 qts. potatoes, cubed
2 lbs. hamburger
½ c. chopped onions
2 t. salt
¼ t. pepper
1½ c. sour cream
2 cans cream of mushroom soup

2 c. french fried onions
1 (16 oz.) pkg. cheese slices
3 c. finely crushed B-B-Q chips
¼ c. red or green peppers (optional)

Cook potatoes until tender and drain. Fry hamburger with onions, salt and pepper. Drain. If using peppers cook them with the potatoes. Pour hamburger and potatoes into large casserole dish. In another bowl combine sour cream and mushroom soup; use ½ soup can of milk and stir well. Pour over mixture in casserole and stir together. Put a double layer of cheese on top then crumble french fried onions on top of that and layer with B-B-Q chips. Bake uncovered at 350° for approx. 30 min. or until edges begin to bubble.

# Hamburger Potato Casserole

*Mrs. Vernon (Polly) Beechy*

1½ lb. hamburger, browned
  and drained
Add ½ pkg. taco seasoning
8 med. potatoes, boiled,
  peeled, shredded
4 T. melted butter
2 c. grated cheese

1 t. salt
1 small onion, chopped
1 pt. sour cream
1 can cream of mushroom
1 can milk
2½ c. crushed cornflakes

Put hamburger in a greased cake pan. Combine all the other ingredients except cornflakes. Pour potato mixture over hamburger. Mix together 2½ c. crushed cornflakes with ¼ cup melted butter. Spread crumbs on top of potatoes. Bake at 350° for 45 min. May be prepared ahead and refrigerated until ready to use.

# Hamburger Rice Casserole

*Mrs. Milo (Lorene) Yoder*

1 lb. hamburger, browned
1 c. uncooked rice
1 c. diced carrots
1 c. onions, chopped
2 cans tomato soup

2 c. boiling water
1 qt. tomato juice
1 t. salt - pepper to taste
cheese

Combine in casserole. Cover and bake 2 hours at 325°. Sprinkle with 1 c. grated cheese 10 min. before done.

# Hash Brown Quiche

*Mrs. Freeman (Mabel) Yoder*

4 c. cooked shredded potatoes,
  or hash browns
⅓ c. butter or margarine
1 c. diced, fully cooked ham
1 c. shredded cheddar cheese

¼ c. diced green peppers
2 eggs
½ c. milk
½ t. salt
¼ t. pepper

Press potatoes in the bottom and up the sides of an ungreased 9" pie plate. Drizzle with butter. Bake at 425° for 25 min. Combine the ham, cheese and green peppers; spoon over crust. In a small bowl beat eggs, milk, salt and pepper. Pour over all. Reduce heat to 350°; bake 25-30 min. longer or until knife inserted near the center comes out clean. Allow to stand for 10 min. before cutting.

*After all is said and done,*
*there is more said than done.*

## Hess Mess

*Mrs. Noah (Amanda) Lehman*

1½ lb. hamburger
1 large onion, chopped
salt and pepper to taste
1 can tomato soup
1 can cream of chicken soup
1 can cream of celery soup
1 can cheddar cheese soup
10 oz. spaghetti
4 oz. grated mozzarella cheese

Brown hamburger, onion, salt and pepper. Add soups, combining well. Cook spaghetti and add to meat mixture. Put in 9 x 13" pan and top with cheese. Combine ½ c. milk and 1 can of mushroom soup and spread over the top. Bake at 350° for 20-30 min.

## Impossible Cheeseburger Pie

*Mrs. Sam (Viola) Miller*

1 lb. ground beef
1 c. chopped onion
½ t. salt
1 c. shredded cheddar or
mozzarella cheese
½ c. Bisquick (or any other
pancake mix)
1 c. milk
2 eggs

Cook together: ground beef, onion and salt until beef is brown; drain. Spread in pie plate and sprinkle with cheese. Stir remaining ingredients with fork and pour over meat and cheese. Bake at 400° for 30 min.

## Jiffy Pizza

*Miriam Yoder*
*In Memory of Katie*

2 c. flour
1 T. baking powder
1 t. salt
²/₃ c. milk
¹/₃ c. salad oil

Sift flour, baking powder and salt. Add milk and oil. Mix together and pat dough in bottom of pan. Put pizza sauce on top. Crumble browned meat and put on. Add mushrooms, olives, peppers or whatever you wish. Bake at 425° for 25 min. Cover with shredded mozzarella cheese and bake a few min. longer. Serves 6.

*It's never right to do wrong,*
*And it's never wrong to do right.*

## Lazy Day Overnight Lasagna

*Mrs. Toby (Martha) Yoder*

1 lb. ground beef
32 oz. prepared spaghetti sauce
1 cup water
16 oz. cottage cheese
2 T. chopped fresh chives,
 or 1 T. dried chives
½ t. oregano
1 egg
8 oz. uncooked lasagna noodles
16 oz. sliced mozzarella cheese
2 T. grated Parmesan cheese

In large skillet, brown ground beef; drain. Add spaghetti sauce and water; blend well. Simmer 5 min. In med. bowl combine cottage cheese, chives, oregano and egg. In bottom of ungreased 9 x 13" pan, spread 1½ c. meat mixture; top with half the noodles, ½ the cottage cheese mixture and ½ the mozzarella cheese. Repeat with remaining noodles, cheese mixture and mozzarella cheese. Top with remaining meat mixture. Sprinkle with Parmesan cheese. Cover and refrigerate overnight. Heat oven to 350° and bake uncovered 1 hour or until casserole is bubbly. Let set 15 min. before serving. Yield - 12 servings.

## Marinated Carrots

*Mrs. Eldon (Katie) Nisley*

5 c. sliced carrots
1 sm. green pepper (optional)
1 med. onion
½ c. salad oil
1 t. salt
1 t. pepper
1 t. Worcestershire sauce
1 c. sugar
¾ c. vinegar
1 (10 oz.) can tomato soup or
 ketchup

Cook carrots till tender but not soft. Drain and cool. Cut onions and peppers in round slices and mix with carrots. Mix other ingredients and pour over vegetables. Cover and marinate in refrigerator for 12 hours. Drain and serve. Save marinade and put back on leftover carrots. Will keep in the fridge at least 2 weeks.

## Marinade for Meats

*Mrs. Freeman (Mabel) Yoder*

1½ c. stir-fry oil
1 t. sugar
1 T. liquid smoke
¼ c. red wine vinegar
1 T. soy sauce
2 T. A–1 steak sauce
1 T. Tenderquick
4 T. water
¼ c. Hickory B-B-Q sauce

Combine all ingredients in a large bowl, stir well. We use this mostly for pork chops. Is enough for 2-3 lbs. meat and is great for grilling. Should marinate meat for 24 hours but overnight is fine, too. White chicken meat and steaks do well with this, too. Add salt just before meat is done on the grill. *Note: Stir-fry oil is hard to find, but can be found in the Ethnic Food section of most grocery stores.*

# Meatballs

*Mrs. Alvin (Katie Mae) Yoder*
*Mrs. Leland (Orpha) Yoder*

3 lbs. hamburger
1 c. oatmeal
1 c. crackers
1 c. milk
2 eggs
Sauce:
2 c. ketchup
1 c. brown sugar
½ t. liquid smoke

½ c. onions
½ t. garlic salt
2 t. salt
½ t. pepper
2 t. chili powder

½ t. garlic salt
¼ c. onions

Roll hamburger mixture into balls. Put into oven about 15 min. or until crusty. Pour sauce over meatballs, then bake at 350° for an hour.

# Meat Loaf

*Mrs. Orva (Marietta) Yoder*

4 lbs. hamburger
2 pieces bread
¼ lb. crackers
2 eggs
Topping:
2 T. mustard
4 t. ketchup

¾ c. milk
1 t. pepper
3 t. salt
2 t. Tenderquick

4 T. brown sugar

Mix hamburger with salt, pepper and Tenderquick. Crush crackers until fine; add rest of ingredients. Put topping on after ½ hour in oven. Bake at 350° for 1 hour.

# Mexican Chicken Wings

*Mrs. Ivan (Arlene) Bontrager*

10 chicken wings (about 2 lbs.)
¾ c. baking mix (such as Bisquick)
2 T. cornmeal
1 T. chili powder

½ t. salt
¼ t. pepper
½ c. buttermilk
¼ c. margarine, melted

Heat oven to 425°. Separate chicken wings at joints. Discard tips. Mix baking mix, cornmeal, chili powder, salt and pepper. Dip chicken into buttermilk then coat with cornmeal mixture. Arrange in an ungreased 13 x 9" pan. Drizzle margarine over chicken. Bake 35-40 min., uncovered, till light brown and crisp.

*We love ourselves with all our faults,*
*so why can't we love others?*

# Mexican Cornmeal Pizza

*Mrs. Freeman (Mabel) Yoder*

1 c. coarse yellow cornmeal
1 c. water
1 c. milk
1 t. salt
¼ c. flour
¼ c. Parmesan cheese, grated
1 small egg, beaten
1 T. oil

Mix water, milk, and salt and bring to a boil. Stir in cornmeal with wire whisk and remove from heat; add Parmesan, flour, egg and oil. Knead until smooth. Spray or oil a 12" deep-dish pizza pan. Oil your hands and press dough into pan and up the sides. Bake at 400° for 20-25 min. Then spread with ½ **c. pizza sauce, 1½ lb. browned crumbled hamburger with 1 pkg. taco seasoning,** ¼ **c. chopped onion, and 2 c. shredded cheese, cheddar or mozzarella.** Bake 20 min. longer; just before serving sprinkle **2-3 c. crushed taco chips** over pizza. Toppings may be varied to suit your taste.

# Mexican Lasagna

*Mrs. Herman (Elsie) Mullett*

1 lb. ground beef
1 can (16 oz.) refried beans
2 t. dried oregano
1 t. dried cumin
¾ t. garlic powder
12 uncooked lasagna noodles
2½ c. water
2½ c. picante sauce or salsa
2 c. sour cream
¾ c. chopped onion
1 can (2.2 oz.) sliced black
   olives, drained
1 c. shredded Monterey Jack
   cheese

Brown beef; add beans, oregano, cumin, and garlic powder. Place four of the uncooked lasagna noodles in the bottom of a 13 x 9 x 2" baking pan. Spread half the beef mixture over the noodles. Top with four more noodles and the remaining beef mixture. Cover with remaining noodles. Combine water and picante or salsa. Pour over top. Cover tightly with foil and bake at 350° for ½ hour or until noodles are tender. Combine sour cream, onions and olives. Spoon over casserole and top with cheese. Bake uncovered until cheese is melted. Yield: 12 servings.

# Mexican Salsa Casserole

*Mrs. Freeman (Mabel) Yoder*

1½ lb. hamburger
1 can (15 oz.) refried beans
1 pkg. or 2 T. taco seasoning
2 c. sour cream
10 flour tortillas
2 cans cream of mushroom soup
2 c. cheddar or American
   cheese slices
1 c. chopped tomatoes
3 c. chopped lettuce
2 c. mild or med. salsa

Fry hamburger. Add beans and taco seasoning; set aside; mix sour cream and cream of mushroom soup. Spread half on bottom of a med. sized casserole dish. Divide hamburger mixture evenly on each tortilla and roll up. Put on top of sour cream mixture and spread the other half of sour cream mixture on top of burritos. Bake at 350° for 30 min. or until heated through. Before serving, top with cheese, lettuce, tomatoes and salsa. Return to oven a few min. until cheese is melted. Delicious!

# Mock Ham Loaf

*Mrs. Freeman (Mabel)Yoder*
*Mrs. Elmer (Wilma) Beechy*

3 lbs. hamburger (I like to
  use ground turkey)
3 lbs. wieners, ground
6 eggs

½ lb. white crackers (3 cups
  crushed fine)
3-4 t. salt

Mix together. In another bowl mix:

2½ T. vinegar
2 T. prepared mustard

2½ c. brown sugar
¾ c. water or slightly more

Pour half of this over meat mixture in bowl and mix well. Put meat mixture in baking pan and flatten out. With edge of hand make 4 dents on top of meat. Then pour the rest of juice over meat. Bake in slow oven, 325° to 350°. Brown sugar in syrup will make it burn more easily so a slower oven is important. Bake 1½ hours or until done.

# Mock Onion Rings

*Mrs. Freeman (Mabel) Yoder*

1½ c. chopped onions
1 t. salt
2 t. baking powder
2 T. cornmeal, heaping

1 T. sugar
1 c. flour
½ c. milk, scant

Mix dry ingredients together, then add milk; batter will be thick. Add onions last. Blend well then drop spoonsful into hot oil and fry till golden brown on both sides. Serve with ketchup.

# Mock Pizza

*Mrs. Eli (Martha) Mullet*

1½ lb. sausage or hamburger
1½ c. pizza sauce

3 c. shredded cheese

Fry meat, drain fat and add sauce. Line a 9 x 13" cake pan with sliced bread. Spread with meat mixture (optional: mushrooms, peppers, onions) and shredded cheese. Cover with another layer of bread slices. Beat together and pour over all: **3 c. milk, 5 eggs and 1 t. salt**. Bake at 400° for 45 min. or until golden brown.

# Mock Steak

*Mrs. Vernon (Polly) Beechy*
*Mrs. Leroy (Sara) Yoder*

1½ lb. hamburger
1½ c. finely crushed white crackers
¾ c. milk
1½ t. salt

½ t. black pepper
Add: 1 can cream of mushroom
  soup and ¾ can water
  (mushroom can)

Mix together and shape in loaves to chill. Slice; fry in shortening. Sprinkle with flour and put in small roaster. This can also be made into patties and fried right away. Bake at 350° for 1 hour.

## Mushroom Brunch Casserole
*Mrs. Ezra (Mary) Miller*

Beat 18-20 eggs
add 2½ c. milk

1 can mushroom soup
salt and pepper to taste

Put buttered bread in bottom of cake pan. Pour egg mixture over bread. Put meat of your choice on top and bake at 350° for an hour or until done; add **cheese** just before done.

## No-Fuss Lasagna
*Mrs. Lonnie (Norma Mae) Bontrager*

1 lb. hamburger
¼ t. salt
¼ t. pepper
1 (24 oz.) cottage cheese

½ c. grated **Parmesan cheese**
1 egg, beaten
10 uncooked lasagna noodles
1½ c. shredded mozz. cheese

Brown hamburger; season with salt and pepper. Then stir in **2½ pts. spaghetti sauce** and set aside. In another bowl, combine cottage cheese, Parmesan cheese and egg. Spread 2 c. meat sauce over bottom of a 13 x 9 in. baking dish. Arrange 4 lasagna noodles lengthwise in single layer. Place fifth noodle across end of baking dish, breaking to fit. Spread entire cottage cheese mixture over noodles. Sprinkle with 1 c. mozzarella and top with 1½ c. meat sauce. Arrange remaining noodles in single layer; press lightly into sauce. Top with remaining meat sauce. Bake at 375° for 45 min. or until noodles are tender. Sprinkle remaining mozzarella on top. Tent lightly with aluminum foil. Let stand 15 min. before cutting into squares.

## One-Dish Meal
*Mom (Rosa) Bontrager*

4 large potatoes, diced
1 qt. canned green beans
Sauce:
2 c. milk
½ lb. soft cheese

1 lb. wieners, cut up
½ onion

½ c. flour
1 T. salt

Three batches fill a big stainless steel roaster. Heat milk enough to melt cheese. Add flour and salt; pour over potato mixture. Bake at 300° for 2 hours. Yield: 12 servings.

## Our Favorite Sausage
*Mrs. Mervin (Emma) Yoder*

35-40 lbs. pork
¾ c. Tenderquick
2 T. liquid smoke

1¼ T. black pepper
½ c. salt

Grind together and stuff casings or make patties. Cut casings in desired lengths and roast in oven then process. Divide excess grease in cans then fill jars with water. Process at 10 lb. pressure for ½ hour.

# Overnight Sausage and Egg Casserole

*Mrs. Freeman (Mabel) Yoder*

8 slices homemade bread
  or french bread
2 c. shredded or American
  cheese slices
1½ lbs. bulk pork sausage
4 eggs

2½ c. milk
1 T. prepared mustard
1 can (10¾ oz.) cream of
  mushroom soup
½ c. chicken broth
¼ t. salt

Place bread cubes in a greased 13 x 9" pan. Sprinkle with cheese; set aside. In a skillet brown sausage over med. heat; drain fat. Crumble sausage over cheese and bread. Beat eggs, milk, mustard, soup and broth and pour over sausage. Cover and refrigerate overnight or 2-3 hours before baking. Remove from refrigerator ½ hour before baking. Bake at 350° for 50-60 min. or just until set.

# Perfect Baked Chicken

*Mrs. Christy (Anna) Bontrager*

⅓ c. flour
1 t. paprika
¼ t. garlic powder

1 t. salt
¼ t. pepper
2½-3 lbs. chicken

Put flour and spices in a bag and mix. Melt butter. Dip chicken in butter then put in bag and shake until covered. Bake at 350° for 1-1½ hrs.

# Pizza Meat Loaf

*Mrs. Leland (Orpha) Yoder*

2 lbs. ground beef
1 c. cracker crumbs
1 c. milk
¼ c. onion, chopped

½ c. Parmesan cheese
2 eggs
2 t. seasoned salt
1 t. oregano

Mix all ingredients and spread in a 9 x 13" cake pan. Bake at 350° for 1 hour. The last 10 min. spread with pizza sauce and 1-2 c. shredded mozzarella cheese.

# Pizza Casserole

*Mrs. Owen (Verna) Hershberger*

2 lbs. hamburger
1 med. onion
1 pack wide noodles or
  macaroni
1 small can mushrooms
1 qt. pizza sauce

2 cans cream of mushroom soup
1½ c. chopped ham, beef, or
  wieners
Velveeta or mozzarella cheese
  (amount of cheese can vary)

Fry onions and hamburger. When done put in a roaster and put cut up mushrooms on top. Cook noodles until done; drain and put on top of meat. Add other kinds of meat on top of noodles. Heat pizza sauce and mushroom soup until hot and pour over everything in roaster. Top with cheese. Bake at 350° for 30 min. You can mix everything together except cheese or fix in layers. Very filling and scrumptious!

## Pizza Casserole

*Mrs Ora N. (Orpha) Miller*

2 lbs. hamburger, browned
½ green pepper, cut up fine
1 med. onion, cut up fine
1 can pizza sauce
8 oz. noodles, cooked 5 min.

1 c. mushroom pieces
1 c. Parmesan cheese
1 c. cream of mushroom soup
Velveeta cheese or any kind of
   melting cheese on top

Mix all together and place in a casserole or roaster and bake at 350° for approx. 45 min. or up to bubbly point. Add cheese on top a few min. before taking from oven.

## Pizza Casserole

*Mary Miller*

2½ lbs. hamburger
1 onion
½ cup spaghetti (measure
   then cook)
1 qt. pizza sauce
Crust:
1½ c. flour
2 t. baking powder
⅔ t. salt

1 c. sour cream
mix with 3 T. salad dressing
   and 3 c. grated mozzarella
   cheese

½ c. milk
¼ c. oil

Fry hamburger and onion together till done then add rest of ingredients and pour over crust. Bake at 350° for 30 min.

## Pizza

*Mrs. Ervin (Clara) Yoder*

2 c. flour
½ t. salt
1 T. instant yeast

1 T. oil
1½ c. very warm water
1 T. sugar

Put water in bowl - should be fairly hot but not too hot. Add all the other ingredients and whip with wire whip. Should be sticky and gooey. Add more flour till a soft dough forms. Let rise till double then divide and roll out and put on greased pans. Makes 2 (12") round pizzas. Top with ½ **c. pizza sauce** on each. Add favorite toppings such as chopped onions, green peppers, pepperoni, hamburger, sausage or any kind of cheese. It is best to prebake crusts 15 min. at 375° and then add the toppings whenever you are ready. Bake near top of oven at 400°.

*Where there is a human being,*
*there is an opportunity for kindness.*

## Polish Sausage
*Mrs. Harry (Edna Mae) Bontrager*

10 lbs. chicken meat,
  cut off of bones
2 c. non-fat dry milk
6 T. salt
1 T. sugar

½ t. Tenderquick
1 T. black pepper
1 t. garlic salt
1 heaping t. marjoram
2 lbs. water

Grind the meat as you would for chicken bologna. Add all the other ingredients and mix well. Freeze and put in jars and pressure cook, like any other meat. 1½ hours at 10 lbs. pressure.

## Poor Man's Steak
*Mrs. Marvin (Ruby) Shrock*

1½ lbs. ground beef
½ c. fine bread crumbs or
  cracker crumbs
½ c. water

2 t. salt
½ t. pepper
2 small chopped onions

Mix all ingredients together. Pat out ¾" thick in pan. Refrigerate overnight or at least 8 hours. Cut into pieces. Roll in flour and brown in a small amount of fat. Lay pieces in baking dish. Pour over meat: 1 can mushroom soup. Bake in preheated oven at 300° for 1½ hours.

## Pop-Over Pizza
*Mrs. Leland (Orpha) Yoder*

1 lb. ground beef
1 can cream of mushroom soup
1 pint pizza sauce
any cheese you like that melts

1 c. Bisquick
2 eggs
1 c. milk

Brown ground beef with some onions and 1 T. veg. oil. Put in bottom of a cake pan and put pizza sauce over hamburger and top with cream of mushroom soup and cheese. Mix Bisquick, eggs and milk and pour over top and bake at 400° for 30 min. I like to put a layer of green beans or french fries in, too. I put them on the hamburger before adding the rest of the ingredients.

## Poppy Seed Chicken
*Mrs. Simon (Martha) Schmucker*
*Mrs. Marvin (Ruby) Shrock*

2 lbs. chicken (boned
  and cooked)
1 can cream of chicken soup
1 c. sour cream

1½ c. crushed Ritz crackers
½ c. oleo, melted
1 t. poppy seed

Arrange in a buttered 9 x 12" baking dish. Mix soup and sour cream and pour over chicken. Mix oleo with cracker crumbs until crumbs are well coated. Stir in poppy seeds and spread crumb mixture over chicken. Bake at 350° (325° if using glass dish) for 35-40 min.

## Pork and Bean Pizza

*Mrs. LaVern (Martha) Yoder*

1 (31 oz.) can VanCamps
   pork-n-beans
1 (14 oz.) jar pizza sauce
8 English muffins, split, toasted,
   (regular bread may be used)

Favorite pizza toppings such as
chopped onions, chopped
green peppers, sliced ripe
olives, 2 cups mozz. cheese

Combine beans and pizza sauce. Spoon ¼ c. bean mixture onto each muffin half. Top with 1 or more of your favorite pizza toppings. Sprinkle with 2 T. cheese. Broil 5-6" from heat or until cheese begins to bubble and melt. Yield - 16 mini pizzas.

## Potato Casserole

*Mrs. Ezra (Mary) Miller*

8 lbs. potatoes
3½ lbs. ham
9 c. milk
1 c. flour

⅓ lb. margarine
7½ t. salt
½ t. black pepper
2 lbs. Velveeta cheese

Wash and cook potatoes; peel and cool. Cut up ham and heat. Heat the milk with margarine, then make a paste with flour, salt and black pepper and add this to your boiling milk. Now put your cheese into this. Put your potatoes through shoe stringer, and mix everything in an 8 qt. roaster. Bake at 350° for 45 min. to an hour.

## Potato Cheese Puffs

*Mrs. Allen (Elsie) Bontrager*

1 c. mashed potatoes
2 eggs, beaten
½ c. milk
¼ t. baking powder

2 c. shredded cheddar cheese
½ c. flour
salt and pepper to taste
salad oil for frying

Combine ingredients except for oil. Mix well. Pour about 2" of oil in a saucepan and heat to 375°. Drop batter by T., 4 or 5 at a time, into the hot oil. Fry 3-4 min. or until golden brown. Serve immediately. Yield: About 24 puffs.
This is a good way to use up leftover mashed potatoes.

## Quiche

*Mrs. Ivan (Arlene) Bontrager*

4 eggs
1 can cream of celery
   or onion soup
½ c. cream
1 c. cheddar cheese, shredded

½ c. diced ham or diced cooked
   chicken
½ c. broccoli, cooked, drained
   and chopped
1 (9") unbaked pie shell

Beat eggs. Gradually add soup and cream, mixing well. Sprinkle meat, cheese and broccoli evenly over pie crust. Pour soup over top. Bake at 350° about 50 min. or until set. Let stand 10 min. before serving.

## Ranch Potato Casserole

*Mrs. Lester (Verna) Bontrager*

6-8 med. sized potatoes
½ c. prepared Ranch
  style dressing
½ c. sour cream

¼ c. cooked, crumbled bacon
2 T. minced fresh parsley (or 1
  T. dried flakes)
1 c. shredded cheddar cheese

Topping:
½ c. shredded cheddar cheese
2 c. slightly crushed cornflakes

¼ c. butter, melted

Cook the potatoes until tender; peel and slice. Combine dressing, sour cream, bacon, parsley and 1 c. of cheese. Place potatoes in a greased 9 x 13" baking dish. Pour sour cream mixture over potatoes and gently toss. Top with ½ c. of cheese. Combine cornflakes and butter; sprinkle over casserole. Bake at 350° for 40-45 min.

## Ranch Potato Casserole

*Mrs. Vernon (Polly) Beechy*

8 med. potatoes
¾ c. sour cream
¾ c. prepared Ranch
  style dressing

1 lb. bacon, fried and crumbled
2 T. minced parsley
1 c. shredded cheese

Topping:
½ c. shredded cheese
2 c. crushed cornflakes

¼ c. melted butter

Cook potatoes until tender; slice or quarter, leaving skins on; and put in greased 9 x 13" pan. Combine sour cream, dressing, bacon, parsley and 1 c. of cheese, then pour over potatoes and mix gently. Top with ½ c. cheese. Combine cornflakes and butter; sprinkle over casserole. Bake at 350° for 45 min.

## Raw Vegetable Casserole

*Mrs. Melvin (Mary Esther) Shrock*

thick slices of cabbage
coarsely cut potatoes
celery, onions, carrots

flavor with salt and pepper
  as you layer it

When you have what you need, add **raw hamburger** (mixed) on top and bake at 350° for 1½ hours (covered); add **cheese** after it is done. Wash all vegetables and leave dripping wet. On bottom of roaster or pan put in order as written above. Only cabbage once on bottom. This forms its own juice. You can make any amount for your size family. (A bit of water doesn't hurt.) This can be put in a frying pan and cooked on top of stove, slowly. I add cauliflower or broccoli, too, or whatever.

## Rice Casserole

*Mrs. Elmer (Wilma) Beechy*

1 lb. hamburger
1 c. diced celery
1 chopped onion
1 c. rice or more

1 can cream of chicken soup
1 can mushroom soup
2 soup cans water
1 t. soy sauce

Fry hamburger and onions together. Boil the rice to almost tender; mix with other ingredients and bake for 1 hour at 300°-325°. A good potato dish replacement.

## Rocky Mountain Chicken

*Mrs. Daniel (Esther) Yoder*

2 cans (16 oz. each) green beans
2 c. cubed chicken
1 can cream of chicken soup
½ c. mayonnaise

1 T. lemon juice
1 c. shredded cheese
1 c. bread crumbs
¼ c. melted butter

In 9 x 13" pan layer green beans, then chicken, then mixture of soup, mayonnaise and lemon juice. Top with cheese. Mix bread crumbs with butter and sprinkle with cheese. Bake at 350° for 1 hour or until browned. May substitute broccoli for beans. I use salad dressing instead of mayonnaise and lemon juice.

## Sassy Zucchini

*Mrs. Ivan (Arlene) Bontrager*

1 lb. fresh gound beef
1 med. onion, chopped
2 c. cut up fresh tomatoes
¾ cup water

1 env. spaghetti sauce mix
1 t. salt
1 c. precooked rice
4 c. cut up zucchini

In a large skillet, fry ground beef with onions till beef is browned. Mix in undrained tomatoes, water and sauce; mix and salt. Stir in rice and zucchini. Cover tightly and simmer 15-20 min. or until zucchini is tender. Serves 6.

## Sausage

*Mrs. Sam (Martha) Schrock*

40 lbs. meat
  (⅓ of it being beef)
1 c. salt
1 T. black pepper
1 t. dry mustard

1 t. ginger
1 t. allspice
4 T. liquid smoke
1 lb. brown sugar
1 c. cornmeal

Combine all ingredients, mixing well with hands. May be frozen or packed into jars and processed for 1½ hours at 10 lbs. pressure.

## Savory Sausage and Potato Pie
*Mrs. Freeman (Mabel) Yoder*

5 med. potatoes
1 t. salt
1 egg
Filling:
1 lb. sausage
½ c. green pepper, chopped
2 t. flour

½ c. chopped onion
½ c. cornflakes
2 t. parsley flakes

1 can cream of mushroom soup
1 c. corn
1 c. shredded cheese

Crust: Cook potatoes in boiling salted water until tender. Drain and mash; stir in egg; add onions, cornflakes and parsley. Spread in greased 10" pie plate.

Filling: Brown sausage in skillet. Remove and drain on paper towel. Pour off fat, reserving 1 T. Add green pepper and sauté for 5 min. or until tender. Stir in sausage and flour. Add soup and corn; blend well. Turn mixture into potato shell and sprinkle with cheese. Bake at 400° for 25-30 min.

## Skillet Beef Macaroni Casserole
*Mrs. Reuben (Martha) Yoder*

2 T. melted butter or margarine
1 lb. ground beef
1½ c. uncooked macaroni
1 c. cut up onion
½ c. green pepper
1 t. oregano
1 t. salt

¼ t. black pepper
1 cube beef bouillon
1½ c. boiling water
1 T. flour
1²/₃ c. milk
¼ lb. grated cheese (approx. 1 c.)
2 T. finely cut pimiento

In a 10 in. skillet combine the first 8 ingredients in order given. Cook and stir over low heat until meat is browned. Dissolve bouillon in boiling water. Stir into meat mixture. Bring to a boil and cover. Cook over low heat 20 min. or until macaronis are tender and water is absorbed. Sprinkle flour evenly over meat mixture and mix. Stir in milk, cheese and pimiento. Cook about 5 min., stirring now and then. Serves 6-8. If you prefer a sausage casserole, add 1 lb. sausage instead of beef and omit the beef bouillon but add the water. The rest of the ingredients are just the same.

## Sloppy Joe Bake
*Mrs. Sam (Viola) Miller*

1 lb. ground beef
1 c. chopped onion
1 can tomato sauce (15 oz.)
½ c. ketchup
⅓ c. packed brown sugar

2 t. mustard
1½ c. Bisquick (or any
   pancake mix)
1 c. milk
2 eggs

Brown ground beef and onion together; drain. Stir in tomato sauce, ketchup, brown sugar and mustard. Heat to boiling and spoon into ungreased cake pan. Stir Bisquick, milk and eggs together with a fork and pour over beef mixture. Bake at 400° for 25 min.

## Sloppy Joe Potato Pizza Casserole

*Mrs. Christy (Anna) Bontrager*

2 lbs. cooked shredded potatoes
1 can (11 oz.) cheddar cheese soup
  or cook your own soup
Cheese Soup Recipe:

| | |
|---|---|
| **2 T. flour** | **1 egg** |
| **2 T. butter** | **½ t. pepper** |
| **¾ c. milk** | **1 t. salt** |
| **1¼ in. Velveeta cheese** | |

Put flour, butter, milk, and cheese in saucepan and heat, stirring, until cheese and butter are melted. Then add egg, salt and pepper. Mix into potatoes and put in casserole. Bake 20-25 min. at 450°.

Meanwhile, brown 2 lbs. hamburger and drain. Add pizza sauce to taste and simmer 5 min. Put on top of potatoes and sprinkle cheese on top. *Variations: Put chopped lettuce or tomatoes on top.*

## Spanish Rice

*Mary Miller*

| | |
|---|---|
| **¼ c. butter** | **1 qt. tomato juice** |
| **1 med. onion, sliced thin** | **1 t. salt** |
| **1 stick celery, diced** | **⅛ t. pepper** |
| **1 c. rice** | **1 lb. hamburger** |

Heat butter in large saucepan. Put in tomatoes, onions, celery, seasoning and fried hamburger. Bring to a boil and add rice. You have to brown hamburger separately. Cover and simmer for 30 min., stirring occasionally. Add a little water yet, and sugar, if desired. This is good with spaghetti or macaroni too, instead of rice.

## Spicy Meat Loaf

*Mrs. Mervin (Gertie) Eash*

| | |
|---|---|
| **1 slightly beaten egg** | **2 T. chopped onion** |
| **1 c. milk** | **2 t. salt** |
| **1 c. dry bread crumbs** | **½ t. pepper** |
| **2 lbs. ground beef** | **¼ c. ketchup** |

Combine egg and milk; add bread crumbs and allow to soak until milk is absorbed. Add beef, onion, salt, and pepper and blend. Place in 9 x 5 x 3" loaf pan or shape into loaf in a shallow baking dish. Spread top with ketchup. Bake 1½ hours at 350°.

*God without man is still God.*
*Man without God is nothing.*

## Swedish Meatballs and Gravy

*Mrs. Lester (Verna) Bontrager*

1 lb. ground beef
1/3 c. bread crumbs
1 egg
1½ t. salt
Sauce:
1 can cream of mushroom soup
1 (8 oz.) pkg. cream cheese

1/3 c. milk
2 T. chopped onion
½ T. Worcestershire sauce
½ t. black pepper

½ c. water

Mix meatball ingredients and shape into 2" balls. Place in a baking dish and bake at 375° for 20 min. Meanwhile, heat sauce ingredients, then pour over meatballs and continue baking for another 30 min.

## Taco Casserole

*Mrs. Leland (Orpha) Yoder*

1 lb. ground beef, mixed with
  1 pkg. taco seasoning
2/3 c. salad dressing and
  1 c. sour cream, mixed together
2 T. chopped onions
1 c. chopped green peppers
3 c. chopped tomatoes

1 c. shredded cheddar cheese
tortilla chips (crushed)- may use
  B-B-Q chips or Doritos
½ c. water
2 c. Bisquick-may use a reg. biscuit dough recipe instead

Heat the oven to 350°. Grease baking dish. Brown beef and mix with taco seasoning according to pkg. Mix Bisquick and water and pat into pan and ½ in. up the sides. Layer beef, tomatoes, onions and peppers on dough. Next put sour cream and salad dressing mixture on. Bake 25 - 30 min. Put cheese on after it has baked awhile. Put crushed chips on top after it is done and just before serving.

## Tater Tot Casserole

*Mrs. Ray (LeEtta) Yoder*

1 lb. hamburger
salt and pepper to taste
1 sm. onion, diced
1 (12 oz.) can peas and
  carrots, drained

1 sm. can Mexicorn, drained
1 can cream of mushroom soup
½ soup can milk
1 pkg. Tater Tots

Brown hamburger with salt, pepper and onion. Drain off any excess fat from hamburger. Place browned hamburger in bottom of 9 x 13" pan. Combine soup and milk. Add peas, carrots and corn to soup mixture. Pour over hamburger. Place Tater Tots on top. Bake in 350° oven for 1 hour.

## Tater Tot Casserole

*Mrs. Marvin (Ruby) Shrock*

2 lbs. Tater Tots
1 pt. sour cream
2 cans cream of chicken soup
1½ soup cans milk
½ c. chopped onions
2 lbs. hamburger
1 lb. Velveeta cheese
1 t. salt
½ t. pepper
2 c. cornflakes or
   crushed Ritz crackers
½ c. melted butter

Put Tater Tots in bottom of roaster or pan. Mix together sour cream, soup, milk, onions, salt and pepper. Pour this over Tater Tots; top with cheese and fried hamburger with onions. Sprinkle with cornflakes or cracker crumbs mixed with melted butter. Bake at 350° for 45-60 min.

## Tater Tot Casserole

*Mrs. Lester (Verna) Bontrager*

1 bag frozen Tater Tots
1½ lbs. ground beef, browned
½ c. chopped onions
1 (8 oz.) pkg. cream cheese
1 can cream of mushroom soup
¼ c. milk
1 t. salt
¼ c. ketchup

Brown onions and ground beef together; place in small roaster with the rest of ingredients, except Tater Tots. Mix everything together; put a layer of American cheese on top, then add Tater Tots on top of cheese and bake in a 350° oven for 45 min. or until Tater Tots are done.

## Tenderquick for Turkey or Chicken

*Mrs. Merlin (Mary) Lehman*

1 c. Tenderquick
2 T. liquid smoke
10 c. water

Soak whole chicken overnight. Drain and bake in covered roaster at 350° for 1½ hours or until tender. Soak whole turkey for 3-4 days; drain and bake in covered roaster at 350° for 4 hours. It takes 2 batches for a turkey.

## Texas B-B-Q Sauce

*Mrs. Marvin (Ruby) Shrock*

Mix in saucepan:
1 T. paprika
2 T. brown sugar
1 t. salt
¼ t. chili powder
1 t. dry mustard
⅛ t. cayenne pepper
2 T. Worcestershire sauce
¼ c. vinegar
½ c. water
1 c. tomato sauce
¼ c. ketchup

Simmer 15 min. or until slightly thickened. Very good on pork steaks or spareribs when grilled or baked.

## Turkey Loaf

*Mrs. Mervin (Emma) Yoder*

Mix together well:
1 egg, beaten
1 t. prepared mustard
Add:
1 lb. ground turkey or chicken

1 c. soda crackers
1 T. vinegar
⅓ c. brown sugar

⅓ lb. ground wieners

Mix well with hands. Put in cake pan or casserole dish. Drizzle ¼ to ½ c. water around the edges of meat. Cover and bake at 350° for 1 hour. Very easy and delicious.

## Turkey Meatballs

*Mrs. Freeman (Mabel) Yoder*

1½ lbs. ground turkey
1 c. butter flavored crackers
1 egg
¼ c. chopped onion
½ t. ginger
1 c. shredded mozzarella cheese
4 T. Dijon mustard

1¼ c. pineapple juice
¼ c. chopped green pepper
2 T. honey
¼ t. onion powder
½ t. salt
⅛ t. pepper

Combine first 6 ingredients and 3 T. mustard, salt and pepper. Form into balls and place in a greased cake pan. Bake at 350° for 20 min. In saucepan combine 1 T. mustard, pineapple juice, green pepper, honey and onion powder. Bring to a boil and cook for 2 min, stirring constantly, then pour over meatballs and bake 45 min. more or until done. Very tasty.

## Welsh Rabbit Potatoes

*Mrs. Toby (Martha) Yoder*

2 T. butter
2 T. flour
1 c. milk
1 c. shredded cheese
1 t. spicy brown mustard

6 large baking potatoes
2 med. onions, sliced & halved
garlic salt
crumbled bacon (6 slices)
chopped green onions

Cheese Sauce: In a small saucepan over med. heat, melt butter and add flour. Cook, stirring, 1 min. Gradually stir in milk and cook until boiling, stirring constantly. Simmer 1 min. Remove from heat; stir in mustard and cheese until cheese melts. Cut each potato almost through crosswise in ¼" slices and place in center of heavy-duty aluminum foil. Insert 4 onion half slices evenly spaced into each potato. Sprinkle with garlic salt. Wrap each potato and cook in covered grill over medium heat about 1 hour or bake in 350° oven. Reheat cheese sauce. Just before serving open each packet and top with cheese sauce, bacon and green onions. Yield: 6 servings. NOTE: If I don't have Dijon mustard on hand I use reg. prepared mustard.

## Western Meat Loaf

*Regina Miller*

3 lbs. ground beef
1½ c. milk
1 c. rolled oats
1 c. cracker crumbs
2 eggs
Sauce:
¾ c. brown sugar
¼ c. chopped onion
2 T. ketchup

½ c. chopped onions
1 t. garlic powder
1 t. salt
1 t. pepper
1 t. chili powder

1 t. garlic powder
½ t. liquid smoke

Mix all ingredients well and bake at 350° for approx. an hour. Mix sauce and put on meat ½ hr. to 20 min. before meat is done. Meat can also be made into balls, instead of a loaf, and baked.

## Wet Burrito Casserole

*Mrs. Allen (Elsie) Bontrager*

1 lb. hamburger
1 onion
1 green pepper
1 pkg. taco seasoning
1 can refried beans
½ c. hot water

½ c. salsa
1 can cream of mushroom soup
1½ c. sour cream
10 med. soft flour tortilla shells
2 c. taco flavored cheese
2 c. marble cheese

Fry hamburger, onion and green pepper. Add taco seasoning, refried beans, water and salsa. Combine soup and sour cream. Pour half of soup mixture into a 9 x 13" pan. Lay out the tortilla shells. Divide hamburger mixture on shells. Roll up and place in pan, side by side. Top with rest of soup mixture. Bake for 20 min. at 350°. Add cheese and bake 10 min. more. May be served with shredded lettuce, tomatoes and sour cream. Yummy! Servings: 10.

## Yum-E-Setti

*Mrs. Daniel A. (Ida) Miller*

1 lb. hamburger
1 can cream of chicken soup
1 can tomato soup
1 c. celery

1 sm. onion
salt and pepper to taste
1 pkg. noodles
1 lb. Velveeta cheese

Fry hamburger, onions and celery in skillet. Cook noodles in water until tender, but not soft. Mix tomato soup in hamburger and chicken soup in noodles. Put hamburger in casserole and noodles on top. Cover with cheese and bake in slow oven (250°-300°) for 1 hour.

## Zucchini Casserole

*Mrs. Ivan (Arlene) Bontrager*

4 slices bread, cubed
2 T. butter, melted
1 med. zucchini, grated
  but unpeeled
1 tomato, peeled and sliced

1 sweet pepper, cored and
  grated
1 large onion, peeled and sliced
sliced American cheese
salt and pepper

Toss bread cubes with melted butter. In a greased casserole dish, layer zucchini, tomato, pepper, onion, bread and cheese. After each layer of vegetables, sprinkle with salt and pepper. Bake 1 hour at 350°.

*Does your faith move mountains or
do mountains move your faith?*

# Helpful Hints

When boiling eggs add a few drops of vinegar to the water. It will help keep shells from cracking.

If cheese becomes moldy, trim off ½ inch of cheese on all sides where mold is visible. Then it is fine to eat. For best flavor of any cheese, slice and let sit at room temperature for 30 minutes before serving.

Add ½ c. of honey to any coleslaw recipe and "you'll be amazed".

When making jelly, just before you remove from heat, drop in a T. of butter or oleo. As it melts it will make the jelly very clear - and skimming unneccessary.

Store whole lemons in a tightly sealed jar of water in the refrigerator. They will yield more juice.

Celery will keep fresh longer if wrapped in a paper towel then in tinfoil and kept in refrigerator.

Put frozen bread loaves in a brown paper bag and place for 5 minutes in a 325° oven to thaw completely.

While peeling apples, peaches and pears, place slices in slightly salted water. They will retain their natural color.

When canning sweet corn, put corn in jar; add water, 1 t. salt and 1 t. sugar. Add 1 t. lemon juice or a slice of green tomato on top of corn.

A pinch of salt added to cream before whipping strengthens the fat cells and makes them more elastic. This helps the cream to stiffen more quickly.

Sunlight doesn't ripen tomatoes; it's the warmth that makes them ripen. So find a warm spot near the stove where they can get a little heat.

Cream cheese and sour cream can be added to mashed potatoes; improves the flavor and are more fluffy.

A white of an egg is easiest to beat at room temperature.

Lettuce and celery will crisp up fast if you place it in a pan of cold water and add a few sliced potatoes.

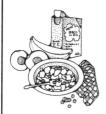

# Cereals,
# Pancakes,
# & Syrups

*Many things are opened by mistake - but none so frequently as the mouth.*

*Being confident of this very thing, that he which hath begun a good work in you will perform it until the day of Jesus Christ.*
*Philippians 1:6*

# Notes....

## Blueberry Sour Cream Pancakes   *Mrs. Allen (Elsie) Bontrager*

½ c. sugar
2 T. cornstarch
1 c. water
Pancakes:
2 c. all-purpose flour
¼ c. sugar
4 t. baking powder
½ t. salt
2 eggs

4 c. fresh or frozen
 blueberries

1 c. sour cream
⅓ c. butter or marg., melted
1 c. fresh or frozen
 blueberries
1½ c. milk

In a medium saucepan, combine sugar and cornstarch. Gradually stir in water. Add blueberries and bring to a boil over medium heat. Boil for 2 min., stirring constantly. Remove from heat; cover and keep warm. For pancakes combine dry ingredients in a bowl. In another bowl beat the eggs. Add milk, sour cream, and butter and mix well. Stir into dry ingredients just until blended. Fold in the blueberries. Pour batter by ¼ cupfuls onto a greased hot griddle. Turn when bubbles form on top of pancakes. Serve with blueberry topping and/or regular syrup. Yield: About 20 pancakes and 3½ c. topping.

## Century Griddle Cakes   *Mrs. Alvin (Katie Mae) Yoder*

2 well beaten eggs
1 t. salt
1½ c. buttermilk or sour milk
1 T. sugar

2 c. flour
1 t. soda
1 T. butter, melted

Beat mixture thoroughly. Add melted butter last. Yield: around 8 pancakes.

## Overnight Pancakes   *Mrs. Freeman (Mabel) Yoder*

1 T. or 1 pkg. yeast
¼ c. water
4 c. flour
2 t. baking powder
2 t. soda

2 t. sugar
1 t. salt
6 eggs
1 qt. buttermilk or sour milk
¼ c. veg. oil

In a small bowl combine yeast and water; let set. Meanwhile in a large bowl combine dry ingredients, then beat eggs, buttermilk and oil. Stir in yeast mixture. Stir into dry mixture just until moistened. Cover and refrigerate overnight or 8 hours. To make pancakes, pour batter by ¼ cupfuls onto a hot griddle until bubbles form on top. Turn and fry until second side is golden brown.

## Pancakes   *Mrs. Clarence T. (Ruby) Yoder*

1¼ c. flour
1 c. whole wheat flour
1 t. salt
¼ c. sugar
2½ T. baking powder

4 T. salad oil or melted butter
2 well beaten eggs
2 c. milk
a handful sunflower seeds
 (optional)

Mix together in order given and fry. Yield: About 2 doz. pancakes.

# Pancakes
*Mrs. Eldon (Katie) Nisley*

2 eggs, beaten
1 c. whole wheat flour
1 c. white flour
2 T. sugar
2 c. milk

1 t. salt
2 t. baking powder
1 t. soda
2 T. veg oil

Mix well and fry on hot griddle. Serve with maple syrup or syrup made with
**1 c. brown sugar, 1 c. white sugar, 1 c. light corn syrup and 1 c. water.**
Heat till sugar is melted, then add maple flavoring.

# Pancakes
*Mrs. Vern (Irene) Schlabach*

2 eggs, beaten
2 c. sour milk
1 t. soda
2¼ c. flour

2 t. baking powder
1 t. salt
4 T. melted butter
2 t. sugar

Beat eggs until light and add the sour milk and soda. Sift flour with baking
powder, salt and sugar. Beat flour mixture into eggs and milk mixture. Add
melted butter and beat until smooth. Bake on a hot griddle.

# Pancakes
*Miriam Yoder (In memory of Katie)*

2 c. flour
½ c. whole wheat flour
  or cornmeal

½ t. salt
3 level t. baking powder
2 c. milk

Mix dry ingredients together. Gradually add milk till the right consistency.
Bake on hot skillet.

# Pancakes
*Mrs. Emmon (Edna) Schmucker*

3 egg yolks
1 T. sugar
1 c. flour
1 c. milk

2 heaping t. baking powder
pinch of salt
2 T. melted butter
3 egg whites, beaten stiff

Beat egg yolks and milk together. Add dry ingredients which have been sifted
together. Then add melted butter. Fold in egg whites just before baking. Bake
on a hot griddle.

# Homemade Syrup

½ c. white sugar
½ c. brown sugar

½ c. white Karo syrup
½ c. sweet cream

Melt, but do not let it boil.

## Potato Pancakes
*Mrs. Freeman (Mabel) Yoder*

4 c. cooked shredded potatoes
½ c. finely chopped onion
¼ c. minced fresh parsley
   or 1 t. dried parsley
2 T. milk

2 eggs, beaten
¼ c. flour
1 t. salt
cooking oil

Place potatoes in a large bowl; add onion, parsley, milk, eggs, flour and salt; mix well. In a skillet heat ¼" of oil over medium heat. Drop batter by ¼ cupfuls into hot oil. Fry until golden brown on both sides. Drain on paper towels.

## Sourdough Starter for Pancakes
*Mrs. Ora N. (Orpha) Miller*

1 c. flour
½ T. yeast

2 T. sugar
1 c. warm water

Mix together and place in a glass container and let set in warm place overnight. Cover, but not too tightly. Next day move to cooler place and stir every day until mixture seems spongy and sour like. Ready to use.

## Sourdough Pancakes

Take above mixture and add: **3 c. flour and 3 c. milk.** Cover loosely and set in a warm place, preferably overnight. Before adding the following ingredients remember to take out some mixture (2 full cups) for your starter next time. Keep in a cool place. **3 eggs, ½ t. salt, ⅓ c. cooking oil, 1½ t. soda, 5 t. sugar.** Mix thoroughly but quickly. Fry on hot griddle.

## Waffles
*Sister Elvesta*

2 c. flour
¾ t. salt
1½ c. milk

2½ t. baking powder
2 eggs, well beaten
5 T. melted shortening

Mix dry ingredients. Then beat eggs well. Add milk and shortening, then add to dry ingredients. Bake on a hot iron.

## Corn Crunch Cereal
*Mrs. Owen (Verna) Hershberger*

4 c. cornmeal
4 c. flour
2 c. brown sugar
2 t. salt

2 t. baking powder
2 t. soda
1 qt. buttermilk or sour milk

Mix all dry ingredients. Stir in milk. Spread in pan. Bake at 350° for 35 min. Put through screen and toast like grape nuts. This recipe will make 2 (13 x 9") cake pans.

## Graham Granola

*Mrs Freeman (Mabel) Yoder*
*Mrs. Harry (Edna Mae) Bontrager*

10 c. quick oats
4 c. finely crushed
  graham crackers (2 packs)
1 c. brown sugar
2 c. coconut

1 t. salt
1 c. crunchy peanut butter
½ c. wheat germ
½ c. honey
½ lb. butter or margarine

**(For a fat-free cereal omit the margarine.)**

In a large bowl, mix all the dry ingredients then add peanut butter and honey. Mix well with hands; melt oleo or butter and mix well. Pour into large roaster and toast slowly at 300° for 45 min., stirring occasionally. Store in an airtight container when cereal has cooled thoroughly. *Variations: 2 c. wheat germ, 1 c. sunflower seeds, and slivered almonds may be added.*

## Granola

*Mrs. Milo (Lorene) Yoder*

12 c. quick oats
6 c. wheat germ
1 c. oil or melted margarine
1½ t. salt

3 c. brown sugar
2 c. coconut
nuts or raisins, optional

Mix together all dry ingredients then add melted margarine or oil. Spread evenly on cookie sheets and toast lightly in oven. Add raisins after it has been cooled. Store in tight container. For bigger crumbs add ½ to ¾ c. water before toasting.

## Granola Cereal

*Mrs. Vern (Irene) Schlabach*

10 c. quick oats
2 c. wheat germ
1 c. whole wheat flour
2 c. coconut

1 large T. salt
1 c. raw sugar
1 c. brown sugar
½ lb. oleo, melted

Mix all ingredients, then toast in oven for 20 min. at 350°, stirring a few times to toast evenly. Cool, and add 1 box slightly crushed cornflakes.

## Granola Cereal

*Mrs. Martin (Katie) Wickey*

6 c. oatmeal (quick or reg.)
1 c. wheat germ
1 c. bran
1 c. brown sugar
1 c. sunflower seeds
½ c. shredded coconut, opt.

½ c. water
1 c. vegetable oil
2 T. vanilla
½ c. honey
1 c. chopped nuts (optional)

Mix until evenly coated. Bake 1 hour in 350° oven, stirring frequently. Raisins and/or cornflakes may be added when cool.

## Grape Nuts
*Mrs. Sam (Martha) Schrock*

5 lbs. brown sugar
2½ qts. buttermilk or sour milk
¾ lb. oleo, melted
1½ t. maple flavoring
2 T. vanilla
8 lbs. whole wheat flour
4 t. soda
1¼ T. salt

Mix in order given. Divide in 5 greased cake pans or 2 greased cookie sheets and 1 cake pan. Bake at 350° for 30 to 35 min. Cool. Then crush grape nuts and store in an airtight container in a cool place. Makes 15 lbs.

## Heartland Cereal
*Mrs. Elmer (Wilma) Beechy*

10 c. oatmeal
1½ c. brown sugar
2 c. coconut
2 c. wheat germ
½ c. honey
½ c. oil
1 t. salt
2 t. vanilla
add nuts or whatever you wish,
sunflower seeds may be
used or small choc. chips

Mix and put in pans and toast in oven until golden brown. 275° - 300°.

## Peanut Butter Granola
*Mrs. Freeman (Mabel) Yoder*

½ c. wheat germ
1 c. raisins
¾ c. sunflower seeds
5½ c. quick oats
4 T. margarine
½ c. honey
1 t. vanilla
¾ c. peanut butter

Mix oatmeal, wheat germ, and sunflower seeds. Heat margarine and honey in a saucepan over low heat. Remove; add vanilla and peanut butter while warm. Combine with dry ingredients. Pour on a cookie sheet and bake at 225° until golden brown. Stir often; add raisins after granola is cooled so they do not harden. Store in an airtight container in a cool dry place. This recipe freezes well.

*A man is rich according to what he is,*
*not according to what he has.*

# Candies & Snacks

*The recipe for a happy family includes a heaping cup of patience.*

*A soft answer turneth away wrath: but grievous words stir up anger.*
*Proverbs 15:1*

# Hints For Candy Making

Temperature tests for candy making: There are two different methods of determining if candy has been cooked to the right consistency. One is by using a candy thermometer in order to record degrees; the other is to use the cold water test. The chart below will prove useful in helping to follow candy recipes.

| Type of candy: | Degrees: | Cold Water |
|---|---|---|
| Fondant, Fudge | 234° -238° | Soft Ball |
| Divinity, Caramels | 245° - 248° | Firm Ball |
| Taffy | 265° - 270° | Hard Ball |
| Butterscotch | 275° - 280° | Light Crack |
| Peanut Butter | 285° - 290° | Hard Crack |
| Caramelized | 310° - 321° | Caramelized |

In using the cold water test, use a fresh cupful of cold water for each test. When testing, remove the candy from the fire and pour about ½ t. of the candy into the cold water. Pick the candy up with fingers and roll into a ball if possible.

In the Soft Ball Test the candy will roll into a soft ball which quickly loses its shape when removed from the water.

In the Firm Ball Test the candy will roll into a firm but not hard ball. It will flatten out a few min. after being removed from water.

In the Hard Ball Test the candy will roll into a hard ball which has lost almost all plasticity and will roll around on a plate when removed from water.

In the Light Crack Test it will form brittle threads which will soften on removal from water.

In the Hard Crack Test the candy will form brittle threads in the water which will remain brittle after being removed from the water.

In Caramelizing, the sugar first melts then becomes a golden brown. It will form a hard brittle ball in the cold water.

## Baby Ruth Candy Bar
*Mrs. David (Rachel) Plank*

1 c. syrup
1 c. sugar
1½ c. peanut butter

1 T. marshmallow creme
1 c. peanuts
4 c. Rice Krispies

Bring sugar and syrup to a boil; add remaining ingredients. Pour into greased 9 x 13" pan and cool. Cut into desired pieces (1 x 3") and dip in chocolate.

## Basic Fondant
*Mrs. Elmer (Ida) Yoder*

2½ c. white sugar
½ c. whipping cream
¼ t. cream of tartar

½ c. milk
2 T. butter or margarine

Combine above ingredients in a Dutch oven. Stir together then place on heat. Cook without stirring to 236° (not higher) then pour on cookie sheet. When cool work with fingers till it sets up. Let rest 25 min. then knead it in a bowl. Put ½ t. flavoring and coloring in. Form into any shape you wish and coat with chocolate. Is best to let set a week before eating.

## Butterscotch Bon Bon Double
*Mrs. Herman (Elsie) Mullett*

2 (6 oz.) pkg. of butterscotch chips
1 c. peanut butter

3 c. cornflakes
2 c. miniature marshmallows

Melt peanut butter and butterscotch chips in double boiler. When melted add the cornflakes and marshmallows. Mix well then drop on wax paper on cookie sheets. Chill.

## Bun Bars
*Mrs. Freeman (Mabel) Yoder*

2 c. peanut butter
2 squares unsweetened choc.

12 oz. chocolate chips
12 oz. butterscotch chips

Melt together in a heavy saucepan then spread ½ of mixture in a 10 x 15" greased pan. Freeze. Set other ½ aside.

¼ c. instant vanilla pudding
½ c. evaporated milk

Mix together in a saucepan and add 1 c. butter. Heat slowly until the butter is melted. Remove from heat and add 1 t. vanilla and 1½ lb. powdered sugar. Beat well and spread over chocolate in pan; put in cool place and add 12 oz. peanuts; top the other half of chocolate mixture and spread over top. Store in a cool place.

## Candy Snack Squares
*Mrs. Freeman (Mabel) Yoder*

2½ c. broken pretzels
2 c. Corn Chex
1½ c. M&M's

½ c. butter or margarine
⅓ c. creamy peanut butter
5 c. miniature marshmallows

In a large bowl combine pretzels, Corn Chex, and M&M's. In a large saucepan over low heat melt butter, peanut butter and marshmallows. Cook and stir until marshmallows are melted and mixture is smooth. Pour over pretzel mixture; stir to coat. Press into a 13 x 9" cake pan. Cool before cutting. Makes about 3 dozen.

## Cinnamon Candy

*Sister Elvesta*

2 c. sugar
1 c. white Karo syrup
½ c. water

⅓ t. cinnamon oil
food coloring

Cook first 3 ingredients together until hard ball. (Test in cold water.) Add flavoring and coloring. Pour in greased pan. Set in cool place to harden. Break into bite size pieces.

## Cinnamon Popcorn

*Mrs. Ezra (Mary) Miller*

8 qts. popcorn
1 c. butter or oleo
½ t. salt

½ c. Karo
8 oz. red hot cinnamon hearts

Put butter or oleo, Karo, salt, and hearts in a heavy pan. Place on medium heat; bring to a boil and boil for 5 min., stirring constantly. Pour over popcorn (mix well). Bake 15 min. at 250°.

## Chocolate Caramel Candy

*Mrs. Freeman (Mabel) Yoder*

1 c. milk choc. chips
¼ c. butterscotch chips
Filling:
¼ c. butter or margarine
1 c. sugar
¼ c. evaporated milk
1½ c. marshmallow creme
Caramel Layer:

¼ c. creamy peanut butter

¼ c. creamy peanut butter
1 t. vanilla
1½ c. chopped salted peanuts

**1 pkg. (14 oz.) caramels**
¼ c. whipping cream or ready-to-whip non-dairy whip topping
Icing:
1 c. milk choc. chips
¼ c. butterscotch chips

¼ c. creamy peanut butter

Combine first three ingredients in a small saucepan. Stir over low heat until melted and smooth. Spread onto the bottom of lightly greased 13 x 9" pan. Refrigerate until set. For filling, melt butter in a heavy saucepan over med.–high heat. Add sugar and milk. Bring to a boil; boil and stir for 5 min. Remove from heat; stir in marshmallow creme, peanut butter and vanilla. Add peanuts. Spread over first layer. Refrigerate until set. Combine the caramels and cream in a saucepan; stir over low heat until melted and smooth. Spread over the filling. Refrigerate until set. In another saucepan, combine chips and peanut butter; stir over low heat until melted and smooth. Pour over caramel layer. Refrigerate for at least 1 hour before serving.

## Chocolate Cheese Fudge
*Mrs. Ervin (Clara) Yoder*

1 lb. milk chocolate
1 8 oz. cream cheese
1 c. chopped walnuts

Melt chocolate over hot, but not boiling, water. When melted take off of the burner and beat in cream cheese until smooth and shiny. Add nuts. Spread in buttered 8 or 9" square pan. This is such a simple recipe that anyone can make it, and it always turns out perfect and delicious.

## Chocolate Pretzel Rings
*Mrs. Freeman (Mabel) Yoder*

50 round pretzels
¼ c. M&M's
8 oz. pkg. milk chocolate
kisses, plain

Place pretzels on a greased baking sheet. Place a chocolate kiss on the center of each ring. Bake at 275° for 2-3 min. or until chocolate is softened. Remove from oven. Place an M&M on each one, pressing down slightly so choc. fills the ring. Cool well before storing in an airtight container. For Christmas, use red and green M&M's; for Valentine's Day, use pink and red, using different colors for each season.

## Crispy Crunchy Corn Chips
*Mrs. Clarence T. (Ruby) Yoder*
*Mrs. Owen (Verna) Hershberger*

1 c. yellow cornmeal
½ c. flour
½ t. baking soda
½ t. salt
¼ t. Lawry's seasoning salt
3 T. veg. oil
½ c. lowfat milk

Mix together cornmeal with flour, soda and salts. Gradually stir in oil that has been mixed with milk. Form into a ball and knead 2 min. Break off small bites and roll out thin. Put on cookie sheets and bake at 350° for 8-10 min. until golden brown.

## Delicious Caramel Corn
*Mrs. Leroy (Sara) Yoder*

2 c. brown sugar
1 c. butter or margarine
½ c. dark Karo syrup
1 t. salt
½ t. baking soda
5 - 6 qts. popped corn
1 or 2 c. salted peanuts
(optional)

Combine sugar, butter, syrup and salt. Boil 5 min. Remove from heat and stir in soda. Pour immediately over corn and nuts, mixing well. Use large roaster pan to mix in. Bake in a 250° oven for 1 hour, stirring every 15 min. Remove from oven and spread on large surface to cool. Will not stick. Light Karo may be used if you do not have dark Karo on hand.

### Finger Jello Jigglers
*Mrs. Freeman (Mabel) Yoder*

1¼ c. boiling water; do not add cold water
1 pkg. 8 oz. serving size any flavor jello

If using a jello mold, oil mold slightly and set aside. Stir boiling water into gelatin in a medium bowl at least 3 min. until completely dissolved. Pour into mold to ⅛ inch from the top. Refrigerate at least 3 hours or until firm (gelatin does not stick to fingers when touched). Dip bottom of mold into warm water about 15 sec. Unmold. This is a never-fail recipe and very flavorful. Can be put in an oiled cake pan and cut into squares.

### Mint Patties
*Sister Mary Yoder*

2½ lbs. powdered sugar
8 oz. cream cheese
4 T. butter
1½ t. peppermint extract
a couple drops green food coloring

Mix all the ingredients together. Shape into balls and press down. Dip into chocolate coating.

### Party Mix
*Mrs. Simon (Martha) Schmucker*

½ c. butter or oleo, melted
1½ t. Worcestershire sauce
½ t. garlic salt
⅛ t. hot sauce
3 c. corn chips
3 c. cheese crackers
12 oz. can mixed nuts
3 c. popped corn

Stir together first 4 ingredients in a bowl. Set aside. Combine corn chips and next 3 ingredients in a large roasting pan. Add butter mixture, stirring to coat. Bake at 250° for 1 hour, stirring every 15 min. Spread on paper towels to cool. Yield: 8 cups.

### Party Mix
*Mrs. Noah (Amanda) Lehman*

1 box Corn Chex
1 box Rice Chex
1 box nacho cheese crackers
1 box veg. thins crackers
4 c. pretzels
4 c. potato sticks
3 c. corn chips
1 lb. butter
½ c. Worcestershire sauce
2 t. Lawry's salt
2 t. table salt

Melt butter; add salts and sauce. Pour over snacks. Mix real well and put in oven at 250° for 1½ hours. Stir every 15 min.

### Peanut Butter Cups
*Mrs. Vernon (Polly) Beechy*

1 lb. butter or oleo, melted
1 lb. peanut butter
2 lb. powdered sugar

Melt butter; stir in the peanut butter while it's still warm, then add powdered sugar. Stir in Rice Krispies to make it crunchy (if desired). Shape into balls and dip in melted chocolate. You have to use your hands to mix this.

## Pecan Pralines

*Mrs. Freeman (Mabel) Yoder*

1 T. butter
2 c. sugar
½ c. brown sugar
1 c. half & half or top milk
pinch of salt
2 c. pecans
1 t. vanilla

Cook first five ingredients together until it forms a soft ball in cold water. Remove from heat and add vanilla and pecans. Cool mixture in a pan of cold water till cool before the final beating. Beat till mixture loses its glossiness and is stiff.

## Peppermint Patties

*Mrs. Glen (Lydia Mae) Miller*

4 c. white sugar
1¼ c. white corn syrup
½ c. water

Cook to a hard ball (260°). Pour over **4 beaten egg whites** and beat while pouring - like frosting! When cool add **1 stick oleo, a little cream and 1 bag of powdered sugar,** or more if not stiff enough, and 1 t. peppermint flavoring, or to taste, then dip in chocolate.

## Pizza Popcorn

*Mrs. Toby (Martha) Yoder*

½ c. margarine
½ t. Italian seasoning
garlic powder or salt
6 qts. popped corn
onion salt
3 T. Parmesan cheese

Keep popcorn hot until mixed. Melt butter; add Italian seasoning and garlic as much as is desired. Pour over popcorn and mix. Sprinkle with onion salt and Parmesan cheese.

## Pretzel Seasoning

*Mrs. Ezra (Mary) Miller*

1 c. oil
½ t. garlic salt
½ t. lemon pepper
1 T. dill weed
1 pkg. Hidden Valley Ranch
  dressing mix
30 oz. pretzels

Mix oil, garlic salt, lemon pepper, dill weed and Hidden Valley Ranch mix, and pour over pretzels. Let set a few hours then they are ready to eat.

## Rice Krispie Candy

*Mrs. Freeman (Mabel) Yoder*

6 c. Rice Krispies
½ c. butter or margarine
10½ oz. marshmallows

Melt marshmallows and butter in a double boiler just until marshmallows are melted. Then pour over 6 c. of Rice Krispies in a bowl. Stir to coat then pour in a greased cake pan; cool and cut into squares.

## Rice Krispie Caramels

*Mrs. Mervin (Emma) Yoder*

¼ lb. butter

3 c. marshmallows

3 c. Rice Krispies

Melt together and press in a 13 x 9" cake pan. Then in double boiler: Melt **40 caramel candies, 1 sm. can Eagle Brand milk and ½ c. butter.** Pour this mixture over Rice Krispie mixture. Let cool. Then make another batch of the first layer and place on top of caramel mixture. Eat as is or can be cut into squares and dipped in melted chocolate.

## Scotcheroos

*Mrs. Freeman (Mabel) Yoder*

1 c. Karo syrup or honey

1 c. sugar

1 c. peanut butter

Mix into **6 c. Rice Krispies**. Put into ungreased 9 x 13" pan.

Topping:

Melt **1 c. chocolate chips** and **1 c. butterscotch chips** and spread over the top. Very good!

## Soft Pretzels

*Miriam Yoder (In memory of Katie)*

2 c. warm water

2 t. salt

2 T. yeast

2½ c. whole wheat flour

¼ c. butter

4 c. white flour

½ c. brown sugar

Knead thoroughly and let rise for ½ hour in a warm place. Divide dough into 24 pieces. Roll and shape into pretzels. Dip in 2 cups hot water and 4 t. soda. Place on a greased pan. Sprinkle with pretzel salt. Bake at 325° for 20 min. Dip in or brush with browned butter.

## Soft Pretzels

*Mrs. Melvin (Mary Esther) Shrock*

2 c. warm water

6½-7½ c. flour

½ c. sugar

2½ T. instant yeast

2 t. salt

Add yeast to flour

¼ c. soft oleo

1 egg yolk

1 egg

2 T. water

Measure water, sugar, salt, egg and oleo into bowl and stir until dissolved. Add 3 cups flour w/ yeast added and mix until smooth. Add enough additional flour so it isn't sticky. Cover bowl tightly and let rise. Put ½ of dough on lightly floured board and roll out. Cut into 16" strips and twist into pretzels. Beat the one egg yolk and water and brush over pretzels and sprinkle with pretzel salt (very coarse). Let rise and bake at 350° for 15 min. or until done. (Put on greased cookie sheets.)

## Soft Pretzels
*Mrs. Elmer (Wilma) Beechy*

4½ c. flour
2 T. yeast
2 t. brown sugar (heaping)
¾ t. salt
1½ c. warm water

Mix dry ingredients; add warm water and mix well. Take a small amount of dough and roll out and form into a pretzel shape. Dip into hot soda water. **4 T. soda and 3 c. water.** Put on greased pan and bake at 450° till golden. Dip in melted butter and sprinkle with salt or garlic salt. Also, you can just make pretzel sticks instead of pretzel shape.

## Sugar Pecans
*Mrs. LaVern (Martha) Yoder*

1 egg white
1 t. cold water
1 lb. pecans
½ c. sugar
¼ t. salt
½ t. cinnamon

Beat egg white and water till fluffy. Pour over pecans and stir well, then mix sugar, cinnamon and salt. Pour over first mixture and stir till pecans are well coated then put on cookie sheet. Bake at 225° for 1 hour, stirring and turning every 15 min.

## Turtle Candy
*Mrs. Elmer (Wilma) Beechy*

2 c. white sugar
¾ c. light Karo
¾ c. butter or oleo
2 c. cream
1 T. vanilla
pecans

Put all of syrup, sugar and half of cream in pan and bring to a boil. Stir mixture constantly. Add rest of cream and butter slowly so mixture doesn't stop boiling. Boil to soft ball on candy thermometer. Add vanilla and pour over pecan halves. Have pecans ready, single layer on buttered pan. Melt chocolate and pour over candy.

## Twix Candy Bars
*Mrs. Vernon (Polly) Beechy*

½ c. brown sugar
½ c. white sugar
½ c. butter or margarine
¼ c. milk
1 c. crushed graham crackers
Club crackers
½ c. peanut butter
1 c. choc. chips
½ c. butterscotch chips

Line a 9 x 13 in. pan with a layer of Club crackers. Simmer for 5 min. in a 3 qt. pan on the stove: Brown sugar, white sugar, butter and milk. Add crushed graham crackers to heated sugar mixture and spread over Club crackers. Add another layer of Club crackers. Melt over low heat: Peanut butter, choc. chips and butterscotch chips. Spread over last layer of Club crackers. Cool and cut into squares. Taste like Twix candy bars.

## Valley Taffy

*Mrs. Glen (Lydia Mae) Miller*

2 c. white sugar
2 c. canned milk or cream
¼ c. water

2 c. light Karo syrup
1 pkg. Knox gelatin

Put gelatin in cold water. Put all other ingredients in kettle and boil 15 min. Then add gelatin and continue boiling until a hard ball forms when tested in cold water. Put in pie pans and cool enough to handle. Have 2 people pull it until it gets nice and light colored. Cut into desired lengths and wrap in wax paper.

## Valley Taffy

*Miriam Yoder (In memory of Katie)*

4 c. white sugar
2 c. light corn syrup
2 c. cream

1 T. Knox gelatin
paraffin (size of a walnut)
½ c. water

Mix everything together except gelatin dissolved in water. Bring to a boil and boil 15 min. Then add gelatin and continue to boil until about hard ball stage (250º). When cool enough take out and pull until white and stretchy.

## White Trash

*Mrs. Edwin (Annie) Ropp*

6 c. Crispix cereal
4 c. small pretzels
2 c. dry roasted peanuts

½ lb. M&M's
1¼ lb. white chocolate
a few sprinkles of paraffin

Mix together in a bowl, except paraffin and white chocolate which are melted together. When it is melted, pour over other snacks. Put on cookie sheets to cool. Break in pieces and put in airtight containers.

*Life is too short to belittle. (or) To belittle is to be little.*

# Canning & Freezing

*For every minute you frown you lose 60 seconds of happiness.*

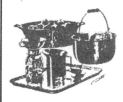

*Be patient therefore, brethren, unto the coming of the Lord. Behold, the husbandman waiteth for the precious fruit of the earth, and hath long patience for it, until he receive the early and latter rain.*

*James 5:7*

# A Table Grace

God bless the food before us
And these with whom we share it,
The ones who helped to grow it,
To harvest and prepare it.
We thank you, dear Lord Jesus,
That you did provide it.
We bid you to be with us
Now as we divide it.  Amen

## Apple Pie Filling

*Mrs. Owen (Verna) Hershberger*

10 c. water
4½ c. sugar
1½ c. clear jel
2 t. cinnamon
¼ t. nutmeg

1 t. salt
14 c. apples (shredded
   or sliced)
2 T. ReaLemon juice

In a large saucepan heat 8 c. water and 3½ c. sugar. Mix 1 c. sugar with clear jel and spices, then add 2 c. water. Add this to the kettle of boiling water. Stir until it thickens. Remove from heat and add lemon juice. Pour over apples; stir well, then put in jars. Cold pack 20 min. This comes in handy to bake pies. Or for a quick dessert, crush graham crackers and put pie filling on top then whipped cream on top of the filling.

## Aunt Annie's Ketchup

*Mrs. Allen (Elsie) Bontrager*
*Mary Miller*

4 qt. tomato juice
3 garlic buds or
   3 t. garlic powder

3 onions, chopped
1 hot pepper or ½ t.
   red pepper

Put in large kettle and cook 2 hours. Then put through sieve. Put on stove and add:

3 c. white sugar, scant
3 T. salt
3½ t. dry mustard, moistened
   with vinegar

1 T. pickling spice
1 T. ketchup spice*

Tie spices in bag and drop into kettle. Cook together one more hour. Then thicken with **3 lg. T. clear jel** and cook 1 min. more. Bottle and seal.
*It's OK to substitute more pickling spice for the ketchup spice as sometimes the ketchup spice is hard to find.

## Brine to Can Peppers
### (Sweet or Hot)

*Mrs. Martin (Katie) Wickey*

1 qt. vinegar
½ c. water

½ c. brown sugar
¼ c. salt

Prepare peppers (wear rubber gloves). If you prefer very hot peppers leave seeds in. Fill jars with whole, fine or diced peppers. Removing the seeds will give a milder taste. A salsa master works well when peppers are cut up fine for pizza, sandwiches, etc. Mix ingredients but do not heat. Pour cold liquid over peppers. Put lid on tight and they are ready to store. (No heating, no sealing.) Try it. You'll like it unless they are too hot!!

## Cabbage Slaw to Freeze or Can

*Mom (Rosa) Bontrager*

4½ qts. shredded cabbage
6 med. carrots, fine
3 onions, fine
3 green or red peppers, fine
Mix and let set 1 hour. Boil:

3 t. salt
2¼ c. veg. oil
1 T. mustard seed

1 c. vinegar
3 c. sugar

1 c. water

Add 1 large box lemon jello. Cool and add to cabbage. Put in canner long enough to seal.

## Catsup

*Mrs. Eldon (Katie) Nisley*

2 gal. tomato juice,
cooked with some onion
2½ c. vinegar

8 T. salt
20 drops each of cinnamon
and clove oil

Boil down till only ⅔ of it is left. Mix 6 c. sugar and 6 heaping T. Mir Clear or clear jel and stir into juice and bring to a boil again. Put in jars and seal. The oils can be bought at a drug or health food store. You can add 1 t. red pepper which will help keep it if the jars don't seal.

## Chili Soup (to can)

*Mrs. Marvin L. (Erma) Miller*

5 lbs. hamburger
2 c. onions, chopped
salt and pepper
1 gal. kidney beans
1 gal. tomato juice

1 c. pickle relish
1¼ c. brown sugar
2 T. chili powder
1 t. garlic salt
1 qt. water

Brown the hamburger with the onions. Add salt and pepper to taste. Mix with the rest of the ingredients, adding water to suit. Pork and beans can be used instead of the kidney beans. Cook in pressure cooker for 75 min. with 10 lbs. pressure.

## Crisp -N- Easy Pickles

*Mrs. Freeman (Mabel) Yoder*
*Mrs. David (Rachel) Plank*

5 qts. sliced pickles
6 med. onions, chopped
1 red pepper, chopped
2 green peppers, chopped
1½ c. vinegar

1½ c. water
5 c. sugar
1½ t. turmeric
1½ t. celery seed
3 t. salt, rounded

Combine salt, pickles, onions and peppers. Let stand. Combine sugar and water, vinegar and spices. Add to first mixture and bring to a boil. Put in jars and seal. More pickles and less onions may be used.

## Deer and Chicken Bologna

*Mrs. Ora (Susie) Miller*

10 lbs. ground chicken
20 lbs. ground deer venison
1 lb. Tenderquick
4 T. ground coriander
1 T. garlic powder
1 t. mace

2 t. salt petre
3 T. black pepper
2 oz. mustard seed
2 qt. water
1 qt. Karo

Mix and stuff like you would any other bologna, in casings. May be put in quart jars and canned like other meat. 10 lbs. pressure for 1½ hours.

## Dill Pickles

*Mrs. Freeman (Mabel) Yoder*

1 c. sugar (scant)
1 c. canning salt (scant)

2 qts. water
1 qt. vinegar

Bring to a boil; remove from heat. Pack clean whole 2 to 4" cucumbers into qt. jars, with 1 garlic bud, 1 slice onion and lots of homegrown dill, 2 to 3 large heads. Makes around 5 qts. Put water into the bottom of a cake pan and set jars in water. Water bathe in oven at 250° for 20 min. Wait 1 month before opening a jar. When you open a jar, pour out approx. half of brine, fill with cold water, and shake slightly to mix. These taste like the store-bought Milwaukee dills, firm and delicious.

## Dilly Chips

*Mrs. Ezra (Mary) Miller*

1 qt. sliced pickles
sliced onions
2 heads dill

1 t. salt
¼ t. alum
1 garlic clove

Boil the following:

1 pint water
1 pint cider vinegar

2½ c. sugar

Put 1 clove garlic in each jar. Pack pickles and onions alternately. Heat brine on stove. Put alum in jars. Pour hot brine over pickles. Hot water bathe for 15 min. to seal.

## Freezing Corn

*Mrs. Sam (Martha) Schrock*

4 qts. corn, cut off the cobs
¾ c. sugar

4 t. salt
1 qt. water

Bring to a boil and simmer for 10 min. Cool as soon as possible. Put corn and liquid in containers and freeze. Ready to eat when thawed out.

*A gentleman is a gentle man.*

# Garlic Dill Pickles

*Mrs. Glen (Lydia Mae) Miller*
*Mom (Rosa) Bontrager*

3 c. sugar  
2 c. water  

1½ c. vinegar  
2 T. salt  

Boil this together till sugar is dissolved. Slice pickles, not too thin, and don't peel. Soak in good salty water (I put 1 c. salt to a 13 qt. bowl) for 1 hour. Put dill and 1 garlic bud in bottom of a qt. can; fill with sliced pickles and fill with the above mixture. Enough vinegar mixture for 3 qts. Then to help your cans to seal, cold pack for just a few min. or pressure up to 5 lbs.

# Hot Pepper Butter

*Mrs. Marvin (Katie) Wickey*
*Mrs. Ervin (Clara)Yoder*

40 hot peppers  
6 c. sugar  
1 qt. vinegar  

1 qt. yellow mustard  
1 T. salt  

Remove seeds from peppers. (Always wear rubber gloves when working with hot peppers.) Grind peppers and mix with ingredients. Boil 10 - 15 min. Mix 1½ c. flour and 1½ c. water. Slowly add to the above mixture. Boil 5 min. Stir thoroughly as it sticks easily. Put in bottles and seal while hot. We like our mustard hot! I use only 5 c. sugar rather than 6. I leave many of the seeds in. To make the thickening, I use **1¼ c. flour, 1 c. water and ½ c. of vinegar.** A good sandwich spread.

# Pickled Red Beets

*Mrs. Ora N. (Orpha) Miller*

2 c. sugar  
2 c. vinegar  
2 c. water  

1 T. cinnamon  
1 t. cloves  
1 t. allspice  

**(Use water in which beets were cooked in.)**

Cook red beets until tender in water. Cold dip and slip skins off. Cut up to desired pieces. Mix the above pickling syrup; heat to boiling enough to dissolve sugar and spices. Cover beets with mixture and let simmer 15 min. Can immediately and seal.

# Pizza and Spaghetti Sauce

*Mrs. David (Rachel) Plank*

6 qt. tomato juice  
1 c. sugar  
¼ c. salt  
½ T. paprika  
½ T. chili powder  

¼ T. red pepper  
1 T. garlic salt  
1 T. oregano  
3-4 onions  
½ c. parsley flakes (optional)  

In a large kettle cook the tomato juice, parsley and onions. (More or less parsley and onions may be used.) Add rest of ingredients. Now thicken the juice with 1 c. clear jel. (More or less depending on how thick you want it.) Fill jars and seal.

## Pizza Sauce
*Mrs. Lester (Mary) Lehman*

4 qt. tomato juice
1 onion, chopped
1 t. garlic salt
1 t. oregano

1 t. black pepper
½ t. Tabasco sauce
2 t. salt or to taste

Put together and bring to a boil. Dissolve 4 T. clear jel in cold water. Stir in tomato mixture and bring to a boil; put in jars and cold pack ½ hour.

## Pizza Sauce
*Mrs. Leroy (Sara) Yoder*

1 pint tomato juice
½ t. oregano
1 t. prepared mustard

1 T. Worcestershire sauce
1 t. garlic salt

Cook sauce 15 to 20 min. May add a little cornstarch or clear jel (mixed with a little cold water) to thicken it to pizza sauce consistency.

## Red Beets to Can
*Mom (Rosa) Bontrager*

3 c. sugar
1½ T. mustard seed
1½ T. celery seed

2 T. salt
1 pint vinegar
1 pint water

Boil this together then add 4 qts. cooked beets. Boil again and can. I put mustard seed and the celery in a cloth. I just open-kettle can them but you could cold pack them just long enough to seal them.

## Salsa
*Mrs. Lester (Verna) Bontrager*

In a large pot combine:

6 qt. peeled, ripe tomatoes, chopped
6 c. chopped bell peppers
6 c. chopped onions
½ c. vinegar
3 - 6 oz. cans tomato paste

½ c. sugar
6 T. salt (scant)
2 T. chopped garlic
1½ t. red pepper (add more to suit taste)

Cook 1 hour. Pour boiling hot into jars; add lids and seal. Or, let salsa cool a bit, then put in jars and water bathe for 10 min.

## Spaghetti Sauce
*Mrs. Christie (Anna) Yoder*

2⅔ gal. tomato juice
3 lbs. onions
2 c. vegetable oil
5 T. Italian seasoning
1½ c. white sugar
½ c. salt
1 T. garlic powder

4 hot peppers
3 green peppers
2 t. chili powder
½ t. paprika
1 t. pizza spice
1 bunch celery

Mix and boil 1 hour. Add 48 oz. tomato paste. Bring to a boil. Thicken with Perma–flo then cold pack 10-15 min. Approx. 10 lbs. pressure. 1 batch makes 28 pints. To make 1½ batch use scant 4 gal. juice; this makes 42 pints.

## Sweet Dill and Garlic Pickles
*Mrs. Emmon (Edna) Schmucker*

3 c. sugar
2 c. vinegar

2 c. water
1 t. salt

Bring to boiling point. Put pickles in cans. Put 1 garlic bud in bottom and 1 on top. Put 1 t. dill in bottom and 1 on top. Cold pack. Bring just to the boiling point. Let stand in water 5 min. before taking out.

## To Can Fruit Pie Filling
*Mrs. Edwin (Annie) Ropp*

3 qts. fruit; peaches,
blueberries, raspberries, etc.
9 c. water
4 c. sugar

¼ t. salt
6 T. jello
1¾ c. Perma-flo

Bring water, sugar, salt and Perma-flo to a boil, then add jello. Add the berries last. Put in jars and cold pack. Bring to a rolling boil. Boil 5 min. then turn off and let stand 15 min. then take out. Use any kind of berries and jello you want.

## Tomato Soy
*Mrs. Ervin (Clara) Yoder*

1 pk. ripe tomatoes
8 onions
½ c. salt
1 qt. vinegar
1 t. cloves

1 t. cinnamon
1 t. ginger
1 or 2 t. dry mustard
½ t. pepper
2 lbs. sugar

Peel and slice tomatoes into a large stainless steel or granite kettle. Slice onions into tomatoes. Sprinkle salt over vegetables and mix in. Let stand overnight. Next morning drain, rinse and drain again. Add vinegar and spices. Cook slowly for 2 hours. When nearly done add the sugar. Ladle into hot sterilized jars. Process in hot water bath for 20 min. Serve with meat. Especially good with roast.

## Vegetable Soup to Can
*Submitted by Mrs. Owen (Verna)*
*Hershberger (In memory of Melvin Edna Ellen and Aunt Anna Mae)*

1 qt. beans, green,
navy or kidney
1 qt. carrots
1 qt. corn
1 qt. celery

1 qt. potatoes
1 qt. peas
1 qt. onions
1 qt. macaroni

In a large stockpot, cook all vegetables in salt water till not quite done. Then add ½ c. sugar, 2 T. chili powder, 2 qts. water, 4 qts. tomato juice and add salt to your taste. Stir together well then put in jars and seal. Cold pack 2 hours. I also add some fried hamburger.

## Zucchini Pineapple

*Mrs. Clarence T. (Ruby) Yoder*

2 gal. diced or cubed zucchini,
  peeled and seeded
2 c. sugar
1 t. oil of pineapple (optional)

1½ c. ReaLemon juice
1 (46 oz.) can pineapple juice
  or 3 pt. water & 1 c. pineapple jello

Combine all ingredients in large kettle and bring to a boil and simmer 10 min. Thicken with ½ **c. clear jel mixed with a little cold water**. Pack in jars and cold pack 5 min. Variation: Can be cold packed ½ hour to keep better and eat as a fruit. Yields: 7 qt.

## Zucchini Squash Relish

*Mrs. Owen (Verna) Hershberger*

10 c. zucchini, ground
4 c. onions, ground

2 c. peppers, ground

To the zucchini, onions and peppers add **8 t. salt** and let stand 2 hours. Rinse in cold water and drain. Add: **5 c. sugar, 1 T. celery seed, 1½ c. vinegar, and green cake coloring, optional.** Mix and put in large kettle. Cook 15 min. Put hot in jars and seal. Serve with hamburgers, hotdogs, or omelets.

# Helpful Hints

Strawberries keep in a colander in the refrigerator; wash just before serving.

A rib of celery in your bread bag will keep your bread fresh for a longer time.

Store your cottage cheese carton upside down; it will keep twice as long.

Chicken will fry more crispy and brown quicker if a little baking powder and paprika is added to the flour.

When cooking dried beans, add salt after cooking. If salt is added at the start it will slow the cooking process.

Rice will be fluffier and whiter if you add 1 t. lemon juice to each quart of water.

When cooking vegetables, bring water to a boil before adding vegetables; it will help preserve the vitamins.

Add a bit of sugar (without stirring) to milk to prevent scorching. Pan will be much easier to clean if first rinsed with cold water.

Use a pizza cutter to cut bars or bar cookies into nice, smooth squares in half the time.

To keep granulated sugar from lumping, place a couple of salt crackers in container and cover tightly.

Soften "hard as rock" brown sugar by placing a slice of soft bread or half an apple in the package and closing tightly. In a couple hours the brown sugar will be soft again.

For fluffier omelets, add a pinch of cornstarch before beating.

For soup and stew that is too salty, add a raw potato and discard after cooking.

To improve an inexpensive cake mix, add one T. butter to the batter for a richer tasting cake.

A fresh egg sinks in water and lies on its side. If it stands on end it's getting old. If it floats, get rid of it.

Brush the inside of your bottom crust with egg white when making fruit pies to prevent juice from soaking through.

# Misc., Jams & Jellies

*Happiness is like jam; you can't spread even a little without getting some on yourself.*

*Now unto Him that is able to keep you from falling, and to present you faultless before the presence of His glory with exceeding joy.*
*Jude 24*

# A Happy Home Recipe

4 cups of love
2 cups of loyalty
3 cups of forgiveness
1 cup of friendship
5 T. of hope
2 T. of tenderness
4 qts. of faith
1 barrel of laughter

Take love and loyalty; mix thoroughly with faith. Blend it with tenderness, kindness and understanding. Add friendship and hope. Sprinkle abundantly with laughter. Bake it with sunshine. Serve daily with generous helpings.

## Apple Butter (in a big kettle)
*Mrs. Sam (Viola) Miller*

25 gal. apple snitz
50 lbs. sugar

3 T. cinnamon
3 T. allspice

Put 15 gal. water in kettle then measure with a yardstick. Put in applesauce then boil down to stick measure. Put spices in sugar, then put sugar and all into apples and cook down again to the stick measure. Variations: A little less sugar and a little more spices can be used.

## Cheese Spread
*Mrs. Edwin (Annie) Ropp*

2 c. milk
2 lb. box cheese (such as Velveeta)

¹/₃ stick oleo

Heat milk, then add cheese; after it is melted add oleo, stirring constantly. You can also put in pints and cold pack for 15 min.

## Clay
*Sister Elvesta*

Boil 2 c. water; add 2 t. powdered alum, 1 t. oil and ½ c. salt. Pour over 2¼ c. flour. Stir. Put on a warm burner until it feels like clay. Add desired food coloring. Store in a tight container and in a cool place.

## Homemade Baby Wipes
*Mrs. Freeman (Mabel) Yoder*
*Mrs. Christy (Anna) Bontrager*

1¾ c. water
1 T. baby bath
1 T. baby oil

1 roll Bounty towels, rinse and reuse

Cut towels in half; remove center cardboard. In a 5 lb. peanut butter container mix the first 3 things together then put towels in. Cut a hole in the lid and thread the towels through the hole. These wipes smell wonderful. Do not use a cheap brand of toweling; nothing works like Bounty.

## Homemade Laundry Soap
*Mom (Rosa) Bontrager*

10 c. cold water
9 c. melted fat
½ c. ammonia

3 T. borax
1 can lye

Mix in order given; sprinkle lye in last. Let stand 10 min. then stir frequently for the first hour and a half. After that once every hour throughout the day. Avoid inhaling fumes. Let this set a couple of days, then put in tight container so it will not dry out. This gets crumbly and will readily melt in wash water. Note: May add ½ oz. citronella for fragrance.

## Homemade Noodles

*Mrs. Harry (Edna Mae) Bontrager*
*Mrs. Lonnie (Norma Mae) Bontrager*

2 c. egg yolks
1 c. egg white

1 c. boiling water
3½ lbs. flour

Mix yolks, whites and boiling water. Add all the flour. Will be very dry and crumbly, but just cover it and let it set for ½ hour or more. Then knead with hands till it's nice and smooth. Will take very little kneading. Add more flour if needed. Put through a noodle chef.

## Marshmallow Creme

*Mrs. Mervin (Emma) Yoder*

2 c. white sugar
1 c. water
2½ c. white Karo
c. white Karo

1 c. egg whites
1 t. vanilla
1 sm. box jello (optional) any   ½
flavor

Cook first 3 ingredients to soft ball (almost 250°). Meanwhile put the following in a large bowl: ½ c. Karo and egg whites. Beat slowly until mixed, then beat hard until fluffy. Then add hot syrup in a fine stream while beating. Beat hard for 3 min. Cool; stir occasionally while cooling. Yield: approx. 3 lb.

## Mock Raspberry Jam

*Mrs. Leland (Orpha) Yoder*

5 c. chopped green tomatoes
4 c. sugar
raspberry jello (1 lg. pkg. or 2 sm. pkg.)

Combine chopped tomatoes and sugar; let stand until juice starts coming out of tomatoes. Then put in a saucepan and cook 15 min. Watch carefully so it doesn't burn. Stir slowly all the while. Add jello and stir until dissolved. Pour into sterilized jars. Keep in refrigerator or put in hot water bath for 10 min.

## Pineapple Jam

*Mrs. Lloyd (Edna) Raber*

4 c. sugar
2½ c. Karo

1½ c. pineapple (crushed)
a little water

Cook sugar, Karo and water till thick, soft ball stage. (See candy section for info. on soft ball stage.) Add pineapple; again cook for 4 min.

## Popsicles

*Mrs. Christie (Anna) Yoder*

1 pkg. jello (3 oz.)
1 env. Kool-Aid (of your choice)
1 c. sugar

2 c. boiling water
2 c. cold water

Mix all ingredients and pour into molds. Freeze.

## Rhubarb Jam
*Mrs. Mervin (Gertie) Eash*

5 c. finely cut rhubarb
3 c. sugar

1 c. crushed pineapple w/ juice
½ c. raspberry jello

Combine rhubarb, sugar, and pineapple in large pan and cook 10 - 12 min., stirring occasionally. Dissolve jello in hot rhubarb mixture and stir well. Place in jars to store in refrigerator or freezer.

## Silly Putty
*Mrs. Freeman (Mabel) Yoder*

1 c. Elmer's glue (7⅝ fl. oz.)
½ c. liquid starch (scant)
a few drops food coloring

Place glue in a bowl. Slowly add liquid starch, 2 T. at a time. Stir well after each addition. When glue begins to form a ball and is stringy, take it out of bowl and keep tucking stringy ends under. After kneading 8-10 min. and you're beginning to think it is a hopeless mess keep on for another 5 min. and it will all stick together and crackle and pop. It will be a soft elastic ball that can be divided into small egg size chunks or however you wish, providing many hours of quiet playtime for children. This is not as crumbly as playdough. Store in an airtight container. Does not keep as long as playdough.

## Cooked Playdough
*Mrs. Christy (Anna) Bontrager*

Combine **1 c. flour, ½ c. salt and 2 t. cream of tartar** in a large saucepan. Gradually stir in **1 c. water mixed with 2 T. oil and 1 t. food coloring.** Cook over med. heat, stirring constantly, until a ball forms. Remove from heat and knead until smooth. Store in an airtight container. Enjoy!

*Silence is not always golden -
sometimes it is plain yellow.*

# Helpful Hints

Add a little salt to applesauce; takes less sugar and brings out a richer flavor. Sprinkle apples while cooking with baking soda so they won't turn brown.

Need a pan scraper? Crumple a piece of tinfoil and use in an emergency.

To hard-boil cracked eggs, add salt and pour hot water over them to boil; they peel easier too.

To make your own tartar sauce for fish, mix relish chopped with salad dressing.

A little baking powder added to meat loaf will make it more fluffy and if you add about ½ c. milk to a lb. of hamburger and let it set for 1½ hours before using it, it will be more juicy.

To soften brown sugar lumps, put in a jar with a piece of moist paper towel under the lid, or heat in oven for several minutes.

A full, rolling boil is a boil that cannot be stirred down with a spoon.

Add a pinch of salt to jello; improves the flavor.

An apple cut in half and placed in a cookie jar, cake box or bread box will keep your baked goods fresh and moist.

When baking cookies save the crumbs you scrape from the cookie sheets and add to your graham cracker crumbs.

Roll biscuit dough thin, then fold it before cutting. Makes them flaky in center and split open easily for buttering.

Brush cream, then sprinkle sugar on top of two-crust pies; browns beautifully.

A home remedy for bee stings. Wet the injured area and apply meat tenderizer - it stops the pain immediately.

For burns wet area with cold water. Sprinkle some table salt on the spot - it will stop the burn and will not blister. Do this immediately.

Crushed cranberries make a good poultice for wounds such as dog or cat bites.Drink cranberry juice - good for urinary and bladder infections.

Sorghum syrup in your diet will help dry scalp and dandruff.

Of all the home remedies a good wife is the best.

A good mess of dandelion greens made into a warm salad is a good spring tonic and also good for kidney problems. Dandelion is also good for diabetics.

For bed-wetting: Give the child 1 t. of honey before going to bed. Also let child eat lots of raisins. Parsley tea is also good - drink 3 times a day. 1 heaping t. per 2 c. water.

For cough - colds: Mix the juice of 3 lemons, 1 pt. honey, 3 T. of maple syrup, a pea size chunk of baking soda together. Take as needed.

Garlic is very good for respiratory infections. 1 teaspoon dried garlic in one cup boiling water - drink while warm.

Remedy for severe diarrhea in babies -
   1 c. raw oatmeal (quick oats)
   3 c. warm tap water
Mix this together and soak for a few minutes. Strain off the water and give to child instead of milk. I barely gave them anything else until it cleared up. Put in bottle if they take a bottle. Also very good on diaper rash and eczema. Rub on after diaper change.

For sinus trouble: Take $1/4$ t. soda in 8 oz. glass of tepid water before going to bed and first thing in the morning again. It cleans out your stomach and first thing you know your sinus will be gone.

Add a t. of honey and a t. pure apple cider vinegar to a cup of hot water. Drink first thing in morning upon rising. Good for stomach, colitis and liver trouble; may help get rid of excessive fluid too.

Plain cider vinegar stops itching. Wash the itch with plain water; pat some vinegar on cotton; apply to itch and let the air dry it.

For heart problems: Blue vervain tea is good for the heart, as is rosemary tea brewed 1 t. per cup of water.

# Index

## Meats & Main Dishes

Use the order form(s) below for obtaining additional copies of
*Family Treasures* cookbook.

Please send _____ copies of Family Treasures cookbook @ $9.99 each, plus $1.50 postage and handling per book.

*Ship to:*

Name _____

Address _____

City _____ State _____ Zip _____

*Make check payable and send to:*

        Mrs. Freeman Yoder
        7850 Dutch Bethel Rd.
        Freedom, IN 47431

*Please include payment with order.*

Please send _____ copies of Family Treasures cookbook @ $9.99 each, plus $1.50 postage and handling per book.

*Ship to:*

Name _____

Address _____

City _____ State _____ Zip _____

*Make check payable and send to:*

        Mrs. Freeman Yoder
        7850 Dutch Bethel Rd.
        Freedom, IN 47431